J.D Clark

Sketches In and Around Shanghai

J.D Clark

Sketches In and Around Shanghai

ISBN/EAN: 9783337114152

Printed in Europe, USA, Canada, Australia, Japan

Cover: Foto ©Andreas Hilbeck / pixelio.de

More available books at **www.hansebooks.com**

SKETCHES

In and Around

SHANGHAI,

ETC.

SHANGHAI:
PRINTED AT THE "SHANGHAI MERCURY" AND "CELESTIAL EMPIRE" OFFICES.
1894.

INDEX.

	Page.
The Performances at a Chinese Theatre	1
The City of Shanghai: its Streets, Temples, Prisons, and Gardens	9
Apotheosis of Liu Sing-kau, God of Peace	27
The Manila Cock-Pit, in Bamboo Town	34
The Birthday of the Moon; in Shanghai City by Night	37
The Shanghai Telephone Exchange	41
The Aquarius Company's Steam Factory and Water Distillery	44
Gambling in China	47
The Celestial "Boulevards" of Shanghai, or Foochow Road by Day and Night	49
The Jinricsha and Coolie	64
A Curiosity Stall at the City Gate	69
The Chinese Wheelbarrow and its Coolie	70
Chinese Printers	72
Chinese Legerdemain: The Showmen on Hongkew Wharf	76
Anglo-Chinese Signboards	80
The Chinese Policeman	89
Chinese Boys	91
Chinese Amahs	93
The Cangue and the Chain-Gang	97
Chinese Noises	99
The Mixed Court	103
The Maloo Bridewell	115
The China Inland Mission	118
The Thomas Hanbury School and Children's Home	120
St. Francis Xavier's School	122
The Shanghai Library	125
The Shanghai Museum	127
The Kiang-su Acid, Chemical, and Soap Works	130
The Match Factory	134
A Trip on the Yangtze-kiang from Shanghai to Hankow	136
A Description of Peking	161
Temple of Kwang-ti, Peking	163
A Journey to the West of China	165
A House-Boat Trip to the Hills	181

INDEX OF ILLUSTRATIONS.

Chinese Theatricals	... facing page	6
Chinese Priests	,, ,,	16
Temple in the City	,, ,,	32
The Aquarius Company's Steam Factory and Water Distillery	,, ,,	44
Chinese Wheelbarrow	,, ,,	70
Chinese Amahs	,, ,,	94
The Cangue	,, ,,	97
The Chain-Gang	,, ,,	98
Chinkiang	,, ,,	142
The Hills—Fung-Wang-San	,, ,,	181

INTRODUCTION.

THESE "Sketches," hasty limnings in printer's ink, have for the most part appeared at irregular intervals in the *Shanghai Mercury*, and in some cases have already been published in book form. They are now republished *in extenso*, in the hope that they may prove of some utility, or offer some amusement to that section of the great English-speaking public who take an interest in the peoples and manners of the Far East. They do not pretend to enter into abstruse questions of polity or science, but take up the more familiar matters of daily life, as they present themselves in the microcosm known as Shanghai. It may be said that the Chinaman is many-sided : the Chinese Question decidedly is,—but on that we do not propose to enter. However, the individual, if not many-sided,—for it is out of order to speak of sides in a figure whose complaisant roundness takes the place of European angularity,—to be understood, requires to be painted from many points of view. From one of them, that of the ordinary resident in one of the Treaty Ports, the present "Sketches" are taken. Withal, it is a by no means easy matter for the average European to evolve from his inner consciousness the native of the Middle Kingdom, as the Chinaman loves to call his home. The Willow Pattern is still the predominant image in our imaginations. Faces like the moon, moustaches drawn out and drooping at the ends, eyes set at strange angles with the horizon, long tails, and hats shaped like pagodas are, of course, his predominant features. His surroundings are equally quaint : a pagoda or two, impossible bridges spanning innumerable waterways, trees with blue fruit hanging in huge clusters ; fair ladies, with long fantastic skirts gathered in huge folds about their feet and ankles, and bare-headed urchins fishing in ponds amidst lotus-flowers, and with one foot chronically raised in mid-air. Such are the landscapes conjured up by nine Europeans out of ten when their attention is called to matters Chinese. To the resident, even for a few months, the Chinaman, on the other hand, seems a very ordinary individual,—vulgar, selfish, and by no means cleanly in person or mind. His manners are out of a book, bookish: for every occasion he has a code of etiquette, firm and immutable, but in the ordinary amenities of life he is too often utterly wanting in natural politeness. The fact of his having had laboriously to study his code of artificial propriety,—in fact, has weakened his natural instinct; and the most flagrant breaches of what even a savage learns to respect are openly committed, even by individuals of high rank. High rank is, in fact, no test of accomplished manners; the exact way of bowing or prostrating himself before an equal or superior are, indeed, matters of anxious study, as the least departure from rule would entail heavy penalties in one form or other; but of what we would call the ordinary politeness due from one gentleman to another few traces are left, and the possession of the most graceful manner counts little beside the slavish obedience to precedent in externals. That graceful polish and chivalrous attention to the feelings of others which the social usages of the West require, and more especially the refinement proceeding from the free association of woman and the social equality of the sexes, is in China utterly absent. Of Society as we understand it there is no trace, nor is it easy to convey the idea to a Chinese mind.

We do not, however, propose to enter on the introspective stage: our point of view is essentially an outside one; and our views of Chinese life are distant perspectives, where, we feel, too many of the details are hidden with the mist that the Oriental loves to evolve about him.

Shanghai is, however, in many respects a favourable field for these telescopic views, with which we hope to amuse and, perhaps, in a measure instruct our readers. It is essentially the "show" place of China, and thither resort not merely the eager merchant, but the *jeunesse dorée* of the Empire, who, in the abundance of its pleasures and the freedom of its institutions, seek some relief from that oppressive *ennui* which is the lot of all those in China not actually in office or engaged in the toils of business. Here we meet with the smug-faced and crafty Cantonese, the *beau ideal* of all that is objectionable in the Chinese character. Selfish and ungrateful to a degree, he is to be found aiding and abetting every movement for the supercession of the Foreigner, to whom he owes everything in life. Hither resorts the more decided Fuhkien-man, who, as a colonist in the Straits and elsewhere, has shown himself in many respects worthy of esteem. Here, in numbers, are to be found the more angular natives of Chehkiang, mostly born in Ningpo or Chusan, and who, clannish to a fault, jealous of all external influences, wary and unprogressive in business, may be looked upon as the Scotch of China. Here, too, we may meet with natives of Shansi, a larger race, fond of money for its own sake, enterprising and born financiers, to whom is often given the title of the "Jews of China." Here, too, from the Yangtze Provinces, come the small round-headed inhabitant of Hunan, the soul of China as he thinks himself, whose prowess saved the Empire from the Taipings, and now seeks, under the name of patriotism, to expel the hated Foreigner; who hounds missionaries to death, cuts down telegraph poles and produces such literature as the "Death Blow to Corrupt Doctrines." Hither, too, come the merchants from Tientsin and the North,—stalwart fellows, free and easy in their ways, and little troubled about the questions that agitate their fellows in the South: ready to trade and ready to fight, but withal a more generous race than their fellows in Mid-China.

Still, in spite of these marked differences between the provinces, the Chinese as a nation are wonderfully homogeneous. A common language, common cult, a common dress, a community of family and social institutions, and a common government, have tended to fuse into one the natives from the frontiers of Annam to the heart of Mongolia. The people think in the same grooves, and have the same social distinctions and national aspirations. Notwithstanding dialectic differences, the language as a whole is one, and the *lingua franca* at Shanghai, albeit founded on a jargon, barbarous to northern ears, is readily comprehensible by all, and forms a close bond of union. There is thus no inducement to form outside connections. The Chinese, here as elsewhere, are as distinct as if they belonged to a separate species, and take care to let this be felt. Above all other nations they excel in this particular; and none—not even the Irish in the United States—know so well how to bring into effect these combinations. This forms at once their strength and their weakness,—their strength, as practically giving them the command when divergent interests come into play; and their weakness, by exciting ill-will and rendering them more or less disliked when mixing with other races.

Even their vices are separate and distinct. Their partiality for opium, especially in the form of smoking, is distinctly a national characteristic. Their immorality is marked; yet it is carried on under an outward show of propriety that might give a lesson to others. The streets of the Settlement exhibit no outward signs of vice; the police record is marked by the general absence of crimes of violence; yet pilfering is a national characteristic, and prevails in the highest quarters. Nothing passes through their hand without leaving traces of the passage.

Filthy to an extreme, they yet can talk of sanitation; and the Native who rents from a Foreigner a house within the Settlements will talk as seriously of ill-drainage and bad odours as if for the first time in his life he had been exposed to insanitory conditions. As a nation, the Chinese are not addicted to truth; yet no people will more scrupulously observe its word in matters of business, for the Chinese who deliberately breaks his agreement is a marked man. No nation is less moral in the ordinary ways of life; yet from time to time proclamations, couched in terms of the highest morality, are issued,—too often, it is true, with the intention of reaping a rich harvest from their breach. Still, homage is paid to virtue in the act. "Assume a virtue if thou have it not" is an axiom understood and acted on by China.

But we wander. We started to write an "Introduction," and we have been discoursing of all things. After all it is wonderful how we get on and how we square matters off. Of course, we can only carry on affairs in our unique Settlements by mutual concessions. Our Chinese friends like many of our customs, and, being of a generally tolerant mood, put up with the rest. If we like to air ourselves in the afternoon, so do they; if we like to sport liveries, so do they. They take a mild interest in our races, look with complacency on our volunteers; smile, rather contemptuously than otherwise, when our town band discourses sweet music, and wonder why Chevalier VELA prefers the bassoon to a good, honest gong. They use our gas, appreciate our water supply, and admire, so far as the celestial mind can exercise itself in the effort, our electric light. But they are not going to introduce gas for themselves; nor is one town in

China a whit better governed that they have seen what can be done in the way of policing the Settlements. All these things are well enough for the Foreigner who has been brought up to them, but the man of Han heedeth them not. They are in his idea a passing fancy, and, like all ephemeral growths, will pass away as fast as they came. When, under Octavius, the Roman Empire flashed forth in a coruscation of glory, that of China was already nearly two centuries old. Amidst troubles, it is true, rebellions and changes of dynasty, the Empire, founded by the great Tsin Shi Hwangti, still survives, with its essential principles unchanged. There is no interval in China corresponding to the Dark Ages in Europe: and no such break as separates the Roman Empire from the monarchies of to-day. Even in the short period since European intercourse began many have been the changes. The Portuguese, the first "openers" of China, are now little better than pensionaries in the petty settlement of Macao. The Dutch, who contested empire with them, have now virtually disappeared. The United States flag, that once floated proudly in Chinese waters, has now practically deserted them. Great Britain, that stormed in 1842, now takes a second place. No one then talked of steam-boats or railways, or electric telegraphs or lights. They are only the mushroom growths of half a century; who knows but that in another half century they will have ceased to exist?

It is frequently said of the Chinaman that he does not understand the value of time. This is in some degree true, but, like all truisms, is founded on a mass of error. He is keen in completing a time bargain, and, as is natural in a country where interest is high, understands the evils of delay. He is, however, never in that state of mental high pressure that distinguishes the European, and more especially the American, in these electric days. His nerves are not so tightly strung, and the vibrations take longer in their passage to and from his brain. Who knows that he may not in this be in the right, and that our high civilisation of the nineteenth century may not in itself bear the seeds of internal decay?

Like the French philosopher who told us that all things come to him who knows how to wait, the Chinaman has learnt the efficacy of remaining at ease. A generation or two is but an insignificant increment in the long procession of the past; it will doubtless be equally insignificant in the future. Such is undoubtedly one of the most prevalent ideas in the Chinese brain. "What," said Li Hung-chang, naïvely, when he saw a new British ironclad, "do the English still know how to build ships of war?" It seemed but natural that the new art rapidly acquired should be as rapidly forgotten, and that a space of thirty years was amply sufficient. The "Sketches," slight as they professedly are, may throw some side-lights on these topics, and it is in the hope of enlisting the sympathies of our readers that we now launch them on the stream. Perhaps a waif cast here or there on the bank may prove itself not altogether unworthy of preservation.

J. D. CLARK.

" SHANGHAI MERCURY " AND " CELESTIAL EMPIRE " OFFICES,

Nanking Road,

SHANGHAI, 26th July, 1894.

SKETCHES IN AND AROUND SHANGHAI.

THE PERFORMANCES AT A CHINESE THEATRE.

ACCORDING to a legend which is known to every Chinaman, the Emperor Tong Ming Wang, of the Tong Dynasty, visited the moon in company with his wives, concubines, and all his retinue, and they were there enchanted by witnessing a host of young girls acting tableaus; and to this wonderful legendary expedition of Tong Ming Wang is attributed the origin of what exists to this day as the Chinese theatrical performance of ancient historical plays and modern comedies. In all the towns and cities of the Empire, theatrical performances are conducted either by travelling companies or in regularly established theatres. When the Chinese congregate in any foreign part,—such as San Francisco,—they have their own theatres there too. In this large community of Shanghai, where, in the native City and the Foreign Settlements, about 250,000 Celestials have their abode, the native theatre is a great institution, and is patronised on a very extensive scale. There are at present, we believe, four large theatres in the English Settlement, and one in the French Concession, which are in full swing every day. The natives therefore have no lack of amusement of this particular kind; and though the performances seem passing strange to a foreigner, the Chinese take great delight in them. The theatres are open nearly all day, and from seven o'clock in the evening till midnight, and during all the performances, especially in the evening, the houses are crowded. Some of the theatres employ about 125 actors, all males, and the principal professionals, who have earned some fame in their own sphere, are thought a good deal of by the people; but the large proportion of the young men and boys brought on the stage are only of the lowest order. We visited one of the theatres last night—the Chin Kwai Yuen in the Fuhkien Road—and now give a description of what we saw there. Our party was made up of three or four Europeans, and a Chinese gentleman who acted as interpreter.

The theatre is a large square building, standing off from the side of the street, and the approach to it is by a broad alley, the two-storeyed shops and tea-houses on either hand being lighted up, and the frontage of the theatre itself illuminated; the Fuhkien Road is crowded so densely with Chinamen, that it is difficult to walk along amongst them, and the entrance to the theatre is also crowded—jinricshas and sedan chairs and their coolies being the chief obstructions. The loud beating of gongs, the singing, or rather screaming of actors, and the laughter of the Celestials inside, are heard as soon as we come to the entrance, and our friends are fully convinced that the fun is already going on "fast and furious." In the hall or lobby there are a number of Chinese attendants; the box office and cloak room are amalgamated, and are in form more like a small shop, with a large counter, than anything else. An attendant led the way to a private box, overlooking the right hand side of the stage; the box had to be engaged a couple of days beforehand, and was fitted up in tolerably decent style: to reach it we had to ascend a rather shaky staircase, and walk through the front and right galleries. The area or pit of the theatre is marked off in a square surrounded by a wooden railing; the space is filled by five rows of small tables, five or six in each row; each of these tables is sufficient for the accommodation of four persons, who sit on small wooden chairs. The whole of this part was packed full with Chinese; judging by their appearance the majority were merchants, or shopkeepers, or at least in tolerably good circumstances; they were all well-dressed, the dark purple cloak or jacket being the general array. Outside the rails there is a space around three sides of the building for a cheaper class of seats, and the occupants were one mass of blue cottons. In the galleries, which are only of small breadth, part of the left hand side was occupied by one or two private boxes, and the rest was laid out with small tables and chairs; the front gallery, of considerable length, and greater breadth than the others, had no private boxes at all, but had one row of the tables as the "front seats," and behind them a passage through which we had passed, while further back, and more elevated, there were several rows of tables. The right hand gallery was chiefly composed of private boxes, and the one reserved for our accommodation was close to the stage, and about ten feet directly above the side of it. All over the house the tables were furnished with fruits—pears and oranges; saucers full of roasted watermelon seeds; small green cups for tea, which we drank *a la Chinoise;* and vermilion coloured sheets of paper, on which was printed the programme of the day's performances. Space is reserved between all the rows of tables, and a small balcony is fixed in front of the private boxes for the use of the servants, who continually keep running about with huge black kettles, from which they pour the hot water on the tea leaves in the small green cups, and then it is ready for drinking; or to renew a supply of fruit, or to supply paper lights—for on every table there are the large hubble-bubble tobacco pipes of brass and some of silver;—none of the foreigners in our party had any objection to the *a la Chinoise* as long as it was the tea, or fruit, or cakes, or even the hubble-bubble pipes that were to be tried; but when the coolie came round with a handful of heavy cloths, soaked in hot water, and steaming, he could not get any foreigner in our box to take one and use it as the Chinese do—to wipe the perspiration off their hands and face.

The stage is a wooden platform, standing four feet above the level of the floor of the house, and two huge pillars stand at each corner in front of the stage, for supporting the roof; but they are also made use of for very primitive gas fixtures in the way of footlights, and two or three brackets project from the pillars, giving the light of a few burners to the stage, others to the gallery, and others to the pit; the rest of the house being tolerably well lighted by gas. The pillars are also utilized in another way than for gas fixtures, for about fifteen feet above the stage, a horizontal bar is fixed in them, on which acrobatic performances are given. As

A POWERFUL ORCHESTRA.

seen from the front, there is a large ornamental board stretching across the pillars, and on it there are in huge gilt letters the name of the theatre. There is no scenery about the stage; the back of it is only a partition, composed chiefly of panels, in carved wood. In the centre is a large pier glass—mirrors are charms for the Chinese, but whether this one is meant for a universal charm to all present, we don't know; it is more likely that it is there for use rather than ornament, for the actors change their robes and head-dresses in front of it, instead of retiring to do that off the stage. A number of Chinese scrolls, in vermilion with gold letters, are hung on the partition; and two prominent objects are the American clocks, which are hung up, one on each side of the pier glass, one clock going much faster than the other. On either side of the panelled and ornamented wall are two doors, one for the entrance of the actors to the stage, and the other for their exit; they are open doorways, hung with curtains that once were bright in colour, but now are sadly in need of a wash. Above the clocks, mirror, and ornamented panels, there are four pictures, the only native "works of art" about the stage,—they are not very large pieces, each about four feet square, and the two flank ones are representations of trees and flowers, with a very hazy, grey, watery sort of look about them; the two subjects in the centre are possibly historical scenes, for they are groups of figures and bits of landscape wonderfully mixed up. The middle of the stage is covered with a carpet which might once have been in the parlour of a foreign resident; it is now rather threadbare, and has been patched with canvas in the centre. At the various corners of the stage, and all around it, there are small tables and chairs lying about, handy for utilization in the production of the wonderful stage effects which are to be presented.

The band consists of seven or eight old men, who sit around two tables at the back of the stage; and with drums, gongs, cymbals, flutes, and pieces of hard wood, they were able to make as much noise as any other band on the face of the earth. The leader of the band sat there with a small drum, fixed on the top of a stand, the drum being made of sheepskin stretched over a circular frame of wood, about twelve inches in diameter; he beats this curious drum with a small stick—just like a chopstick or a pencil; while he is beating slowly with the right hand, he has two oblong pieces of rosewood in the left hand, and beats them by shaking his hand, one piece being held firmly and the other loosely attached with a string; but when the leader comes to a part where he is to make a supreme effort, or to do his level best in making a terrific noise, he throws down the rosewood crackers—(analogous to the negro minstrel's "bones")—and with a chopstick in each hand he knocks thunder out of that small sheepskin drum. Behind the leader, an old man stands beating a gong,—he stands because he could not beat the gong if he were sitting down; but he omits no opportunity of taking it easy on his chair, if his gong music is not required for a minute or two. This gong genius is no doubt well up to his duty, and he looks as if he considered *his* part of the performance the most skilful; at any rate he can strike hard enough, and that seems to be the main thing; he can also strike so as to give one distinct peal, instead of the long booming sound produced by the vibration of the gong; he strikes hard, and then puts his hand on the gong, which stops the sound instanter. Another bandsman beats the cymbals, and makes a clattering noise in a most miscellaneous manner. Four fiddlers sit round a table and play their curiously shaped instruments with great power—so far as infernal noise is concerned; a musical friend thought they were playing the same tune all night, and we guess he was pretty correct. An Irishman once said he did not know whether he could play the violin, because he had never tried; but we think anyone could play as well on a Chinese fiddle the first time he tried as the bandsmen of the theatre did; an amateur could certainly play something more like sacred, operatic, or dance music the first time he tried, but he might not be able to come near the Celestial orchestra in head-splitting noises. The man with the gong also makes himself useful at times in producing a loud noise by striking two pieces of hard wood; and another old man shuffles about the stage, at one time shifting the chairs and tables, and again taking part in the performance of the band; his part, too, was highly intellectual,—he held a piece of hardwood in the palm of his left hand, and struck it with another stick he wielded in his right; this old man shuffled about so listlessly that in spite of the tremendous noise he seemed to be half asleep. Occasionally, when there was a cessation in the uproar, some of the bandsmen enjoyed a smoke out of long bamboo-stem tobacco pipes; in fact they did not seem to care much whether they all played together or not, for even when they were executing some grand transcription, one of the head fiddlers would stop all of a sudden and not resume until he had filled and lit his pipe, and we thought it was an improvement,—it would certainly have been more pleasant if they had all followed his example.

The plays presented at the Chinese Theatres are chiefly historical, and some of them go on for years before being completed; the whole history of a dynasty is acted in one play, part of it being given every day. But they have also pieces which are more like the comedy of two or three acts, although they make such pieces all one act, and the whole play is presented without the adventitious aid of scenery; the costumes are studied, and the characters make up their styles with a considerable amount of skill; the dialogue is the main thing, and the spectators stretch their imagination to make up for the want of scenery. The remark made by Sir Philip Sydney in regard to the English drama and the stage in 1583, was applied to the Chinese by Sir John Davis, and it is certainly an appropriate one:—"Now you shall have three ladies walk to gather flowers, and then we must believe the stage to be a garden. By and by we have news of a shipwreck in the same place; then we are to blame if we accept it not for a rock. Upon the back of that comes out a hideous monster with fire and smoke, and then the miserable beholders are bound to take it for a cave; while in the meantime two armies fly in, represented with four swords and bucklers, and then what hard heart will not receive it for a pitched field?"

The play-bill of the Chin Kwai Yuen, for Friday last, was a fairly representative one; it included a portion of an ancient historical play, a trial, a comedy, a farcical piece, another comedy, and finished up with a historical play. The actors at the theatre were all from Tientsin, as is the case also with other three of the native theatres, and a fifth one is conducted by Soochow actors. When we entered the theatre about nine o'clock in the evening, we found that the piece then on the boards was the trial of a man on the charge of murder. The judge was dressed in a richly embroidered robe of blue and white silk; he wore a long white beard coming down on his breast, but neither his whiskers, beard, nor moustache fitted well; they hung loosely about his face, and though these hirsute appendages imparted a patriarchal appearance to the actor when seen at a distance, it was comical enough to see him close at hand, when one could see through between his whiskers and his cheek. The judge's head-dress was a richly embroidered cap, and he wore curious wing-shaped things standing right out from the side of his head. His felt-shoes were enormous, in the thickness of the soles,—about three inches, painted white, and the toes as bluff as the square bow of a native boat. The old judge stalked abóut the stage in a dignified manner, reciting something with a shrieking voice, and his attendants joined him in his declamations, but all their shouting was drowned by the band behind them. The runners and other attendants were dressed very much the same as the subordinates and runners of a native magistrate are,—there was nothing out of place in their appearance; about half a dozen small boys wóre the conical red hat, just exactly the same as we have seen in the retinue of the Taotai or the District Magistrate. The prisoner who was being tried had nothing whatever to say for himself; he was in charge of two runners, who made him lie down on the stage before the judge, who appeared on his bench—three small chairs and a table thrown together;—and after the trial was hurried through, the judge doing all the speaking, the prisoner was dragged up by two runners and his hands bound behind his back. In this way he was led out at one door of the stage and in at another—he had gone from the judgment-hall to the place of execution, and now the two men who had charge of him were black villainous-looking fellows, wearing hideous masks. The wonderful scenic effects which stretch the imagination were again put together—in the shape of two chairs, and an upright post, to which the prisoner was tied for half a minute, and then an executioner flourished a tinfoil sword, dropped a dirty red bag—the culprit's head—on the floor, the old culprit fell down at full length, and was then picked up and carried on the shoulders of four men off the stage, with full power music by the band.

No time was wasted by unnecessary details, such as scene shifting; the band only gave us a moment's relief by stopping their music, and one of the old bandsmen took the opportunity to light his tobacco pipe; then the leader resumed beating his drum,—the gong, cymbals, and fiddles all went hard at work again, and the actors in the next piece came on the stage. This was a comedy in which, as explained by our friend, there was a good deal of interest. A young married pair first came on the stage and sat down beside each other without saying a word. They were plainly dressed, and their reputation as actors was not of much account, for they had nothing to do but sit there quietly. A third party came in who was the chief character in the play; he was a professional thief, and he made a visit to the decorous couple with the avowed intention of stealing something from them. This old thief was shabbily dressed, a threadbare black gown covering him from head to foot, and tied with a girdle of white cotton; his felt-shoes were worn out, the soles being very thin; he wore a long black moustache, his face was disfigured by red paint on his forehead and chin, the tip of his nose shone brilliantly, while under his eyes and over the bridge of his nose there was a layer of white plaster; he had no queue visible—he was either completely bald, or wore a skull-cap very neatly adjusted; at any rate there was not a hair to be seen on his head, and his red cap was too small to stay on, as there was nothing to hold by; his whole appearance was most grotesque. He came forward to the footlights and sang there for a long time, creating great amusement amongst the audience, for he was bouncing about all his smart thieving tricks, and telling them that he was to steal something from the young lady; he was sure he could do it without detection. He then turned to the quiet husband and wife; conversed with them in a half singing, half chanting tone, telling them a great lot of lies about himself, and cunningly obtaining information from the lady as to where she kept all her valuables, money, jewels, and rich clothing; and immediately afterwards he tells the audience that he has stolen several things from her. Two men then come in to protect the house; they were the ghosts of the ancestors of the family! Ghosts! they were more like sea-monsters than anything else. They were short in stature, and each wore embroidered robes in variegated colours; one had long black hair, and the other white hair hanging down his back; but the most remarkable things about them were their heads—such monstrosities, more dolphin-like than human; they were about half the size of their bodies, with earrings like handcuffs; and each ghost carried a huge drum stick in his right hand. The thief pretended to be unaware of their presence, and the ghosts moved about the stage, touching the tip of the old rogue's nose with the leather ball of the drumstick, which made the thief sneeze and look as if he were getting suspicious of coming harm. The head ghost then took a dog chain off his waist, and lassoed the thief while the latter was singing of his exploits; the thief fainted and fell down, and the master and mistress of the house were screaming with terror, while the band played their level best; the ghosts then exhibited their muscular power by lifting up the thief and carrying him off the stage, and reappeared at the entrance in a few moments, with the thief sufficiently recovered to walk on his own legs. Then the ghosts summoned others of their fellow-countrymen, who were soon crowding the stage, and among them was the fellow who acted the part of judge in the former play, and here again he appears as a judge, but in a different garb this time. The tables and chairs are shifted about by one of the supernumerary bandsmen, and a bench is once more thrown up for the ghostly judge. The thief performs the kotow before him, and a few words from the judge are all that are necessary for the trial and condemnation of the accused. The sentence this time is flogging, and a small stout boy, dressed as a runner, with a conical red hat, comes forward with a bamboo stick,—a long, thin, and flat piece. The two ancestral ghosts throw the thief on the stage face downwards, and the runner has meanwhile stripped himself of everything except his pants, and shows a muscular arm which makes the thief shaky. The runner seizes the bamboo stick with both hands, and pretends to give the thief a very hard blow, while the thief yells and rolls about as if suffering great pain. The ghosts let go their hold of the thief, and the latter gets on his feet and beckons to the runner that he wants to speak to him; the two then move off to the side of the stage by themselves, and the thief bribes the runner not to strike hard, but to give the remainder of the blows as gently as he can,—the thief in this part showing by the movement of his hands what he means; the runner eagerly accepts some papers from the thief, and nods, as much as to say that he would make it all right. The judge during all this time is sitting on his bench motionless and speechless. The thief goes down on the floor without fear of his flogging, and the runner now lets the bamboo only touch the thief gently—the proceedings being a caricature of what is frequently done at the Mixed Court here, and the representation evidently took well with the audience. The thief having been subjected to the sham flogging is released, the ghostly court adjourns, and the thief and the quiet man and wife are left on the stage; the thief was presumed to have returned them the articles he was supposed to have stolen; and the parties were so well pleased over this that they invited the old villain to stay with them. Thus ended the amusing comedy, and the actors made their exit.

After this comedy a farce was performed, which seems to be a favourite with the Chinese theatre-goers, for we had seen it performed before at another theatre in the Canton Road, and now it was produced at the Chin Kwai Yuen, and on both occasions the spectators seemed to enjoy

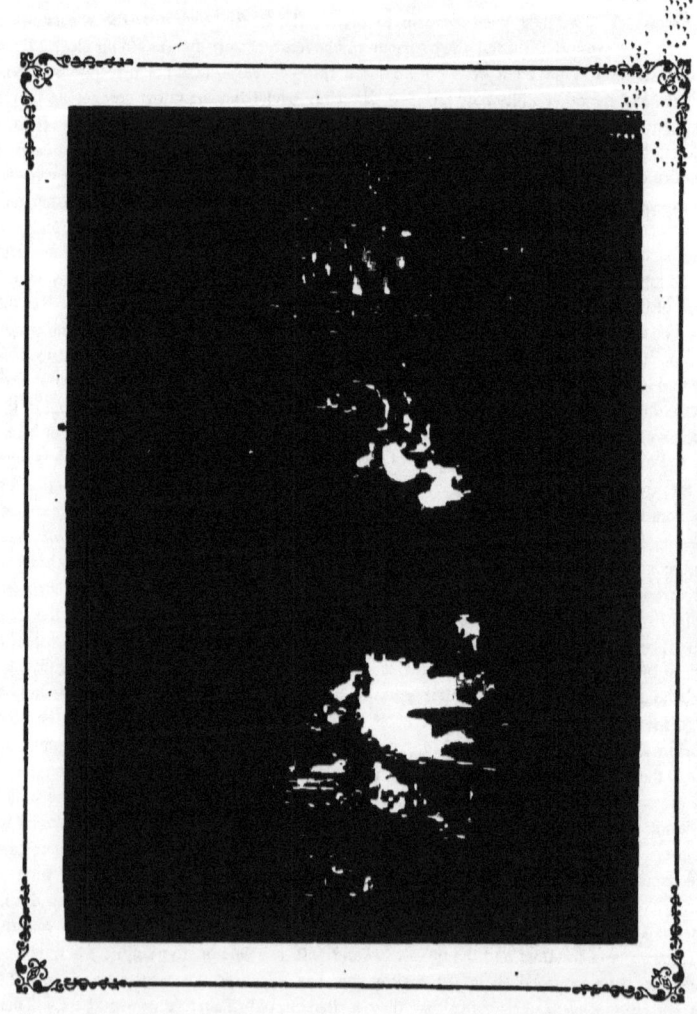

CHINESE THEATRICAL.

it very much, for they were kept in roars of laughter; but the worst feature of it was that the dialogue was of a nature unfit to be laid before European readers. The actors were a lame man, his doctor, and servants, and a concubine and her father and mother, or other aged relatives; and the only thing about the piece we care to describe was the style in which the female was made up. As we have already remarked, all the actors of the Chinese stage are males; the actor who has to take a female part, however, can make up very well in attire, and assume a feminine tone of voice, so that the deception can scarcely be detected. The actor always appears with the small feet of the Chinese lady, and this is secured by the device of wooden blocks, to which his ordinary-sized feet are strapped in an angular position, while the wood is so cut that the bandaged ankle is a true representation, and the small shoe of painted wood is exactly like the most diminutive silken shoe that encases the cramped toes of the fairest "tottering lily." The actor thus standing on pegs represents a rather tall female —taller than the generality of Chinese females are; he walks about the stage with the real tottering gait of a small-footed female; in fact, it is not imitation on his part, for his own natural feet being strapped in an unnatural position to the blocks of wood, he cannot walk otherwise. The pseudo-female actor was dressed in very rich and showy garments,—the wide trousers of purple cloth were not particularly attractive, but the jacket with deep border in beautiful embroidery was really a fine article. His face was naturally brazen, but the application of *rouge* made his cheeks look like those of a female painted to the extreme, as the cheeks of females, Chinese and others, frequently are; his lips were painted a brighter red than they naturally were, and he showed a fine pearly set of teeth. The forehead was large, the wig being worn far back, the jet-black hair parted in the middle, while the artificial decorations, by the hair being twisted in fantastic shapes at the back of the head, and stuck with jewelled hairpins, and the rose-shaped, yellow-coloured ornaments covering the ears, were all true to a nicety as a perfectly made up head-dress of a Chinese lady. The actor who took this part seemed to be one of the principal ones, and there is no doubt he showed a considerable amount of skill. But this is enough for this piece; the quarrel with the old man and his concubine was not an interesting subject.

Another play in one act followed, and there were only two actors; they had the stage to themselves for about half an hour, and their performance was wearisome, although not altogether devoid of amusement; but we were told the dialogue was a very interesting one to the natives. It represented the domestic life of a blacksmith and his wife, who were first on loving terms with each other, then quarrelled and made it up again. The wife came in first, very plainly dressed, and without ever saying a word she sat down on a small stool, made of bamboo, and only about four inches square. An ordinary wooden chair,—Chinese imitation of the foreign style of a common kitchen chair,—was standing on the stage, a few feet in front of the silent spouse of the blacksmith; but who would ever have supposed that that plain article of household furniture, standing all alone, was meant for scenery or spectacular effect? When the old woman was handed a long piece of bamboo by one of the supernumerary bandsmen, or a scene-shifter perhaps, and she began pushing that bamboo stick slowly backward and forward under the chair, we tried to stretch our imagination as much as possible, but were unable to guess what she was supposed to be doing. Oh, her husband was a blacksmith, our Chinese friend told us, and the old woman was working in his shop, drawing out and in the bar of the fire-box, for the Chinese have a curious substitute for the bellows of the village blacksmith, as their box-furnace is worked by pulling out and shoving in a wooden bar, or bars, which by some arrangement or other create a flow of fresh air to fan the flame. The woman kept on at this monotonous occupation, with slow music by the fiddlers, for more than five minutes, and then her husband came in and walked about the stage with rather an operatic air, singing not very unpleasantly if he had not kept it up so long, for he had more than ten minutes of it, during which time his wife had left the fire-box, removed her miniature camp-stool, and sat down in the centre of the stage with her back to the spectators, the little finger of her right hand in her mouth, and looking quite disconsolate. After the blacksmith had had his say he sat down on—a brick. The wife then rose and took an empty bowl and a pair of chopsticks from a table, lifted her stool over beside her husband, and there sat down, while the village blacksmith placed his right hand on her shoulder and looked very pleasantly at her when he saw the rice-bowl and chopsticks. They went through the motions, which is as much as any actors do in having a dinner on the stage, and then the bowl and chopsticks were taken away by a member of the orchestra. A quarrel took place, and very loud screaming words were used on both sides; they rose simultaneously, and the blacksmith picked up his seat—the brick—and threw it at his wife's head; but she was as smart as the catcher at a base ball match, and catching the brick she threw it down on her husband's feet, after which he pretended to have had his corns very severely injured. There was a good deal of yelling over this little domestic riot, but it was soon over, and they sat down again beside each other as pleasantly as ever. Another quarrel occurred, and the offensive was this time assumed by the better-half, who gave the blacksmith a slight push, and as he had only a very precarious seat on the brick, he rolled backwards on the stage. While this second quarrel was proceeding a man came in hawking wearing apparel, and the blacksmith bought a new suit of clothes for himself and made his exit from the stage, his wife following him in a very slow and unconcerned manner, and the spectators saw them no more.

During the whole time occupied by the preceding piece, preparations were being made on the stage for a grand historical representation—the concluding part of the evening's performances. The orchestra had to remove their tables and chairs from the back to the right-hand side of the stage in order to make room for the erection of a grand piece of scenery—the most magnificent thing in its way produced that night. Throughout the evening we had noticed a heap of wooden frame-work and canvas lying at one corner of the stage, and fully expected that it was to be utilised for something or other. Some of the bandsmen and other scene-shifters set to work to put these wooden frames together, while the gong-genius laid down his musical instrument, and, climbing up on the top of a table, put one of the American clocks a quarter of an hour forward, to bring it up to the hour indicated by the other time-piece—eleven o'clock. The stage carpenter and his subordinates, with assistants from the orchestra, first put up one piece of wooden frame work, which was exactly like a "punch and judy" box, and other two or three smaller pieces were placed alongside of it, each separate piece being constructed with four or more upright posts, and numerous cross-bars and supporting brackets; the whole had a front elevation of about ten feet in length, and eight in height; and the frontage was covered with canvas, painted dark green, with flowers and figures in lighter colours. The green waterproofs of two or three jinricsha coolies would have made a better bit of scenery. A box, something like a dovecot, was fixed on the top of the frames, and in another a large pole was placed, resting on the stage and towering above the frame-work and canvas; a good deal of hard work was required to get all the pieces fixed together. The "punch and judy" box was finally surmounted by a square frame with an arched piece of bamboo attached to the front bar, and from it a piece of canvas was hung, which completed the representation of a grand arched window or doorway; another canvas-covered frame was placed in front of the whole erection, and possibly it was meant for a range of steps, or a balcony,—in fact, it might have been meant for a garden or anything else; at any rate the upper half of the "punch and judy" box was left open, except that a loose curtain hung over it, and it was evidently meant for a window or doorway. And what did all this rickety pile or wood and canvas represent? Why, it was a palace, of course; and an imperial palace! After it had been all put together, the actors of the last comedy were just making their exit,—the band had settled down in their new position and seemed to be making more noise than ever—(for they were now right in front of our box)—and the actors in the concluding piece came on the stage. We were told it was to be an historical play; the first part of it certainly wasn't, but we had seen the same sort of thing in Chinese historical plays before—a curious mixing up of acrobatic feats, tumbling somersaults, sword exercise, fighting, singing, and everything mixed together. The first lot of actors who now came in were four acrobats, who went through a lot of manœuvres, striking attitudes, and moving about the stage in a manner somewhat approximating to certain movements in dancing a Scotch reel; and they were singing all the time. They afterwards tumbled somersaults, and one of the chief actors was the individual who had appeared in the farce as a small-footed lady; he still wore the artificial small feet, and he showed considerable ability as an acrobat when he tumbled somersaults and lighted on the awkward wooden pegs which represented the small feet of a Chinese lady. Another actor came carrying in his hands a small wooden board—it might have done for a knife-board—and he went through some very strange evolutions; he laid down the board on the stage, in an angular position in front of the palace, and then drew himself up in a peculiar attitude and walked over the board; his dress was a very strange mixture of bright colours, and he wore a white mask, with black beard and moustache; what he was meant for we don't know, and it took some considerable time before we discovered what he meant by lifting about that wooden board. The tumblers having retired, four young men came in, carrying the body of another on their shoulders; in coming forward they all walked over this mysterious board, and then went up in front of the palace and shoved the fellow they had on their shoulders in at the "punch and judy" box window; he had barely room to get through it without bringing the whole erection down, but he soon reappeared behind it and walked out at the door by which he had half a minute before been carried in. The old white-masked fellow picked up his board and walked out too—his board was meant for a bridge! Another acrobat then came in, and kicked about on the stage for some time, throwing his feet very high in the air till he touched his toes with his hand; he kicked himself about at one corner of the stage, struck a bold attitude, waved his arms about promiscuously, rushed to another corner, and went through the same jumping and kicking performance. Then other four acrobats came in, threw themselves about on the stage, tumbling somersaults and jumping over each other; the one with the small feet "brought down the house" when he walked round the stage on his hands; two tables were next placed one above the other at the pillar at the left hand side of the stage, and two tables in the same way at the right side; two of the acrobats went to each side, scrambled up the tables, and got on to a horizontal bar fixed between the pillars, the four of them going through various feats on the bar all at the same time, and they descended one after the other by throwing back somersaults from the top of the tables,—coming down on the stage with great force, and almost breaking it down. They next had a small table placed on the stage by itself, and the four made a rush at it, tumbling somersaults over the table without touching it, and then made their exit. Well, this was all very well for acrobatic performances, but what was the imperial palace there for? We were anxious to see something of this piece which they called an historical play, but it was now about half-past eleven, and the band had given us a headache. The white-masked fellow came in again with his board and laid it down with solemnity; he was followed by four men, who crossed his plank, climbed up the front of the palace, and went down through the roof; one of them reappeared at the top, hung a red bag —meant for a head—on the big pole, and then he tumbled a somersault from the top of the palace wall; his comrades came out by the "punch and judy" box part of the palace, one of them carrying a female with dishevelled hair; she was lashed to his shoulders with ropes. This looked something more like a play. While the palace was thus entered by three or four fellows, several of the old men from the band, and others on the stage, had to come and hold the framework steady, else the whole palace would have toppled over! The ruffians who stole the female ran out at one door and in at another several times; three of them were armed with tinfoil swords, and the burden-bearer—the one who carried the female—was protected by them; he did not seem to have a very heavy burden, and the female was most likely only a bundle of rags. Another party of four or five armed men came to the palace, and seeing the red bag hanging on the pole, one climbed up and threw it down, tumbling a somersault after it; others entered the palace and rushed out again, raising a hue and cry, and they set off in pursuit of the other party. The offending party came on the stage again, and the white-faced fellow laid down his board for a bridge to let them pass over, but lifted it so that the others could not overtake them. The opposing parties increased in numbers, and kept rushing on to the stage and off again; at times half a dozen or more would engage in a fight and brandish swords and spears, dancing about the stage, and kicking up an awful row; the acrobats would come in and tumble somersaults in the middle of the opposing armies; and they kept up this sort of thing so long, without any appearance of coming to a crisis, that at a quarter to twelve o'clock we left them to fight it out.

THE CITY OF SHANGHAI; ITS STREETS, TEMPLES, PRISONS, AND GARDENS.

VISIT to Shanghai City is of very great interest to a foreigner when he has a Chinese friend with him who knows everything about the place, and although most foreigners here have been in it once or twice, there are very few who can say they have seen everything in it that is actually worth seeing, for many a one may only take a listless walk through some of its streets, pick up a few curios at the stalls, and, getting disgusted with the whole place, leave it as soon as he can possibly find his way out,—which is rather difficult to do sometimes,—and vow that he will never go within its walls again. On a Sunday afternoon we made up a party of three or four foreigners, and two Chinese friends. One of the latter knew the labyrinth of the City streets as well as a London hansom cab-driver knows the way from Cheapside to Piccadilly, and the other, who acted as interpreter, was a highly intelligent Chinese gentleman, educated at Yale College, U.S., and who is proud of being a naturalized American citizen. We entered the City at half-past two o'clock in the afternoon, and a beautiful day it was too— fine, clear, and the roads dry. The early winter is always the best season for exploring the City, because its sanitary state is then less obnoxious than in the heat of summer weather. The day was therefore in every respect favourable as far as the auspices were concerned; it was the seventeenth day of the 10th Moon. Whether it is set down in the Chinese Calendar as a favourable day for making a journey we don't know; at any rate we did not consider that much at the time, but from what we saw were convinced that the day was a special one with the Chinese, for the city seemed to be *en fête*, and one might go twenty times without seeing so much as was crowded into our visit extending over two and a half hours. We entered by the New North Gate, and at once proceeded towards what are known as the Tea Gardens. In our way thither we had to traverse about a dozen narrow streets, some leading south, others west, east, in fact in all directions; first we passed through a long street lined with shops and warehouses on each side; then by the side of a dirty stagnant creek, with shops on one hand; over a small bridge and along narrower streets, with the sky obscured from view by the wooden and canvas signboards and ornamental tablets stretching from one side of the street to the other; then over another bridge; through narrow and crowded streets, till we came to more open ground by the side of a creek, where there were crowds of licensed beggars,—male, female, old, maimed, and blind, and each of them holding out a basket with a few cash in it, while the poor creatures implore every passer-by to give them cash. The blind ones know when a foreigner passes, by his heavy tread, and the noise of hard-heeled boots on the rough granite blocks, for a Chinaman might walk over them in his felt-soled shoes without a blind man knowing that he passed. We never saw any of these beggars getting anything from a native, and when a foreigner gives them anything, he is sure to be followed by dozens of them all the way through the City—a mistake which we avoided, at least at this stage of the journey. The ground here is more open, and on both sides of the creek there is room for Celestial showmen and acrobats, fortune-tellers, and gamblers; but further on when we come to the large pond surrounding the old Tea House, there is quite a large market square, or "garden" as it is called. On this occasion every part of it was occupied, and the scene was almost as lively as Hampstead Heath on a Bank Holiday. A casual glance was all we had time to give them, but it was sufficient for our purpose. The first performer whose proceedings attracted our notice was an old man, who was surrounded by about fifty Celestials of all ages and both sexes; the old show-man had monopolised a small strip of ground by the side of the creek, and the eager spectators crowded round the performer on all sides, but still preserving a limited open space for him. He was a man who looked as if fifty years had passed over his head; his hair was becoming grey, and precious little tail left; he was stripped bare to the waist, but had on as much threadbare blue cottons—their original colour bleached out of them, and now only a mass of patches—in the shape of wide, very wide trousers, as would have made suits for two or three men; his old felt-shoes were in a very dilapidated state, and the excessive amount of cotton rags he wore for stockings, made his ankles of elephantine proportions. He now walked backward and forward on his strip of ground, throwing his arms about like a maniac; he smote his breast with his right hand, then with his left, stretched out both arms, and clenched his fists; walked round and then dropped his arms; walked round again with his hands hanging down, while he was looking anxiously for cash to be thrown into his ground; he then made a great effort, which was about all he could do,—he picked up an iron bolt, that any child might have lifted, threw it down, sticking it into the earth, and once more went on the walk round. He was a fraud, and though the Celestials might be content to look at him all day doing that, it is not probable that he made much money by it. Close by there was a small booth or tent, of bamboo and canvas, inside of which about half a dozen Chinamen were sitting. The proprietor of this concern was a fortune-teller and phrenologist. The old patriarchal humbug sat at the back of the tent; behind him the extravagant pictures of some Chinese worthies were hung in paper on the canvas; in front of the fortune-teller was his small table, with writing materials, joss-sticks, and other paraphernalia; and all round about there were eager observers, listening to the wonderful man reading the fortune of a well-to-do native, and watching the movements when the phrenologist placed his fingers on the bumps of his customers' craniums, then put on a long and sage countenance, and uttered profoundly wise sayings; put forth his hand to draw in the wealth just deposited by his constituent, while the latter tabled another five cash, and was determined to hear more of his fortune, at any expense. When we had passed the fortune-teller we came within sight of the "garden" where most of the shows were being held. There were about half a dozen peep-shows, in foreign style, the large ornamental box standing on a table, and the little peep-holes in the box through which the Celestials peered and witnessed the wonders of the world; several of the peep-shows had a decided appearance of foreign manufacture, in the showy glass cases with which they were surmounted, with pictures of palaces or international exhibition buildings, but we did not turn aside to see what they were. There was one old man there, amongst a crowd of itinerant fruit-sellers and confectioners, whose little game for obtaining chash in exchange for roast chestnuts was rather peculiar; he held in one hand three spikes of bamboo about six inches long, and to the end of one of these sticks a red silk thread was attached, but the sticks were so held that there was as much chance of winning in the "three card trick" as in choosing the bamboo with the thread; he manipulated for our benefit by picking up a cash and placing it on one of the sticks, then pulled the stick out, but it had no thread, repeating the trick several times, sometimes placing the cash on the stick with the thread attached, and at other times putting it on the wrong ones; then shifting them about till it was impossible to tell which was which; the evident arrangement being that a Celestial paid a few cash for a trial,—if successful he got a few roast chestnuts, and if unsuccessful—why then he didn't.

In this Celestial Vanity Fair there were numerous stalls for the sale of sweetmeats, pears, oranges, and cooked sweet-potatoes; stalls loaded with toys; stalls covered with classical literature; stalls of curios, with anything on them from valuable jade-stone ornaments to old nails and champagne corks. Hundreds of natives were loitering all over the place, many of them patronizing the peep-shows; the confectioners and sweetmeat stall-keepers appeared to be doing a good trade, to judge by the piles of cash lying on their tables; but it was at the open air performances of the acrobats, where there was no compulsory payment, where there were very few cash tossed into the ring, and where the sending round of the hat would have been the most effectual method of dispersing the crowd, that the natives gathered in the largest numbers. Near to a small temple or joss-house, on the east side of the Tea House lake, there was a crowd of people, and on looking over the shoulders of some of them, we could see that the attraction was gambling with dice; but close by there was another and much larger crowd, surrounding a couple of acrobatic performers, who were marching to and fro, striking peculiar attitudes, and evidently preparing for the execution of some feats of strength, tumbling, juggling, or some other mountebank tricks; but they were too much like the old man already described, making a great pretence and doing nothing, so that a momentary glance was all that we gave them. The joss-pidgin seemed to be at a discount in this Vanity Fair, for in the small Temple a few red wax-candles were burning at the shrine, but there was no devotee there save the old man in charge of the place.

We next turned our attention to the old Tea House and its artificial lake! Such a dirty dub of stagnant water to be called an artificial and ornamental lake! The small expanse of filthy water, with a skimming of green weeds on the surface, is enclosed by a wall coming up to the level of the ground round about; the lake, pond, or dub, is about thirty yards square, and in the centre stands the Hu-sing-ting, a public Tea House, which may be called the best and most airy institution of its kind in the City, as it is in a comparatively isolated position; but still there is nothing very refreshing in its situation,—the surrounding stagnant and fetid water makes its position little better than if it was in a small street with cook-houses on every side of it. The Tea House is approached by a long and zig-zag viaduct, which we were told was built fifteen hundred years ago; each pier is composed of two columns of grey granite, standing about three feet apart; on their top is laid a transverse block, and from it to a similar block, on the next pier, three huge slabs of the same everlasting rock are laid, forming a narrow pathway; the whole bridge being provided with low railings of strong woodwork, which must have been a work of more modern days. Granite blocks also form the foundations on which the Tea House is built, but the house is not nearly so old as the bridge. This Tea House is a fair specimen of Chinese architecture, but only on a small scale; it covers a very limited area, and rises to the height of two storeys, surmounted by a highly ornamental roof; in the lower apartment there is nothing but windows between the supporting pillars, the windows being of that peculiar translucent substance which the Chinese used in all their houses for glass until the glass of Western countries was introduced, and which substance they still prefer to use in many cases; the wooden frame-work against which the glass is placed in small squares, and the opaque whiteness of the glass in the sunlight, give a good appearance to the Celestial arrangement in windows; when lighted in the interior by the ancient rushlights in red wax, the illumination must have a beautiful effect; the old Tea House would then look like a big lantern. The place was evidently shut up on the occasion of our visit, so we followed the line of the zig-zag viaduct till we had gone over the "lake" from the south-east corner to the north-west, and landed in a small, narrow, and dirty path, unpaved and covered with mud puddles even in this dry weather. A few steps brought us out of that disagreeable part of the "garden" into a very small street, and while passing along we were amused at the display in one shop. It seemed to be a regular theatrical property store, such as is to be seen in the *purlieus* of Drury Lane, only the costumes and paraphernalia were Celestial and not barbarian. Here there were all kinds of ancient weapons,—some real, others only tinfoil imitations,—masks, wigs, and fancy dresses that might be of service at a masquerade ball or amateur theatricals. Our guide led the way, and though we then thought we had seen all the amusements of the Celestial Vanity Fair, we were mistaken, for he led us into another "garden," only a little to the west of the Tea House and lake, but which was not in view before. Business and pleasure were here combined; it was a regular fair. At one place there were hundreds of bird-cages laid out and piled above each other in rows; the Mocking Bird was the most largely represented species, and there were also many Rock Miners, and other birds which can be taught to speak; hundreds of pretty little birds—names unknown to us— were to be found there in their small wooden cages. Their chirping and singing would have been merry enough if they had only done it by turns, but the aggregate of their musical notes forcibly reminded us of ornithological exhibitions at home, or of the bird stalls in Leadenhall Market. In a small public tea house—the lower tea-room all open door-ways—where there were numerous customers sitting at the tables, bird-cages were to be seen on almost every table, and the house appeared to be a regular mart for the sale of birds. Other kinds of business were being done at other parts of the grounds, where there were great displays of toys and useful as well as ornamental articles in carved wood, laid out on mats on the ground. Our guide fancied one small wooden box, circular, and with a glass lid, which he purchased for eighteen cash. At another of the stalls all the toys were composed of lead,— tiny articles of household furniture, tea services, steamboats, junks, and numerous other things in miniature, all of native manufacture, and many of them wonderfully well done. We could easily have identified the steamboat or the junk, but one small curiously shaped thing was a mystery, and we asked what it was meant for. It was oval in form, had an odd number of legs—about half a dozen—neither head nor tail, but three or four spikes stuck out from each side; the back painted in coloured stripes. This was meant for a crab, and a friend suggested to the toy-dealer that he ought to attach a label to each of them to let people know what they were meant for; but of course the Celestial toy-dealer could not appreciate the joke. Close by the toy stalls, and lining a pathway on either side, there were numerous sweetmeat stalls kept by confectioners who had taken up their stand there for the day, while an itinerant cook might also wait there for a short time and and cater to a hungry Celestial, and then move off with his cook-shop to some other place. The book stalls were also here, and one was more a display of "fine art" than of literature, for though the stall-keeper had a large pile of pamphlets, his speciality was in the sale of pictures of mandarins, painted in water colours on white paper; and various specimens of these native works of art were laid out on the dry ground with four stones on the corners of each picture to prevent their being blown away. The pictures were of the commonest description, not worth a cent, and we guess the print-seller did not do much trade either with natives or foreigners. At this side of the square, too, there were two or three different crowds watching the gestures of acrobats; in one ring, there were four performers, but neither of them able to do anything further than kick up their legs till they touched the toe of their boot with their hand. Another old man was trying to get up a sensation by beating a small gong, while he had half a dozen or more long seats formed into a square for the convenience of those who honoured him with their patronage; the seats were already nearly all occupied, and the old man walked backward and forward beating his gong, but there was nothing to be seen which could give the slightest indication of what was going to come off; a small boy tried to trade amongst the occupants of the seats by going round with a bundle of sewn pockets, which the Celestials wear round their waist, but he couldn't trade; the occupants of the benches did not sit down there to spend money, and we guess if the showman requested them to give him a slight contribution towards defraying his expenses or for the support of his family, they would clear out at once, and go round to some of the other open-air shows; they seemed to be enjoying themselves for the time at least, and sat there quietly smoking long bamboo pipes, and had no other thing to engage their attention than to re-fill their pipes when a few puffs spent one "fill;" they were of the poorer class, coolies probably, and if we had offered five cents to anyone to carry a parcel, we would have had the whole crowd offering their services.

After leaving the acrobats and stall-keepers of the fair, we proceeded on our journey through the streets of the City, but had not gone very far before we came to a street corner where a wood carver had his shop, and some of our friends, who were now on their first visit to the City, were anxious to see some of the curios and to take with them a *souvenir* of their visit. The small corner shop was quite open on two sides, and on the counter in front were displayed, in a small glass case, ornamental and curious articles, which were specimens of the workmanship of the natives employed there, some of whom were at that moment engaged in their skilful labour over the carving of some piece of wood, in beautiful designs, with great intricacy and delicacy of finish, requiring much time and labour,—and the whole article when completed only to fetch a few cents. In the glass show case there were several ornaments carved in olive-stone, others in ivory, bamboo, and walnut-shell; the majority of them were small images of Buddhistic appearance, while there were also miniature junks carved in olive-stone and in bamboo; the walnut-shells were engraved all over with representations of Chinese landscape, with temples, pagodas, and figures of Celestials. Any one of the small articles could have been bought at from fifteen to twenty-five cents, and one of our friends traded with the manufacturer of graven images to the extent of half a dollar, receiving a joss or idol, a junk, and an engraved walnut-shell for that sum, while others of the party bought a few of the curios also, and the Celestial artificer seemed very well pleased at doing such a big trade.

While we were at this shop, for only two or three minutes, quite a large crowd of the natives gathered round us, and the narrow street was completely blocked; one old native, who was going home from the fair with some toys in his hand—a little drum, and a miniature jinricsha—had some difficulty in pressing his way through the crowd, but he held his purchases high and aloof from his greasy fellow-citizens lest they should be broken, and his little boy be deprived of the pleasure of disturbing his neighbours by the drum being smashed. Before we had got clear of this crowd, an itinerant cook came along the street; it is bad enough to meet a sedan chair in the narrow streets, or a coolie carrying a couple of buckets of water or two jars of samshu, but the itinerant cook with the whole of his apparatus on his shoulders is even more awkward to pass. Every one here of course has seen the itinerant cook or confectioner, but for the benefit of home readers who never have seen one, we will describe his compendious arrangement in bamboo, earthenware, charcoal, and cooking utensils, which he carries about with him from place to place. This portable cookshop is somewhat comical in appearance, but it is a good specimen of Chinese ingenuity. It stands on four pieces of bamboo, like the legs of a long stool, and they are joined in pairs at the top to another piece; in front, several pieces of the same useful material are formed into a quadrant-shaped bracket, upon which a box is placed; inside the box is an earthenware fire pot or brazier, with an opening in front of it for fanning the fire; charcoal is the fuel, and the box contains a day's supply, while over the fire box is a large round vessel of tin, in which anything can be cooked; in rear of the stand, other pieces of bamboo are twisted upwards and form a quadrant similar to that in front, and upon them is placed a frame containing four or five drawers; and surmounting the whole erection there is a double rack for holding bowls, cups, and saucers. In the forward bracket, under the fireplace, the cook keeps a supply of firewood; in the rear, under the drawers, he has an empty bucket, used for obtaining a fresh supply of water; in the drawers, he has rice, potatoes, fruits, and all the requisites for cooking. The space between the four-legged stand is open, and when on the move the itinerant cook puts his right shoulder under the cross-bar fixed to the top of the four legs, lifts the whole concern quite easily, and goes along, while he heralds his own approach by striking a hollow joint of bamboo with a longitudinal opening in it, and this substitute for a gong is a fixture on a front leg of the stand, the sound produced by every stroke being of loud and grave tone. These itinerant cooks are very numerous in the City and in the Chinese quarters of the Foreign Settlements, and their occupation seems to be a good one for those engaged in it. When we had passed the cook, we moved on a little further till a medical friend had his attention attracted by an exhibition at the door of one of the small shops—a couple of trays full of human teeth. These were at a dentist's shop, and we went in to see how he did business. The dentist showed us the instrument with which he operates on the jaws of the natives,—such a clumsy, rusty pair of iron forceps we never saw before; they were more like the tool with which a farrier extracts nails from a pony's hoof than anything else; there was no doubt that he would be able to pull out the biggest tooth in the head of any native with them, if he only once got hold of the tooth, but the danger would be that he might pull out two or three at one time. He said he charged the natives from fifty to one hundred cents for extracting a tooth; if he got that price for each of the teeth in the pile on the trays, and could turn out as many within the next year, he would make a small fortune. In one corner of his shop there was a large square couch, which looked something like the couches upon which

CHINESE PRIESTS.

the Celestials recline when they smoke opium; probably it was used for this purpose by the dentist when he had toothache himself, if not oftener, and when his patients were to be operated upon with these clumsy iron forceps, he would require to have them strapped down there. The old dentist was quite well pleased to see us taking an interest in his professional affairs, and re-echoed onr "chin-chin" when we took leave of him. We were making slow progress towards the City Temple, which was one of the chief items on the programme of our excursion, but we were not far from it now; and before entering upon a description of the Temple, there is only one character we will mention—a Buddhist priest. While passing along one of the narrow and dirty streets, we saw the wretched figure of a human being crouching on a small curb-stone. His dirty yellowish gown indicated at once that he was a priest, and when we came closer to him we noticed that he wore a band of brass encircling his head; his dishevelled and matted hair concealed the part at the crown of his head, but over his forehead this brazen rim shone brilliantly, and was the only good looking thing about him. He squatted down in the gutter, with his legs completely obscured by his long robe; his arms lay folded, with his hands on his knees; his face was haggard, misery and wretchedness being imprinted on every feature; he had not washed his face for dear knows how long, but if he had only done so, and shaved the bristles off his chin, his physiognomy might have been transformed into one of tolerably decent appearance. By the side of a blank white wall, and extending a couple of yards from where the squalid priest sat in the mire, there were two rows of printed pamphlets and tracts; his whole wealth was nearly exhausted in the cash, which he placed on these pieces of paper to keep them from blowing away; but in one corner—the one nearest him of course —he had piled a few cash, probably the proceeds of the sale of his literature, or perhaps the donations of some of the passing crowd. The blind and maimed beggars were not so pitiable specimens of humanity as this poor and wretched devotee of Buddha.

When we came to the City Temple, or the Temple of the City god, we entered it by a side way—there are three or four thoroughfares leading into it—which brought us at once in front of the shrine, but we will describe the buildings and all their curious adjuncts, as if we had approached by the main entrance. The Temple is dedicated to the City god, or spirits believed to have charge of all the other spirits who have once been embodied in citizens of Shanghai, and the Temple is of great antiquity. The City god is head of the spiritual kingdom of Shanghai; and he is the oracle which is consulted by the citizens when they wish advice about any private or business affairs. The Temple is in a tolerably decent state of repair, as the citizens annually pay certain contributions to the District Magistrate, towards its expenses and for the purpose of keeping it in repair. The Temple buildings cover an area of about thirty yards in breadth by one hundred yards in length, The outer gate is surmounted by an ornamental roof, like three or four roofs piled on the top of each other, the sloping eaves of the lower part extending furthest, and the others diminishing in order till the top part is only a very small one, but all are highly ornamented with turned-up corners and images stuck on the tiles. The gate itself is a big clumsy door in two leaves, painted with figures of mandarins. The wall of the outer gateway is of great breadth,—or rather there is a house on each side of the archway. A small court-yard lies between this entrance and the main gate; and we ascend one or two steps to it. The building here stretches from side to side of the Temple grounds, and rises to a considerable height; the door-way is very spacious, and the doors, roof, and everything much the same as at the outer porch. Inside this building there must be several rooms down stairs, and the topside as seen from the main court-yard is an open stage for the performance of theatricals on certain great feast days at the Temple; the highly ornamented roof is the canopy of the stage, and the actors while performing would look directly forward to the main building of the Temple, containing the shrine. The main court-yard is spacious, the whole are paved with granite, and on either side there are terraces under long low roofs of the plainest construction. The Temple proper occupies the east end, and is not a very large building; there are two small apartments flanking the main one, and the latter is a large and lofty hall, and from the floor to the roof full of idols and tablets. In external appearance the building is of the ordinary Chinese style,. with ornamental roof and turned up corners; there are numerous inscriptions in large gilt characters on the front of the building, as well as over all the gateways, but as we only gave the place a hurried visit, we had not time to get these translated for us. On going inside the great door-way of the Temple, the first things that meet the eye are four idols placed on the level of the floor and against the wall at the right-hand side, with red candles burning in front of them. These represent the runners of the City god; they are dwarfish in the limbs, but the heads are of very large size, and while the bodies are painted black, the faces are of a bright red, the upper lip carefully blackened, eyebrows complete, and though clumsily carved, they are not very hideous after all. Over our heads there are two war-junks, suspended from the roof; they are flat-bottomed, and from what can be seen of the sides, they appear to be tolerably correct models; they are painted black, and are very dirty looking, and doubtless have a deck load of dust. These are the war junks of the City god. In front of us, and towering aloft, the huge idol of the City god rests on a throne of great size, ornamented at the sides with red tablets and gold characters, curtains and scrolls hang from the top, and it is rather difficult to see what the idol is really like; only one thing is visible—the large, broad, red-painted face. The throne is surrounded by a wooden railing about five feet in height; inside it on either side there are three large idols, the one next the rails about six feet high, the next one more elevated, and standing forward nearer the throne, while the third is larger still, and comes up close to the corner of the throne occupied by the great idol of the City god. The three idols on the other side occupy similar positions; these idols, representing attendants, are as black as they could be, and their shoulders are covered with dust. Inside the rails, and directly in front, there is a high stand, apparently made of iron rods, on which red wax-candles are burned, the top of the stand being a series of three or four rods, rising in tiers, and each one has a large number of spikes for sticking the candles on, the whole of them being smeared with red wax. An old man was standing inside attending to the candles. In the front part of the railing there was a large and very richly ornamented censer, and before it a long cushion lay on the ground. When we entered the Temple there was no one there save the attendants, but an old woman came in and knelt down on this cushion, bowing her head very low, though she could not strictly perform the kotow—by beating her forehead on the ground—as she could not throw her head down between the cushion and the censer. She knelt there for three or four minutes, then took a piece of bamboo, a large joint, which was standing beside the censer, and which she shook with considerable energy, the hollow bamboo containing a large number of long thin pieces of the same material, each piece having characters in Chinese. She selected one stick, and then, paying four cash to an attendant, handed him the stick, upon which he selected a corresponding strip of yellow paper from another bamboo-quiver, and read to the distressed devotee the characters on this piece, which was the reply of the City god to the enquiry on the stick the woman selected. The poor woman again went down on her knees, again shook up the small sticks in the joint of bamboo, selected another, paid four cash more, and received another communication, through the attendant, from the god of the City. The small bamboo sticks were all numbered, and each number corresponded with those on a quantity of strips of yellow paper, about 2 in. by 10 in., which the attendant kept. The writings on these strips of paper are quotations from ancient poets; if the strip selected by the devotee contains good sayings, that is taken as a favourable reply from the City god on whatever subject the devotee may have wished to consult the oracle; it might be a business affair, or a family affair, and if she wanted to do anything, she would consult the oracle, and adapt her conduct according to the guidance received by this manipulation of bamboo sticks and strips of yellow paper. By the side of the censer, a long and capacious piece of bamboo was fixed up as a collection box, and on the advice of our Chinese friend, all the foreigners in our party made a small contribution by dropping coin into this box, upon which the attendant seemed quite pleased. Our presence in the Temple had been noticed by idle Celestials outside, and as they now crowded into the Temple we thought it time to clear out, for we did not wish to cause any commotion which might interfere with the devotions of the poor woman before the shrine.

After leaving the main building of the Temple, we came out to the large open court-yard, near the centre of which stands a huge bronze censer, said to be 3,000 years old. It is used for burning the gold and silver sycee—paper representations of shoes of sycee—as offerings to the City god. The censer stands about six feet high, and the main part of it is a large hollow globe, with an opening at the top; in this goblet the joss paper is burned. The top of the censer is composed of a smaller ornamental globe, resting on flying brackets which come up from the sides of the orifice of the larger globe. On the sides of the large globe there are a thousand of Chinese characters, which are still quite clear and sharply defined. Near to the censer there is an ornamental building, with carved columns in marble, and surmounted by richly carved blocks; the small roof too is profuse in ornaments and decorations; this marble sepulchral-looking erection encases the Tablet of Stone on which is engraven, in very small characters, the record of the life of the City god. The whole of the columns and other parts in marble are richly carved, and curiously shaped griffin figures, a mixture between a bull-dog and a lion, are seen at the base; at other parts of the court-yard, in front of the main building and at the gateways, there are also figures of wild animals couchant, and evidently very ancient pieces of sculpture. The court-yard was like a busy market square; in fact it seemed to be a special rendezvous of itinerant cooks, fruit hawkers, itinerant cobblers, and petty chapmen of all descriptions. At the sides of the court-yard there were stalls where the tradesmen had taken up a permanent position for the day; a restaurant keeper had quite an extensive business, and kept one man cooking sweet potatoes over a charcoal fire, while another was roasting chestnuts in a big pan of black stuff, sand and molasses, over another fire; the gateways were almost blocked with small trades-people and hawkers. One curious old man took up his position close in front of the marble shrine which enclosed the tablet of the City god; he had a small stall for the sale of fruit and toys, but his chief attraction for the natives was—a wheel of fortune, with some peculiar Celestial arrangements worth describing. On a small board he had a circle marked off in about thirty six sections; each section was a long thin strip, and alternately they were painted red or white, while at the inner end there were marks corresponding to the spots on dominoes, and in the whole circle there were three sections of each different kind. From the centre, an upright post bore on a pivot a long bar, equal to the diameter of the circle, and it swept round the whole radius, while to one pole of the bar was attached a needle, dangling by a bit of wire. Round the centre post there was a great variety of small porcelain toys and curious articles. The little game was played thus: a guileless native puts, say, three cash on the section marked with three dominoe spots; and then sets the swinging bar on the move; if the needle attached to one pole comes to rest on either of the three sections bearing three spots, the native wins and receives as his prize the porcelain article opposite the section on which he piled his wealth; the money can of course be increased, by placing four, five, six, or up to twelve cash, on the respective sections; and the chances against the speculator are twelve to one.

From the City Temple we proceeded to the yamên of the Che-Hsien, or District Magistrate, Moh,—the special object of our visit being to see the gaols attached to the yamên, where prisoners under sentence of death are confined. Before entering the outer gate of the yamên we observed a small cell at one corner, where about a dozen dirty faces were pressed close to the big wooden bars that form the front of the cage-like cell; they were peering through the openings, watching the movements of Celestials as they passed—the only thing they could do to relieve the monotony of their confinement. These prisoners were only incarcerated for a few days or so, for very paltry offences, and the chief part of their punishment—that of being exposed to public gaze—was the thing they appeared most to enjoy. On entering the large gate-way we came into a wide court-yard, another gate leading into the chief buildings of the yamên being in front; on the right there were some small houses occupied by runners and retainers; on the left we saw part of a range of small buildings which we afterwards went through. The second gate-way of the yamên was ornamented with pictures on the wood-work of the door; numerous inscriptions and proclamations were posted on the portals, while a clothes-line stretched from two pillars on either side, and blue cottons and grey shirtings were hanging up to dry; but they were certainly not very ornamental bunting for a mandarin to pass under when carried in his sedan chair into the interior courts of the yamên. We had obtained permission from the mandarin in charge of the gaols to visit them, and we first called at his quarters, but found he was not at home. However, one of his servants was aware that we had permission, and he led the way to a small house occupied by the "head thief," and the latter conducted us over the cells. The "head thief," is the oldest prisoner, not in years, but in crime; he had been convicted of some offence and put in a long time as a prisoner before he got promoted to be "head thief," and in that position to fulfil the duties of senior warder. He was a middle-aged man, strongly built, and quite pleasant in appearance. He wore a plain suit of blue cottons, with black jacket, and black skull-cap, without any official indications about him. We were disappointed in this respect, for we fully expected that the "head thief" would have some peculiar uniform of his own, or at least a circular patch on his back proclaiming his exalted rank. The range of buildings mentioned as on the left of the large court-yard are the gaols, and in the front part the small houses are occupied by gaolers and runners. The "head thief" occupied one of these front rooms, and when he received us he led the way through a passage to the back of the range of houses, where we found there was quite an extensive area occupied by smaller houses in squares, and the prisoners were kept there in squads of from twenty to thirty. The first ward to which we were conducted was that occupied by long-term convicts and those under sentence of death. As soon as the "head thief" turned the key in a gate, which admitted us to the interior, we heard the jingling of heavy chains, and such a scene as was then presented to our view will never be effaced from our memory. We were now inside a small square.. At the side by which we had entered was a low wall; in front and on each hand there were some small houses. About twenty prisoners were in the court-yard. One of them was engaged in trying to patch up some worn-out garment, which he had spread on a rude bench standing near the centre of the yard; another was tearing the cotton padding which had lined the old garment, evidently to make it up again for a winter coat; several of the prisoners were sitting down in front of their cells engaged in plaiting straw—some making hempen sandals, others ropes and cash-strings. A good number of the wretched inmates walked about doing nothing; some remained inside their cells. All the prisoners were in irons, the least that any of them had were heavy rings round the ankles, and six or ten inches of heavy linked chain between them; those who were at work necessarily had their hands free, but the prisoners who were walking about were loaded with chains, and some much more so than the others. The majority of them had heavy handcuffs, and similar ornaments on their feet, with a chain from their feet to their hands; some were chained hand and foot, and a long chain fixed round their body, attached to hands and feet, and also round their neck, while an iron bar about twelve inches in length was fixed in the chain from the prisoner's neck and lay across his breast in a most uncomfortable manner; the chains still allowed them a limited freedom—just sufficient to walk in very short steps. One prisoner was doing hard labour in a peculiarly tantalizing manner. He was loaded with chains on hands, feet, body, and neck, while a heavy piece of wood about five feet in height was attached to his right foot, by a short chain, and the top of the log of wood was chained to his neck by a longer piece of chain which would just let the log out to arm's length; but he was obliged to keep it hitched up on his shoulder by another chain, for if he allowed it to fall he would be dragged down with it. The wood was very hard and heavy, evidently the trunk of a young tree, about two inches in diameter, and he would have to keep it with him all day and sleep with it all night; he was the newest arrival in this gang, and had to do his turn with the log of wood as the others had done before him. Some of the prisoners looked cheerful enough, and they had full liberty to smoke in the court-yard, as a good many of them were doing. We looked in vain to see Moh-lee and Ko-ching-gee, the two Shansi men who murdered a Shanghai mountebank in a tea house in the Maloo nine months ago. They paid $150 to the father of the murdered man and satisfied him. How much they paid to satisfy the mandarins is unknown; but it is a notorious fact that prisoners are confined just so long as their friends can be squeezed, set at liberty if a sufficient sum is paid, or executed if they are unfortunate enough to be without any money or friends. That is said to be the case with most of the Chinese officials, and the Maloo affair evidently shows it holds good in this province too. The prisoners in this ward included murderers, robbers, thieves, adulterers, and some convicted of other offences. Some of them were in the last week of their life, for since our visit four we then saw have been executed outside the South Gate of the City. They were, we believe, the men whom we saw sitting plaiting the straw—one was a pirate who had committed murder and robbery at Min-hong, and his head would be exposed at the scene of his crime; another culprit had committed the unpardonable offence of robbing a mandarin's residence; and two were said to be the pirates who robbed an opium shop in the English Settlement nine months ago. About a dozen pirates from the lake district had committed the robbery, but only two were captured. They now sat on a heap of straw, and worked away slowly. They looked wretched and miserable in the day time, and what a night these men would pass, for their cell was a long narrow space, with four small stools standing up amongst the dirty straw which covered the floor of earth—a wretched stall that was not fit for beasts of burden. They worked all day in plaiting and twisting straw, they lay on foul straw all night, but only four times did they pass through their monotonous work of the day, only four times more did they sleep in that wretched stall, until that early morn when the mandarin sent them in a special supply of food—such is the strange mode of intimating to the doomed man that his hour has come—and on that fourth day, two of the culprits received their last meal and were taken out to the South Gate and decapitated by the executioner's sword. When two had gone, the others must have felt apprehensive, and not without cause; after a lapse of two days, and the other two culprits were executed.

The executions take place on the order of the Imperial Board of Punishments. After a prisoner has been convicted, the District Magistrate of Shanghai sends a petition to the Taotai of Shanghai, who forwards it to the Futai of Sunkiang, and the latter reports to the Board of Punishments at Pekin. An Imperial Edict is issued through that Board, and sent back by the same roundabout way to the District Magistrate. Until he receives it, he has no idea what is to be done with the prisoner, but when the order is sent for the execution of the latter, the District Magistrate must see that it is carried out within two or three days, and he never allows any one to know of it till the morning of the event. It is therefore almost impossible for a foreigner to know of such an affair till after the occurrence. We have been told that mandarins sometimes send the doomed man samshu to drink two or three days beforehand, to give him a hintt. At any rate, on the fatal morn, a signal is given regarding which there is no mistake, the mandarin sending to the culprit a special supply of food, consisting of a dish of fried pork, another of boiled lamb or mutton, and three bowls of rice, He cannot touch either of them for excitement, and does not get time even, although he were prepared to eat the whole lot, for he is dragged off to the execution ground in haste, with a small flag stuck on his back, and if he refuses to walk, he is tied to a bamboo pole, and carried by coolies. The mandarins and military officers are present at the execution. They generally number about twenty, all mounted on ponies, and they ride round in a circle, making as much noise as they can by clattering of hoofs and tinkling of bells, until some small crackers are let off, at which signal the executioner cuts off the head of the prisoner with one fell swoop of his sword.

In the first cell we visited, we gave a small contribution for the benefit of the prisoners, being informed that that was customary on the part of foreigners when they are privileged by being shown through the place. The "hard labour" man, who was loaded with chains and burdened by the log of wood, was the recipient, on behalf of all the others, not only in this cell, but in other cells also. He at once handed the money to the "head thief," who gave it to one of his subordinates; we were assured that the prisoners would get the benefit of it in the shape of some dainties,—rather unusual for them—or perhaps tobacco. On leaving the ward, the prisoners "chin-chinned" our party, some of them shaking their hands at us, *a la Chinoise* salutation, which they could do quite well with their handcuffs on; in fact it came all the more natural to them. In passing on to the next department of the gaol, we went through some houses where runners and others were killing time by playing dominoes, and gambling in other games; we also observed a small joss-house, which is for the prisoners worshipping their gods. The second ward we visited was like the former one, a small square, partly surrounded with small houses which formed the cells; the prisoners here, too, were lounging about the small court-yard, all more or less burdened with iron decorations on their ankles, arms, and necks. One man had the tantalising log of wood attached to his right foot by a chain, like his brother in the other ward, but this second one was not quite so heavily laden with iron, and his log of wood was lighter; it was only fastened to his ankle, and not to his neck, so that he was obliged to keep hold of it always in his right arm, to prevent its dragging on the ground. He seemed to have a full appreciation of his comical situation, and no doubt considered the log of wood a great nuisance; the other prisoners smiled at him when he moved about with it, as they were past that sort of hard labour. Many of the inmates here were engaged in making straw ropes, sandals, and at other work similiar to their *confrères* in the first ward. One part of the building was a cook-house, a pretty large, but very empty-looking, dingy, earthen-floored apartment. A boiler was built up in brick, but the fire was out, scarcely any cooking utensils were to be seen, and away in the far-off corner sat the disconsolate cook, for he too was a prisoner; he sat there with his arms folded, and his legs drawn up under his chair, but still one could see that they were uncomfortably attached to each other at the ankles; he was evidently very miserable in his confinement, at least he did not look very pleasant. All the prisoners in this and also in the other department were dressed, not in prison garb of any uniformity, but in the most extraordinary masses of rags and patches,—scarcely a piece of blue cotton about them more than half a dozen inches square; the patches were of the all-pervading blue cotton, but the colour differed according to the age of the respective pieces, and the amount of wear and tear they had gone through; the patch work was also of the rudest description, and it seemed as if every one had to be his own tailor; a large amount of strings were necessary to keep the garments together, and matted pieces of cotton padding stuck out here and there all round their coats and breeches; they all seemed to have plenty of clothes on, and most likely they had to keep them on night and day, for it would have been a laborious task in the case of some of the prisoners to have to tie all their rags together every morning so as to get them to hang round them somehow. Outside this second ward there was a small garden, a little flower plot only a few yards square, and surrounded by a not very high wall. It was the most pleasant part of the whole establishment, for there was a large plot of the yellow *Chrysanthemum* in full bloom; the prisoners keep this garden in order, and it may afford an opportunity to the more intellectual convicts to study botany. We only visited the two wards described, and then took our leave of the "head thief," thanking him for his kindness in showing us round; he had been very courteous, and now he bowed and shook his fists as we went away, going the first three steps backwards, and bowing to us.

From the Chie-Hsien's yamên, we retraced our steps to the City Temple, and on to the Private Tea Garden, open only to the mandarins. On our way, one thing that attracted attention, and which we had never seen before, was worthy of remark,—at the doorstep of a house in one of the streets, there was a Celestial washing his face, and quite a crowd of astonished citizens around him! This Tea Garden is decidedly the most pleasant spot in the whole City of Shanghai, and its beauty is of no ordinary nature; the artificial devices in the construction of rockeries ponds, the ornamental buildings, and the trees and plants, give it quite a charming appearance, more especially in the summer time, when the trees are in full foliage; and though it is rather bleak in the middle of winter, it has still its charms, being so different from the dirty and crowded thoroughfares of the City. In the summer time, it must form a very enjoyable retreat for those who are privileged to resort to it. As far as we are aware, there is only one day in the whole year when this private retreat of the mandarins is open to the citizens; that is on the 15th day of the 3rd Moon, and on that day we visited this beautiful garden. It was then crowded excessively with citizens of all classes, and the great attraction was what would correspond, in Western ideas, to a floral exhibition. But the show was unique in that there was only kind one of plant exhibited, the *Aglaia Octorata*; the chief characteristic of that plant is that there are numerous varieties, but except to those who are very well versed in the botany of China, it is impossible to see any difference between the specimens; the plant consists of a few long grass-shaped blades, of very delicate and graceful form, with a small flowering stem shooting from the green blade; it requires the very keenest perception to detect the varieties, and in the examination of this plant the Chinese generally and especially those who are of a botanical turn of mind, take the greatest delight; but probably most of them at the show did not know anything of botany, and were only there out of curiosity, because they could get there but once a year. We remember that at every stand in the tea houses, where specimens of the plant were exhibited, there were dense groups of Celestials, eagerly looking at the small flower pots, with the graceful, green-leafed plants in them. So dense was the crowd in the garden that day, that it was impossible for any one to see what the place was like, and the narrow pathways under arches of rock, or over small bridges, or up rugged steps of granite, were blocked with Celestials in blue cottons and silks, fans in every hand, and every tongue jabbering, so that it was the best course to beat a retreat, and set down the garden as an object for inspection on some future date. On the occasion of our present visit to the city, we obtained permission to go to this garden, and accordingly we made it the last item in our afternoon's excursion. The entrance to the garden is reached by some very narrow and mazy paths, from the public garden which surrounds the old Tea House already described; our guide evidently knew the way as well as though he lived on the spot, but it would almost defy any of our company to find the way back again. The way by which we entered, is a very narrow doorway in a wall,—the aperture not more than six feet in height, and two in breadth; a knock on the plain deal door, was answered by a voice from within, a short jabbering followed, between our guide and the guardian, and the small door was thrown open, when we saw a feeble old man before us, who welcomed us to visit the place; the door was locked behind us, and for a good half hour, we had the garden to ourselves. We first entered the pavilion, a building which is of the same shape as the chief building of a temple; it is only one large room, open in front, and while sitting inside, the greater portion of the garden is in view before you. There are numerous tables and chairs here, for use in taking a quiet cup of tea; the walls are hung with painted scrolls of Celestial landscapes and waterscapes, ornamental carved panel work, and lettered tablets; on the back wall there is a niche containing a water-colour daub of a portrait, representing the City God; and from the roof there are suspended a great number of ornamental lanterns, made of foreign glass, set in carved framework, and some of them hung with fringes of beads. In front of this pavilion you have a full view of the immense artificial ridge of rocks, with palm trees, willows, etc., in the foreground and on the slopes of the ridge, while ferns and long spear-like grass grow from the crevices of the rocks; the ridge is surmounted by trees in life, though now bare of foliage, and also by what at a distance appear to be rude pillars of rock, but are really fossil trees; a small octagonal pavilion, open all round, the ornamental roof resting on pillars of wood, stands on the highest corner of the ridge, and further back there is a terrace of small houses, the front of which range is elaborately constructed of doors and windows. When we leave the chief building, we walk round by one end of it, and find there is a small square pond here, the boundary wall being fantastically shaped of water-worn rocks; the water is however covered with a skimming of green weeds, so that we have to exercise faith when we are told that the pond is full of curious fish; and reeds rise up to a great height by the side of the pond. The walk round this corner is paved with small pebbles and chips of porcelain; the walls on the left hand contain niches, enclosed with plate glass, and inside there is trellis work in white plaster, while in every diamond, square, and octagonal space formed by the trellis work, there are miniature figures moulded in blue clay, and some of them are very interesting studies,—where in a few ounces of blue clay you may have an emperor and his army of three soldiers; or a temple, pagoda, and priests; a mandarin on horseback; an old man playing a flute; and with each of them a small bit of landscape, a shoulder of a hill, a tree, or bridge thrown in. The next thing on the walk, or over it, is a small archway of rocks. The stones seem to have been taken from some mighty watercourse, as they are worn and scooped out, and while piled above each other to a great height, cemented with blue clay, their configuration is fantastic in the extreme. On the other side of this archway, we come to another spacious sitting room, furnished as a tea drinking saloon. Beside it there is a long white wall, under cover, and built into this wall there are several tablets, some of flint stone and others of slate—all of them being covered with Chinese characters, and some of these mural tablets contain the names of the people who contributed towards the construction of the garden. The greater portion of the wall, however, is taken up with a grand fresco,—a panoramic view of the country from Shanghai City to Loong-hwa; the work is now sadly spoilt, in some parts by the plaster coming off in scales, at other parts by disrespectful and ill-mannered foreigners writing their names over it with black lead pencil, some of the autographs being in a very large scrawling hand—a very reprehensible practice followed by foreigners, Englishmen especially, whenever they have an opportunity of scratching their names on any place which is seldom visited, of difficult access, or of special interest to visitors. The fresco is very much obliterated, but there is still enough of it to be seen to make it an interesting study. In the left hand corner there is a representation in bold outline of the City Wall, in the back ground there is the placid Hwang-poo River, with three or four great junks with broad sails, and at the right hand, the most perfect object in the whole panorama is a representation of Loong-hwa Pagoda; the foreground had evidently been occupied by a representation of the outskirts of the City, and the fields between the City and Loong-hwa, but the work of the Celestial Angelo is desecrated, and this portion of it is almost completely destroyed. After ascending a rudely shaped flight of granite steps, with walls of rugged rocks on each hand, we come to the top of the artificial ridge of rocks. Here we rest for a time and enjoy a cigar in the small pavilion; and among the interesting objects we examined were a petrified column, standing about twelve feet high, which was evidently a fossil tree, and the grain was quite distinct; another column, of honey-combed rock, formed by white pebbles embedded in alluvial soil, which now had a chalk-like appearance; the pebbles having been extracted all round, the column presented a surface of indentations. A third geological curiosity was in the shape of a boulder, rendered smooth by the action of water, and having a hole worn through it. When you struck this stone gently, a musical sound, grave but very pleasant, was produced; and besides those mentioned there were other curiosities of a similar kind to be seen. This quiet little garden of flowers, trees, and rocks, and its pavilions, would be a splendid attraction if it could be transferred to the grounds of the Crystal Palace, for in the way of artificial rockeries it beats anything at Sydenham. When inside it, you see nothing of the dirty City which surrounds it, and our party at any rate considered it was well worth visiting. From this garden we went as straight to the New North Gate as is possible, considering the irregularity of the streets; and after having seen many strange sights, and learned something of Celestial life within the walls of Shanghai, we completed our afternoon's excursion in exactly two hours and a half.

APOTHEOSIS OF LIU SING-KAU, GOD OF PEACE.

THE great ceremony of Dedicating a Temple to the "God of Peace" took place in Shanghai City on Saturday the 13th September, 1879. Liu Sing-kau, late Futai of Kiangsu, and District Magistrate of Shanghai in 1860, was by Imperial Decree created "God of Peace," and a temple had to be dedicated to his honour by the mandarins and inhabitants of the city and district, over whom he had exercised his powers as an official, and who benefited by his devotion to duty and his interest in their welfare. As a magistrate he had dealt justice with a fair hand; even though only a civil officer he won fame in war, for had he not with courage and daring led a party of militia to Pootung, and gained a victory over the rebels? Throughout the whole course of the Taiping Rebellion his actions showed true perfection of patriotism and love for his people; while yet in the flesh he was not passed over without reward, for he was promoted to be Futai of Kiangsu Province; and while holding that rank he departed this life a few years ago. But like many other great men, his worth only became fully acknowledged after his death; yet it was not too late, for could not his name be handed down to succeeding generations by the story of his good life and brave deeds? He had secured a niche in the Temple of Fame, (Celestial department), for, by the easy way the Chinese have of doing things, an Imperial Decree by the Son of Heaven, "him upon whom the dominion of the world has descended," was only necessary for the apotheosis of Liu Sing-kau as "God of Peace;" he had loved peace, although he could also quit himself gallantly in war, and as "God of Peace" he must have a temple in the City where he formerly held his high post, and his peace-loving spirit will shed a benign influence over the rulers and inhabitants. One curious thing about the new god is that he has to be content with a second-hand temple, for the mandarins chose the Temple near the West City Gate, formerly called the Mow-san Temple; the Mow-san idol was removed some time ago to a less commodious Temple in the city; why he had got into disrepute, we don't know; but at any rate the Temple once occupied by Mow-san was to let; it was rapidly becoming dilapidated; and the mandarins resolved, under Imperial sanction, to repair this Temple thoroughly, and dedicate it to the "God of Peace;" and the great ceremony came off on Saturday in presence of all the mandarins of the district.

The chief feature of the day's proceedings was the great procession, which paraded the streets of Shanghai City and also part of the Foreign Settlements. We resolved to see it; there was the choice of entirely different prospects,—we could see it either in the comparatively broad streets of the French Concession, or in the narrow streets of the City; we chose the latter, to which more interest attached, although there was the disadvantage that you could not get an extended view of the line of procession. Accompanied by an interpreter and a guide, we entered the City by the New North Gate about half-past one o'clock in the afternoon, and after following our guide through the labyrinth of narrow streets between that Gate and the City Temple and Tea Gardens, we turned in various directions till none but our guide had the slightest idea whether we were going north, south, east, or west; but by and by after a very long walk, we found ourselves in a long narrow street, evidently one of the principal ones of the City, judging from the appearance of the shops; the street was literally packed with people. It was on the line of march of the procession (after it had been marshalled at the City Temple, gone out of the City by the Old North Gate, round several streets in the French Concession, and re-entered the City by the big East Gate); and the people in this narrow street were now eagerly waiting its approach. We got refuge from the crowd by standing inside a large drug store, a substantially built house with high brick walls, the frontage unbroken except by a large doorway, and the door was a huge one—the outer part of it being composed of large diamond-shaped bricks cemented together;—the building was evidently fire-proof all round. Our guide was apparently acquainted with the shopmen or the master—at any rate we were made welcome to stand inside until the procession made its appearance; the presence of a foreigner in the shop was sufficient to attract the notice of the natives, and the shop soon became crowded with them. At about half past two o'clock, the procession approached, and the street, formerly packed so much that one could scarcely force one's way through the crowd is now kept clear by all the people standing inside the large open fronts of the shops, and in any place where they can squeeze enough room to stand. Hundreds of voices are shouting, yelling, jabbering, laughing; young and old scamper past in a hurry, in eager search of a place to get out of the way; the noise of horses' hoofs is heard on the rude blocks of pavement, and the merry jingling of bells breaks pleasantly on the ear; the sounds become louder and louder, and the excitement of the spectators increases in the same ratio, till in a few seconds the leaders of the great procession ride past; they are the Taotai's cavalry, mounted on palfreys gaily decked with ornamented saddles and bridles, and the riders are dressed in grand uniforms of embroidered silk. A troop of about twenty pass on, abreast; there is barely room for them in the narrow street, but they ride slowly. They are succeeded by half a dozen men on foot carrying red tablets, with gold characters proclaiming the degrees and titles of the great Liu Sing-kau; then there is another troop of small ponies, and in their rear is a crystal-buttoned mandarin, the commander of the Taotai's cavalry. More red tablets are borne slovenly; and these tablets are the Taotai's. Small mandarins with gilt buttons are next in order; they are mounted on ordinary-sized Chinese ponies, and ride in single file, every man holding aloft a long scroll with letters and ornaments in embroidery of rich and varied colours; they all carry swords, but instead of having them drawn, or dangling at the left side, the swords are sheathed, and fixed in the rider's waistband at his back, and in a horizontal position. Then follow a number of mounted flag bearers, but their small flags are fixed in the back of their waist-bands, like the swords of those in advance. A long pause ensues, the processionists lag on their way, and people crowd the street again; and then there is a scampering and yelling, with loud clattering of hoofs, when four mandarins come galloping past at full speed; how they could do it in these narrow streets without accident is astonishing. Another pause, and they come again, but the ponies are held in funereal marching order; two mandarins have each huge rolls, or tubular boxes tied on their backs; they are of crimson with gilt ornaments, and we are told they are for holding signal flags used in battle; then other two small mandarins bear red flags, small square ones, each having a character in black in the centre. Another break in the procession, and coolies block the street for a while, till two executioners ride up at a good pace and clear the way; they are hideously dressed, but their costumes are not more black or satanic in design than those of the next two riders; our interpreter friend called them reporters at first, and we thought of the enterprising members of the staffs of native papers equalling the strategy of a London reporter, who blackened his face and rode on the head of an elephant from the Guildhall to Westminster to enable him to properly describe the progress of a Lord Mayor's Show; but after all they were not reporters—these demon-like fellows just past—they were meant to represent messengers to carry tidings of battles; they, and the executioners before them, were merely impersonations, and our friend has just explained that many of the characters in the procession are merely for the purpose of representing such attendants and subordinates as the great God of Peace should be supposed to have in his yamên; and the characters are represented by merchants or others of the city who have agreed to take part in the procession. This explanation came in conveniently when there was a long pause, after the messengers galloped past, till a lot of "runners" came up on foot—not running, for "runner" is a misnomer;—several of them have bamboo sticks, used for flagellating prisoners, and they hold them in their hand so that one end drags on the granite blocks, making a grating sound, as one might produce with a walking stick. What the meaning of this was it is hard to say. Then follow two symbolical worthies on horseback, carrying long sticks with silk attached, but not in the shape of a flag or banner, and we only got a glimpse of them; these were messengers between the Emperor and the God of Peace. Music is soon heard in the distance—not far off, for the music was not strong—and we are told this is the Taotai's band which approaches, and are also informed that they have been under a French instructor. They pass by, playing a Chinese tune without beginning or ending the instruments consisting of four small side drums, two bugles, and four trumpets. They are followed by the Taotai's Guard or "picked troops"—the same fellows we saw when General Grant arrived at Kin-lee-yuen. About twenty or more of them trudge along slowly, each carrying a long lance, or spiked pole, with a small three-cornered flag; then the martial tread of the men under arms is heard, evidently with heavy boots on, judging by the noise they make; they are marching two abreast; rifles, with sword bayonets fixed, are carried at the slope. The picked troops wear loose blue jackets, and wide trousers; broad red stripes and facings; straw hats, with blue silk lining on the upturned rim, and a broad black band round the hat. The first ten or twelve file past in good order, marching well, but others are gaping round, first at one shop, then at another; and when they see a foreigner alone in the crowd, that's too much for them; the picked troops stop and stare at us, with a big broad smile, some making a "left turn" till they have nearly brought the points of their sword bayonets in the faces of people at the other side of the street; then the fellows in the rear give them a shove forward, but curiosity being once directed towards us, the whole troop as they pass must look round at the door of the drug store. The rear of the guard was brought up by their commander, a crystal-buttoned mandarin mounted on a pony. We had now seen the most improved specimens of Chinese soldiery with foreign weapons; and immediately after them came a lot of men bearing all sorts of curious and ancient weapons; some resembled "catch poles," there were halberds, and spears, and a curious one we noticed particularly was in the shape of a human hand, which was made of brass; the clenched fist, larger than life size, was on the end of a long pole, and a large pen was grasped in the fist, the pen being thus at right angles to the pole. Then comes a great silk umbrella, embroidered in most beautiful designs, but the momentary glimpse we obtained of it was not enough to enable us to describe it; this was followed at a short distance by a smaller red umbrella, ornamented, but not profusely; and there is a third one in the wake—an old shabby thing in drab-coloured cotton, presenting a striking contrast the richly embroidered article. A crystal-buttoned mandarin rides slowly past on his pony, with tinkling bells on the harness, and he sits majestically on his huge and clumsy saddle; he goes at a slow pace, and does not care to risk his own life or endanger the lives of others by galloping in the narrow street, as some have been doing. Another lot of "runners" on foot, and then an umbrella bearer, his huge parachute being of pink silk; and then by the cries of the people we understand something good is coming. There is a herald shouting, and then chair coolies are seen: eight of them are carrying a magnificent altar, in the shape of a sedan chair, for burning incense; it is of beautiful design, the wood work of ebony, or an imitation of it, and profusedly gilded; the carved work is most elaborate, and altogether the altar is a most exquisite piece of workmanship. Sandalwood and incense are being burned on it. Then there are some allegorical representations—the first a little boy on a palfrey, both richly decked with ornaments and embroidery, and then a man on horseback representing some ancient character. A curious squad of men come next; each holds out his right arm, bare up to the elbow, and in his skin are fixed about a dozen brass hooks, from which is suspended by four cords a heavy censer, the whole weight being about thirty pounds; the men put on wry faces—but they pretend that there is a supernatural interference with the laws of gravity, that some god or spirit bears up the weight of the censer, and that the hooks don't hurt them. Another break in the procession; and then a number of men pass by, almost obscured under big straw hats; they are incense burners who carry variously shaped censers in their hands, and we are told they have to kneel and worship at any temple or idol they pass on the route. Their chin-chinning has probably been the cause of the gaps in the procession; for as soon as they pass, the street is for a few minutes occupied by coolies carrying vegetables and samshu!—they were of course not in the programme. Incense burners come again—they had been tarrying in their worship at some place—and then executioners, "runners" with bamboo sticks, and a red umbrella-bearer hurry past on foot. Another crystal-buttoned mandarin appears, and after him come two men on horseback, carrying richly decorated flags and banners;—these flags have been presented by the people of Shanghai to the God of Peace, and proclaim him to be a divinity. Then there is a magnificent umbrella, the ground-work of crimson cloth, richly embroidered and fringed; and round the flounces are hundreds of Chinese characters, all embroidered in blue silk; these are the names of people who have subscribed to present this umbrella to the great God of Peace. A juvenile band follows the gorgeous umbrella,—the band comprising only four urchins, two playing flutes, one striking a hollow piece of bamboo, and the fourth has a triangle, or something of the same kind. Then a lot of shabbily dressed "runners" hurry past, shouting and yelling, for there is something great behind them; it is a dragon chariot, in which sandalwood is burned, and it is carried by eight coolies, like a sedan chair. The sound of a great gong is heard, and the processionists come up quickly and close together; the gong-beater, with powerful arm, beats that huge gong like thunder; the gong is so large that the man carrying it can barely prevent its touching the ground; it is indeed a gong fit for a god. The next in order are "runners" carrying tablets, followed by mandarins on horseback, in elegant robes; and then four sedan chairs are carried past, each chair occupied by mandarins' secretaries or seal bearers.

Another juvenile drum and flute band, "runners," a sedan chair, coolies, bamboo-beaters, umbrella bearers, and small boys, pass in close succession ; and then there are men burning joss sticks, two boys with flutes, and more joss stick burners. Now we have a swellish string band —a private one belonging to some of the big mandarins; there are nearly a dozen men with stringed instruments and flutes, but as they pass now in a crowd without any order, there is only one old man feebly tooting on his flute. More " runners " and others hurry up, and following them is another swell string band playing vigorously some Chinese air. The next thing is one in which the processionists have more interest; it is a board well covered with sweet-meats—not meant for the gods, but for the processionists themselves; and the last of all the long and glorious procession is a huge sedan chair, decorated with carvings and covered with gilt, every part of it elaborated in the highest degree to which Chinese art and skill can attain —this is the chair of the God of Peace, and inside it is his tablet with his name and degrees,— the tablet which is to be placed in his Temple. The chair is borne by eight coolies, and in their wake the crowd of citizens surge to and fro, and thousands keep up a jolting march after the glorious cavalcade.

After the great procession had passed through the street where for upwards of an hour we had witnessed its progress, our guide took the lead to show us the way to the new Temple of the God of Peace, and we were assured that we could be there long before the procession reached it, for the great cavalcade of mounted mandarins, troops, runners, umbrella bearers, chair coolies, and brass and string bands, had to march through many of the streets before they would complete their perambulation and arrive at the Temple. In the streets we passed through first, we were in the wake of the procession; business was being resumed by the shopmen,—they were hanging up their sign-board tablets, which had been taken down to give free passage to the big umbrellas; workmen were busy—blacksmiths, coppersmiths, comb-makers, ivory-carvers, lamp-makers, embroiderers, shoe-makers, and coffin-makers,—all were busy at their work in the open frontages of the shops; the crowd in the streets soon became mixed, so that they were no longer following in one mass after the procession, but were going to and fro on business or pleasure, each pursuing the even tenor of his way, calm, serene, and inoffensive; and the generality of the men on the streets were much better dressed, and more respectable looking than those forming the crowds in Chinese streets in the Foreign Settlements. We followed our guide through many a narrow street, turning first to one side and then to the other, over bridges spanning creeks of dirty stagnant water, through streets with splendid shops, and others with wretched hovels; and on and on we went, asking impatiently where that God of Peace had fixed his abode, till at length we began to get out into the more open part of the City to the west side, when we knew we would soon be in the open grounds there. In most of the streets we had passed, there was no sign that anything unusual was taking place in the city; but occasionally we could see down the vista of a narrow street, and at the bottom of it, a mandarin on horseback rode past, or the great umbrellas might appear to be blocking the way, or the big gong be heard like the sound of stage thunder; we were having a distant view of the procession going in a direction away from the Temple, while we were approaching at the rate of three miles an hour. We walked on a narrow path by the side of a creek, and on the other side, in the garden ground, there were long rows of seats occupied by women waiting patiently for the show. The Temple was now in sight on our right hand, but we had to take a circuitous route till we crossed the creek on a small stone bridge, and then a zig-zag path-way through open fields or gardens brought us up to the building which was formerly the Mow-san Temple, but is now the Temple of the God of Peace. This Temple is one of the most prominent buildings in the City, as seen from the wall on the west side. Its exterior formerly was of a dirty, dingy, orange colour, but it is now whitewashed; the up-turned corners of gables, the roof, and all its external parts look well, and from a casual observation appear to have been made as good as new. When we get close to it, we see crowds of Celestials all round it, "runners" have laid down tablets against the walls, and chair coolies and runners are crowding in hundreds. The great mandarins of the district did not join in the procession, but are now sitting inside the Temple buildings, and the crowd of Celestials here is largely composed of their retainers who have attended them in their private processions to the Temple.

The Temple is of the ordinary design of a yamen; at the frontage is the lofty porch, with great open doorways; passing through it, we come to the main court-yard; in front of us is the Temple, and on either side are long porches; the Temple is open in front, the stone or brick flooring raised by several steps above the level of the court-yard; on either side of the Temple are two large rooms, the walls entirely bare in the interior, and the rooms evidently not yet quite finished. In these rooms, on benches round the side of the walls, are dozens of mandarins in official robes of richly emboidered silk, strings of corals and precious stones; light mushroom straw hat, and peacock feathers, with buttons of various degrees. The chief mandarin present is Lui, the Taotai of the District of Shanghai; and we also identify the Che-hien or District Magistrate, Moh; and also our old friend Chên of the tribunal in the Maloo; it was needless to hunt up a list of them all; suffice it to say that all the high mandarins holding civil and military posts in the district, and many "expectants" who have no posts, were there in full glory. In the main court-yard, there were dozens of sedan chairs belonging to these officials—the Taotai's in green cloth, the others in dark blue. All round the porches of the court-yard, there were ornamental lamps hanging from the eaves—the lamps octagonal or septagonal in shape, composed of glass, and ornamented with fringes of coloured beads The paved flooring, the walls, pillars, roof, and everything appeared to be repaired equal to new,—if indeed the most of the work was not new altogether;—never having been in the place before we cannot say what it was like when Mow-san's idol was there; but it certainly appeared that no expense had been spared to make it a fit abode for the new comer. Before we ascend the steps leading to the Temple, we notice on either side a small wall, built of brick, but spotless in its covering of whitewash; the wall rises about eight feet, the lower half is solid, the upper is in trellis work, and in the openings are beautiful figures moulded in blue clay,—some of these figures—of men, animals, and groups · are really beautiful and interesting works of art.

In the Temple itself, we find in the foreground a huge stand, nearly five feet in height, and on it are placed at the extreme edges two massive candlesticks; the candles burning are of red wax, about eighteen inches in length, and an inch and a half in diameter; then on each side further in on the table are two small candlesticks, with red wax candles of the ordinary tallow-candle size; while in the centre of the stand is a large square box in bronze, filled with earth, and two long pieces of joss-stick are burning in an upright position. From the roof many small-sized octagonal glass lamps, and four very large square ones, are suspended; the pillars which support the roof are ornamented, and long tablets with large gold letters are hanging

TEMPLE IN THE CITY.

in front of them; on the walls are numerous tablets, and on the roof also; all around there are gilt letters eulogizing the great Liu Sing-kau and recounting his virtues. On the wall in front of us, there is a frame work in varnished wood, richly carved; it forms a niche, and the interior is hung with scarlet curtains, a green curtain being stretched along the top. This is the niche in which the tablet of the God of Peace is to rest. Between the incense stand in front and the altar, there is a table covered with dishes of cakes, chestnuts, dates, nuts, and sweetmeats; on the right hand side of this table, a clean-dressed sheep is stretched on a four-legged stand, and on the other side of the table there is a clean-dressed pig on another stand, and both carcasses are laid in angular positions, with their heads pointing to the seat of the god;—the fruit and sweets, and the more substantial food of mutton and pork are for the God of Peace, but he doesn't touch it, and the keeper of the Temple takes these good things as his perquisites after they have lain before his godship for three days.

  The procession arrived at the Temple shortly before five o'clock; the great mass of processionists could not get near the entrance of the Temple owing to the crowd, and so had to deploy into the garden ground all round about. The great mandarins came out and formed in two lines from the entrance of the outer porch to the steps of the Temple proper, and when the great chair of the God of Peace, the last article in the procession, had been brought up through all the crowd outside, the chair and tablet of the great god were carried in between the lines of the mandarins, the Taotai, the Che-hien, all the others in their turn, according to their rank, bowing to the tablet, and making obeisance to their new god. The tablet was then placed in the niches prepared for it as described. Fireworks and crackers were burnt, the bands played, and the chin-chinning was carried on all evening. The wax candles in the temple and porches were all lighted, the mandarins feasted, and the swellish private string bands and the old tin-potty brass bands played time about till a late hour in the evening. The dedication of the Temple to the God of Peace was thus accomplished. We could not afford to wait all afternoon at the Temple to see the whole ceremony carried out, and therefore the latter particulars are from a Chinese informant. As we left the Temple of the God of Peace and made for the West Gate of the City, we passed on our right hand an old, dilapidated building, which we are informed is the Temple of Kwan-ti, the God of War; it certainly presented a very shabby and ruinous appearance on the outside; and as far as a good-looking Temple goes, the God of War can't hold a candle to the God of Peace in Shanghai City.

THE MANILA COCK-PIT, IN BAMBOO TOWN.

IN our cosmopolitan community there are so many nationalities, and so many different customs are in vogue, that we might expect to see anything here. The Municipal bye-laws are assimilated to the police regulations in England; but in a community comprising nearly all the races on the face of the earth, the Police Act of England, or similar statutes of other countries, can only be adhered to in part. Chinese must be allowed to follow their own customs, so far as these do not interfere with the welfare of foreigners, but the western invention of licenses is enforced as a restraint upon some of their institutions, such as public opium smoking saloons; and their gambling houses are strictly prohibited, the same as lower-class gambling is hunted down at home, while in big clubs it is winked at. But other nationals who have settled here, bring with them their national pastimes, and under license from their Consul, and, apparently, beyond interference on the part of the Municipality, practise games which would not be tolerated under the Police Act of England. The particular case we have under notice is the game of cock-fighting, carried on by Spaniards from Manila. Cock-fighting is the chief sport or pastime of Manilamen, and they carry it on in full swing every Sunday afternoon, in the Cock-pit in "Bamboo Town," the north-western part of the American Settlement; and besides Manila-Spaniards, there are numbers of Portuguese, Chinese, and other nationals among the spectators. A short time ago we visited the Cock-pit, just to see what kind of a place it was. Bamboo Town is a quarter thickly covered with small houses, wretched hovels they are, chiefly constructed of bamboo, and this fact accounts for the name. The cock-pit can, we believe, be approached from Tien-dong Road, (the road to heaven!) through a long course of small and dirty streets; a less complicated route is by Chapoo Road until the west side of Bamboo Town is reached, then by a narrow path down between two rows of small houses; the next turn is into a narrow alley, where there is only room for walking in Indian file; this brings us to the back of one of the rows of houses, where there is a creek of stagnant water covered with green weeds; the creek is crossed by the most ricketty erection in the way of bridges that could be found hereabout; the pillars are only bamboo poles, and four or five planks lie over them without any superfluous fixings; first a single plank, then two alongside, and another two; these constitute the bridge, and it is not fit to bear two persons at once. On the other side of the creek, on a long and narrow strip of ground, the Manilamen have their cock-fighting ground. The "pit," as it is called, is a bamboo erection,—a sort of matshed. The roof is supported by bamboo poles; the west side only is enclosed by a high fence and screen to keep out the strong rays of the afternoon sun; all the other sides are open. The arena is enclosed by a low fence, and between it and the high fence on the west side there is a small enclosure, presumably meant for a grand-stand, or private boxes; here the spectators crowd all around, leaning over the fence of the arena; but at the east side there is a platform or stage erected on bamboo poles; the stage is five feet above ground, and reached by a ladder; spectators are standing on this slim erection, and others crouch below it too. There is other and extensive accommodation for the sports; an open square is surrounded by seats constructed of bamboo poles fixed horizontally on short piles, and beyond this there is another space under a roofing of bamboo and mats. These spaces are where the cocks are kept, tethered to small stakes in the ground, and the men sit all around on the seats in the interval between one fight and the getting up of another match. The day we visited the place, the sport was said to be dull; there were only about eighteen fighting birds on the ground, and few of them could match; the birds were moulting, and hence the small turn-out. We were told that some days there might be nearly a hundred cocks brought to the pit, when numerous combats take place. The owners sit on the benches, talking loudly to each other, making challenges or bets; the talking goes on in Spanish chiefly, but a great deal of pidgin English is also used. The Manilamen are dressed in holiday suits, bright coloured, and checks of the "loudest" pattern; a conspicuous sportsman amongst them is dressed in quite a different garb; he is a Parsee, dressed in a long robe of dark grey checked tweeds, with his curiously-shaped *topee* stuck on the back of his head; away in a corner is a quiet and apparently disinterested person, a Marwaree, in long white robe and white turban; beside him an old man with white beard, wearing a Turkish fez minus the tassel; but his blue cotton pants and jacket show he is only an old sailor, and he is more like an Irishman than a Turk; there are also several "packet-rats" and "beachcombers" of the English mercantile marine, who have been discharged at this port and have lounged about here for many weeks.

During the short time we were there three matches were got up, but only one came to anything. A challenge being given, the owners of the birds set them down beside each other in the open square, to see if they show a disposition to fight; then each owner takes up his bird and holds it out to the other; if the birds ruffle the feathers of their neck and show game for fighting, the match is agreed on, and the owners, others helping them, proceed to put on the horrible artificial spurs; for the fighting is not done in a natural way, but with a long steel blade fastened on the right leg of the cock. These spurs vary in length according to the size of the birds, the measure being from the foot to the joint of the leg. The average spur is two inches in length; it is just like the blade of a small knife, bill-shaped at the point, and as sharp as a lance. Some owners have a quiver of such spurs; they take the leather case from their pocket, select a spur, and then proceed to fix it on the leg of the bird. The blade is furnished with a double haft, which is placed against the leg and passes on either side of the natural spur; then great lengths of strong thread are wound round the leg till the blade is firmly secured, and the bird when placed on the ground cannot use the right foot on account of its being so much tied up; the blade meanwhile is covered with a leather sheath. When both combatants are ready, they are taken into the arena; the fence round it is lined with people on the outside, and about a dozen Manilamen are inside getting up bets on the contest. In one match we saw, the birds ran away from each other at the first trial inside the arena; in another, one caved in after the first round; the third fight lasted about ten minutes, which was a most unusual circumstance, as it is said the fights generally result in a kill or a capitulation in the first minute or two. But in this case there was a horrible fight. The backers had been calling for dollars for about five minutes, while the owners were in the middle of the arena with birds in hand; the stakes were about twelve dollars, besides outside betting; the final trial was made, the birds were presented to each other, and each pecked the neck of his opponent; if they had not done that, it was still time for one owner to withdraw and save his stakes; but the the birds are game fellows, and the backers shout with glee at the prospect of seeing a good fight, and at their chance of winning a few dollars. The arena is cleared of all but two or three men; the stakeholder has thrown down the Mexicans on the ground, and with one coin describes a rude circle round each pile of dollars. The sheaths are removed from the spurs of steel; each owner kisses his bird, and then puts it down on the ground, and there is great shouting and excitement amongst the spectators when the poor birds begin their terrible fight for life or death. One is a grey, the other a brown, and both are young Tientsin fowls. They duck down their heads, with their feathers standing on end around their necks like Elizabethean ruffs; then one leaps over the other and attempts to strike his opponent; they turn again and spring at each other; they jump about, till they have been nearly all over the arena; and their feathers are flying through the air; then the grey gets hold of the brown fowl by the neck and drags his head to the ground, but fails to get above him; the brown one rises and seizes the grey; now they have got hold of each other, the bill of one at the back of the neck of the other, and they keep a firm grip for a while, dancing round and round, each trying to gain the mastery. The grey one throws off the brown, and makes him back up against a fence; the grey then springs at the brown two or three times; and the breast of the latter is bare of feathers, covered with blood, and deeply cut. The two birds are getting pretty tired; they come out to the centre of the arena and take things quietly for a time; the grey has stuck his head under the wing of the brown; the brown pecks gently at the back of the grey, and thus they go on for half a minute; then the grey withdraws his head, flies at his opponent, and his opponent flies next; another halt put in by the strange procedure of the grey with his head under the brown's wing; and finally,. after nearly ten minutes' hard fighting has taken place, the grey makes a wild spring at the brown, and in flying over him sends the long steel spur into his neck; the brown runs away; his owner picks him up and sets him down in front of the grey again, but the brown again runs off;—the grey is proclaimed victor, and his owner and backers win a few dollars over him. The brown cock was dreadfully cut, and seemed to be good for nothing but curry; the grey victor did not appear to have any serious wound at all. Such is a faithful description of the shocking cruelty practised in the game of cock-fighting, as regularly carried on by these Manila-Spaniards under the name of "sport!" The sight was so sickening that some European visitors turned away in disgust.

THE BIRTHDAY OF THE MOON; IN SHANGHAI CITY BY NIGHT.

N the Fifteenth Day of the Eighth Moon,* which is celebrated by the Chinese as the Birthday of the Moon, we availed ourselves of the opportunity of visiting Shanghai City at night, as that is a great night with the Chinese in worshipping their gods and burning incense in the streets and public places of the City; the City Gates are open until midnight, whereas on all other days of the year—excepting the eve of the New Year—the gates are closed at ten o'clock. The Chinese call that particular day the Birthday of the Moon, because, according to their legends, the Emperor Ming-Tai-Tso, the first Emperor of the Ming Dynasty, when out with his army and sore pressed for want of supplies to sustain his men, sent out foraging parties on the Fifteenth Day of the Eighth Moon; but the darkness was at first so great that they could not see where to obtain anything in the fields, when the Moon shone out suddenly with great brilliancy, and the soldiers were enabled by her light to go to the fields and gather in crops for food for the army. Why they had not looked after this in daylight, does not appear from the legend; that difficulty is ignored for the sake of the story. · The Emperor was so much pleased by the wonderful appearance of the Moon at what the legend states was an opportune moment, that he ordered the day to be ever afterwards celebrated as the Birthday of the Moon. Another peculiar custom still in vogue has its origin in the story of this Emperor's foraging party, namely, that any one can go to the fields or to the houses of the farmers on this particular night,· and take whatever he pleases, in the way of grain, vegetables, or food of any kind, without let or hindrance. The foragers of Ming-Tai-Tso's army on that eventful night discovered a peculiar root, which, on trial, after cooking, was discovered to be good for food, and a root to be desired to make one enjoy mutton chops; that root was the potato. "Ould Ireland" cannot claim the potato in the face of this legend; but whether the Celestial foragers also found traces of the ancestors of the American potato bug, the legend sayeth not. Another interesting legend is that, on the Fifteenth Day of the Eighth Moon, the Emperor Tong-Ming-Wang, of the Tong Dynasty, visited the Moon, in company with his secretary, wives, servants, and retainers, and in that luminary they saw a party of young girls, of tender years, who were playing musical instruments and acting tableaus and ancient plays. To this legend the origin of Chinese theatres is attributed.

These stories are related by a Chinese friend while we walk through the Foreign Settlements to the Old North Gate of the City, and then we enter upon an exploring expedition such as few foreigners would care to undertake, but which was not devoid of interest to a foreigner, and its narration may be of interest to others. Shanghai City is shunned by the foreigners who have settled here; most of them have perhaps visited it once out of curiosity to

---

* 15th Day, Eighth Moon, 5th year of Kwang Sü; 30th September, 1879, A.D

see if it is actually as bad as it is said to be, and they find there is nothing attractive in it, but many things repulsive,—its narrow streets, and dirty stagnant pools and creeks; one visit is enough for most people, and that too in the daytime. Well, if there is nothing particularly worth seeing in the daytime, what could possess one to go there at night? Curiosity. Without the expectation of seeing anything to repay the trouble and time spent in the nocturnal perambulation of the City, we crossed the bridge over the moat, and followed our guide down the short winding path, bordered on each side by piles of water-kongs, Soochow bath-tubs, and other huge specimens of native pottery of the coarser descriptions; the path, which is a busy scene in the day time, a crowd of people going to and fro, is now almost deserted; there are only a few stragglers between the bridge and the gate; the "old clo'" men, and the curiosity stall-keepers, who are to be seen during the day with collections of rubbish by the wayside, are all gone to their hovels in the City. We pass through the first archway, or outer gate, and then are within the circular tower, with the sky for a roof, which is seen at all the City Gates. In front of us is the watchmen's house, the guard, by the way, being soldiers of much the same class as the Taotai's "picked troops." One of them is standing in the open front of the house, but not as a sentinel or watchman ought to stand; his favourite position most probably is lying down, with a hubble-bubble tobacco pipe to console him and wile away the time; but now this watchman is standing, yet does not look very much like being on duty, even although it is the Birthday of the Moon and a great celebration night. He is standing, stretching out his arms and yawning, as if he had just got up from a sleep and thought of shutting up shop at the usual time—ten o'clock; but this is an extraordinary occasion, and he has still two hours before him to watch the stragglers passing in and out of the gate. The watchman is duly honouring the great occasion of the Birthday of the Moon, for in front of his house there stands a small table, and on it are two large candlesticks, burning huge red-wax candles, and between them there is a pot with a small pile of sandal-wood, smouldering away. The Buddhistic sandal-wood is the incense of China, and its perfume is about as disagreeable as the smoke from an opium pipe. We were to have plenty of sandal-wood smoke that night, and other disagreeable perfumes from dirty streets, and therefore we took the precaution to keep up a continual incense burning of our own, the joss-sticks being Manila cigars. After passing through the second archway, or inner gate, we proceeded along a narrow, dirty street, running parallel with the wall, and in a direction towards the New North Gate. In this street the houses were all wretched hovels—most of them only dwellings, the others small workshops, cookshops, and teashops. In almost all of them the frontage was still open, and feeble attempts at illumination were seen on every hand; the shopkeeper who managed to light six wax candles, took the shine out of his neighbours; but all have sandal-wood burning, though only a stick or two. At one small shop there is an unusual display—bundles of sandal-wood, ornaments in paper work of flags and figures of various kinds, piles of sweetmeats of all colours;—these are for sale, and while the dealer gives a pretty good display, comparatively, in the piles of incense and wax candles he is burning at his own expense, it is more of an advertisement than anything else, to attract citizens to his shop and obtain, ere it is too late, the requisites for worshipping the Moon on this auspicious night. At another shop a little further on, there is even a much greater flare-up than the vendor of joss pidgin requisites could afford to make at his own cost. It is at a small public teahouse, where a lot of natives are sitting round the small tables, drinking tea, smoking tobacco, and listening to the barbarous music of a band—hired at enormous expense for the occasion, and which succeeds in making a most infernal din. In front of this shop are two stands bearing small tubs, and from them piles of sandalwood have been raised up two or three feet high; one of the piles has been burned down, and is now only a bright heap of smouldering ashes, and the other pile has just been fired at the top, and will burn for several hours. There were only a few stragglers in the narrow street, which was feebly lighted by the candles; and the Moon was half obscured in a mackerel sky, so that the street was rather dark; the wretched hovels were bad enough under moonlight, but their wretchedness was also half obscured.

After a pretty long walk from the Old North Gate, we came to the street which leads from the New North Gate, where there is an open piece of ground, in which three or four new fire-wells have just been dug and built up with brick. We then followed our guide through some of the principal business streets of the City, where the best of the shops are situated. All business had been suspended for two or three hours, but many of the shop frontages were still open, where all kinds of lamps were burning brightly, the sandal-wood sending its curling smoke and nauseous perfume upwards to the gods whom the Chinese worship. At the corner of one street we observed a niche in a wall, where there were various ornamentations; several candles were burning, and a pot of the all-pervading incense; small plates of sweetmeats and fruit were also lying in the niche, in front of a picture which represented the God of Happiness; the offering was being made to this deity, and the sandal-wood which was being burnt bore in Chinese characters a dedication to him. We passed on by public streets, through dirty squares, and over creeks, till we came near the City Temple. Our attention was to be first directed to the Temple of Confucius, but we found it shut up, and no illumination there; the only thing near it was a hungry cur running about with his nose to the ground in search of supper; all round by the stagnant pool which surrounds the Tea Gardens, there was scarcely anyone to be seen; and when we passed into the City Temple, from a side or back entrance, we were disappointed there too, for there wasn't even a tallow candle nor a joss stick burning about it; a few urchins were enjoying the unusual privilege of being allowed out so late, by playing in the main court-yard of the Temple; but otherwise there was no one about. There used to be two or three hundred dollars subscribed and spent on celebrations at the City Temple in honour of the Birthday of the Moon, but a subsequent enquiry elicited an explanation which is very satisfactory, and shows that the money was being applied with far wiser discretion than hitherto, for we learned from our guide that the usual fund subscribed by the citizens for illuminations at the City Temple had been devoted by the City Magistrate to the construction of the fire-wells we had just seen at the New North Gate, and for the increase of the number of water kongs throughout the City, for we had noticed too that many new kongs had been laid down at various places. That such precautions are commendable and likely to prove of good service, needs no argument for support; there have been several fires in the City this year, and it is a matter of surprise that they did not work greater havoc. Shortly after leaving the City Temple, we came to the site of one of the recent fires, where about one hundred houses had been destroyed; it must have been a very big fire, and quite beyond the powers of the citizens to cope with it, and it is a wonder the whole City did not go to ruins.

In our further perambulations we witnessed two or three special displays, but only on a very insignificant scale; at one place the God of Wealth was being glorified by an array of red wax candles and a large pile of sandal-wood; and by the side of a bridge over a creek, close to the Roman Catholic Mission chapel, there was another stand surmounted by a fiery pile of sandal-wood. The latter, we learned, was in honour of Mow-san, whose idol at one time occupied the Temple near the West Gate, from which it was recently removed to less commodious premises by the side of this creek, to make room for the God of Peace. In all the streets there were unpretentious displays by the shopkeepers; people were walking listlessly hither and thither; and youngsters were still playing on the streets. We only observed one juvenile group who had got illuminations of their own, and their design was a curious one: a little Celestial of seven or eight years of age had an illuminated representation of some animal,—our guide stretched his imagination and said it was a rabbit, but it might as well have been called a turtle;—the framework was of bamboo, covered with coloured paper, a candle burned inside, and the whole was mounted on wheels, and as one youngster dragged his "show" along the almost deserted street, the silence was broken, only by the gleeful shouts of his companions. At the District Magistrate's yamên, to which we ultimately found our way, there was a considerable amount of incense burning. At the outside of the yamên are the houses of the Magistrate's " runners," and the dingy cells in which prisoners, convicted of paltry offences, are confined. All round about there were primitive illuminations in the never-failing red wax; three or four huge piles of sandal-wood were burning in front of the house of the "head runner," and our guide and friend read on the unburnt sticks of sandal-wood a dedication to the god who presides over the prisoners, by the District Magistrate, Moh. After walking through some of the open courts of the yamên, where petty mandarins have their residences, we turned to make our way out of the City, and by traversing many a narrow street, by many curious turnings, we at length found ourselves at the New North Gate, and were glad to get out again to the wider streets of the French Concession, and on to the Bund, where there was no perfume of sandalwood; we thought the journey had not been quite worth the time spent on it, and that the Birthday of the Moon in Shanghai City was a very poor affair after all.

THE SHANGHAI TELEPHONE EXCHANGE.

OUR local Telephone Exchange, situated in the Szechuen Road, was first started in 1881. It was then worked under the name of the Oriental Telephone Company, whose head-quarters are in London, and of which the present China and Japan Telephone Company, Limited, is a branch, the Great Northern Telegraph Company being the agents. The Oriental Telephone Company has also Exchanges in India, Australia, New Zealand, the Straits, and Ceylon. The Company had to contend at the outset with a strong local opposition here; and so keen was the competition between the opposing aspirants for public favour that the annual subscription, which was originally fixed at $150, dropped in a short time to the low figure of $50. Some six months after starting, the Oriental Telephone Company bought out the opposition, thus becoming sole masters of the field; but the subscription was not altered till the 26th May 1886, when it was made Tls. 50.

In 1885 the Company spent no less a sum than $2,500 in increasing the efficiency of the service, which had previously not been satisfactory, as up to that time it had been worked on the "Law system," by which several subscribers conversed over the same line, each one being able to hear what the other said. It was therefore considered expedient to put up new lines, and now each subscriber has a separate, insulated wire from the Exchange to whatever office in telephonic connection he wishes to communicate with; so that his secret breathings to friends at a distance cannot be heard by his enemies, or be made use of to his detriment.

The merits and advantages of the Telephone service in Shanghai need no eulogy from us, as they are obvious to all who know anything of the matter; but for the information of the general public we give a few of the advantages additional to the ordinary one of being able to communicate on business matters with so many places in the Settlements, either by day or night.

In case of burglary, or visits from midnight prowlers, who shun the light because their deeds are evil, a subscriber is not only able to ring up the Central Police Station, but he can, by conveying a request by telephone to the operator at the Exchange, be placed at once in *direct* communication with Police Station nearest to his domicile, whether in the English or American Settlement. He can also receive, *gratis*, the correct time daily, as communicated by wire to the Exchange from the Observatory at Siccawei. In the summer months he can, if he ask for it, have the dulcet strains of the Town Band telephoned to his house or office free of expense; and by paying a small additional sum he can have Pony crown receivers fitted above his head, so that while reclining gracefully on his sofa, reading, he can enjoy at the same time the soul-subduing music of the Band, without having the trouble of holding up the receivers. If his house should, unhappily, catch fire, by calling the Exchange and giving the operator the locality, every Fire and Police Station in the various Settlements can be warned in a few seconds; and, finally, should a serious accident happen to himself or any of his family (accidents, as everybody knows, will occur even in the best regulated families), or any member thereof be taken suddenly ill, every doctor in the Settlements can be called up; so that even if, say, four or five of the faculty happened to be out at the time, he is still bound to get into direct communication with some medico in a very brief space of time.

The subscribers at present number 223. The Company started with about 25 in 1881. In 1882, the opposition having been disposed of, the number reached 65. On the 30th June 1883, the number of subscribers was 72; on 30th June 1884 it reached 84; and on the same date in 1885 it had gone up to 130. It will thus be seen that, as time goes on, the Exchange becomes more and more appreciated, as it deserves to be. Formerly, before the "Law system" was superseded, when one fellow could hear conversations not intended for his particular "auditorium," complaints from subscribers were perpetual; now they do not average more than a couple per week. The number of calls which the operators at the Exchange have to attend to, both by day and night, average monthly the very large number of 16,000, or more than 500 *per diem*. Three Chinese operators attend to the calls. The man who attends to the night calls puts a switch across to where he sleeps, in an adjoining room, so that whenever a "drop" falls on the switch-board—the signal that a subscriber wants to have a "confab" with somebody—a strong local battery is put into circuit, causing an electric bell to ring close to the operator's head, which instantly rouses him up. We suppose he sometimes pours celestial maledictions on the subscriber's head who awakes him from a pleasant dream. We fancy we should—"curses not loud but deep." An average Native staff of fifteen is kept for both outdoor and indoor work, but when new constructions are in progress a larger number is required. The operators, who must, of course, know English, have to be paid highly.

The Oriental Telephone Company has acquired all the rights of using the patents of the Edison and Bell Companies (now the United Telephone Company) in any part of the world. Our local Company holds three Edison's and two Bell's patents, as well as the Gower-bell Telephone patent, granted to the Consolidated Telephone Construction and Maintenance Company.

The switch-board at the Exchange is well worth inspecting. On this board all the various subscribers' wires, almost as "thick as autumnal leaves in Vallombrosa," converge and find a resting-place. Each subscriber's line, leading from his house or office to the Exchange, is earthed at both ends to complete the circuit. On the switch-board is an annunciator drop for each subscriber,—that is to say, electro-magnets, with plates of brass in front, which conceal the numbers underneath until an electric current, traversing the magnet, releases the plate, which drops and discloses the number of the subscriber calling. Corresponding to these drops there is an equal number of holes, all numbered, and there are 40 plugs for making connections. These plugs consist of two pieces of brass which fit in the holes and are joined together by a flexible wire insulated with silk. When a subscriber rings his magnet bell he sends an electric current through the electro-magnet appropriated to him at the Exchange, causing the drop in front of his number there to fall. The operator then at once shoves a plug into, say, hole No. 20, which puts that line into connection with the Exchange instrument and disconnects it from the earth. He then calls out "Hello!" when the person at No. 20 may say, "No. 50." The operator then puts the plug at the other end into No. 50, which disconnects that from the earth and makes a complete line from No. 20 to 50. At the same time he depresses a key and gives a couple of turns to the magnet, which rings No. 50 bell. No. 50 then turns the handle of the magnet, which rings No. 20 bell, indicating that No. 50 is ready to have a palaver with him. They then proceed to business, receivers in hand and placed against the organ of hearing. Having finished their "confab" they restore the receivers to their original position and give a couple of turns to the handle of their magnets. In the meantime the operator, having pulled over a small lever, causes another drop at the bottom of the switch-board to fall, thereby indicating that they have finished speaking, and he then immediately pulls the two plugs out, the same process being gone through, *ad infinitum*, with other subscribers. There are frequently as many as 30 or 40 people talking at the time, separate plugs being, of course, used for each pair.

The time signal is worked in the following manner:—The current, having been sent along the line from the Observatory at Siccawei, passes through the Exchange, thereby causing a couple of drops to fall. Immediately this occurs, a local circuit is put in which passes through an electric-magnet, which in turn draws up an armature and releases the hammer of a large gong, causing the hammer to drop. Close under the gong is an ordinary microphone transmitter. This is connected to a brass plate, from which there are about 80 plugs, these being inserted into the different numbers of the subscribers who have applied for the time. A few seconds before 12 o'clock they unhook their receivers, through which they can hear, to a fraction of a second, the correct time.

THE AQUARIUS COMPANY'S STEAM FACTORY AND WATER DISTILLERY.

THE spacious and complete establishment of this Company, which in June 1893 commenced to furnish the public of Shanghai with pure water, both still and sparkling, for the table, under the registered trade-mark of "Aquarius," is assuredly one of the most perfectly equipped establishments to be found in any part of the world, consisting of five large buildings subdivided into Boiler-house, Engineers Work Shop, Engine Room, Distilling, Room, Aërating and Bottling Godown, Storage Loft for Distilled Water on upper-floor Laboratory, Chemical Room on upper-floor, Storage Godowns for manufactures, Cork and Label Rooms, Bottle Godown, Office and Managers Dwelling House. Its site, at the junction of the Seward Road extension with the Broadway, is admirably suited for the purpose, well removed from the contaminating odours and contact of Chinese houses, yet sufficiently near the Settlement for the speedy distribution of the waters from the Central Depôt of the Company at No. 4 Foochow Road. The buildings are well in keeping with the very utilitarian character of the work carried on inside, and are solid brick structures, with massive timber fittings inside. The factory is neat in exterior and substantial in nature, and gives an agreeable air of manufacturing progress and busy life to the neighbourhood. The various processes of distillation, aëration, bottling, and wiring are conducted in different departments of the same spacious, airy, commodious, and well-lighted buildings. A brief description of the works may usefully preface an attempt to make known the process of treating the Waterworks water—first, to render it absolutely pure and fit for drinking, and then to charge it with gas. Steam is supplied by two very fine Cornish steel boilers, each working up to 90 lbs. pressure per square inch, and having an aggregate of 60 horse-power. The motive power is furnished by a horizontal tube-girder engine of the Ryder type, capable of working up to 34 h.-p.; it is from one of the best engineering firms in London. The steam-pump used for pumping the water from the Aquarius Company's large covered reservoir (containing 25,000 gallons of the Water-Works Company's Water) is of the double cylinder rotative pattern, and is furnished with 6 gun-metal plungers. The most interesting portion of the machinery is that in the distilling room. This apparatus, which is the latest patent distilling process, is that known as the "Improved Patent Treble Distilling Fresh Water Apparatus." It is one of the most complicated and perfect pieces of machinery yet introduced to Shanghai, and is the first of its pattern ever made. The distilling plant, is capable of turning out over 3,500 gallons of absolutely pure water *per diem*. It consists of three large and four small evaporators, filled with innumerable pipes of block-tin, through which the water passes in the form of steam. Ordinary water, generally speaking, looks pretty well till one has seen it going through the searching and cleansing process in these evaporators, and sees the marvellously bright, clear, silver-spark-

THE AQUARIUS COMPANY.

ling liquid that passes out through the pipes of the distillers into the purified receiving tanks in the upper portion of the building. The supply of water in the distilling apparatus is indicated by duplicate regulators attached to each of the large evaporators. The large reservoir is constructed of concrete and brick, heavily lined with Portland cement, and roofed in. The water from the Waterworks is taken in through a standard hydrant. Once the water has gone through the process of distillation, it passes through pipes made of block-tin only, so as to ensure absolute freedom from contamination. The extensive storage tanks for the distilled water are kept in the upper portion of the building, and, while most effectually ventilated, are most carefully covered in from all dust. They are constructed of the best Bangor slate, imported from England, and the finest quality Portland cement. All the conduit pipes, and in fact every pipe through which the Aquarius water passes, are either made of copper, heavily lined with block tin, or consist entirely of the latter metal, by which all chance of injurious metallic particles finding their way into the water is avoided. Having said so much about the purifying apparatus, we may now briefly describe the aërating process. Nothing, down to the smallest detail, has been omitted to produce water absolutely pure, and the perfect cleanliness and order of the Aquarius establishment speak volumes for the forethought and care exercised in its planning and arrangement. The distilled water is passed down from the storage tanks into the aërating apparatus, where it is mixed with the carbon dioxide gas which is generated in improved chambers. The important parts of the machinery are duplicated, so that a breakdown of one need not stop the work.

Before entering the aërating machine, the gas is filtered through a new pattern gas filter. Once the water is charged with the gas the rest of the work is simple and is done automatically by two steam-bottling machines, from which the bottle is ejected filled, corked, and ready for wiring. The latter operation can also be performed by machinery instead of by the usual hand method. The greatest attention is given to the washing operations. The bottles are first steeped in ordinary Waterworks water for twenty-four hours, after which they are again washed by very effective revolving machinery in hot water, and brushed, after which they are fixed on gun-metal plungers, through which a strong spray of distilled water is ejected, washing all traces of the ordinary water out of the bottles. The arrangements for making sweetened waters are very perfect; the various kinds of syrups, for lemonade, ginger beer, ginger ale, being contained in large covered porcelain jars fitted with silver taps. Only the purest chemicals are used in the manufacture of the syrups, which is carried on in a spotlessly clean laboratory, upstairs, and it is only entered by the manager of the works, who alone has anything to do with this portion of the manufactures. The Chinese staff have nothing whatever to do with the manipulation of the Company's products—a precaution that will be properly appreciated by everyone who knows how oblivious the Natives are about such trifles as cleanliness or careful handling. Everything about the factory is beautifully clean and fresh. The flooring of the main building is of solid concrete and cement, sloping to the four corners so that it can be washed down daily, and the blessing of such a state of things will at once appeal to those who live in a country like this, where dirt and stenches are the ordinary accompaniments of life. The public may rely with confidence upon the purity of the waters sent out by this Company, as the Factory and Distillery are under experienced European control, and they avail themselves of the advice of a leading local medical man, to whose approval and inspection all their waters are submitted. The Company's waters have already become so well known that there is no need for us to dilate upon the inestimable advantages of having such pure waters at our command at a very reasonable price, and in a place like Shanghai, where in Summer cholera sometimes assumes a serious aspect, it is a matter of the greatest importance that the Public should be able to obtain absolutely pure drinking water. No filter will ever make impure water pure. Distillation alone has that power, and the Treble Distilling Process adopted by the Aquarius Company is the most perfect existing at the present time. Boiling does not free water from inorganic matter, such as silica, lime, and other Mineral substances held in solution, and therefore invisible to the eye. This inorganic or stony substance, however, is precipitated by Treble Distillation or in other words, is left behind in the stills when the water which contained it has passsed into steam. The work undertaken by the Aquarius Company has proved to be one of the benefits of our East. The Company have produced the first drinkable and pure water ever seen in Shanghai. The Registered Trade Mark of this Company is a most appropriate one as it is the sign of the Zodiac representing the water bearer.

GAMBLING IN CHINA.

THE greatest evil which afflicts the Chinese people is not their fondness for the soothing *papaver somniferum*, but their ineradicable passion for gambling. In China, it is hardly necessary to point out how wide-spread and universal is the habit, neither class nor sex, nor age being free from the vice, which enters everywhere—into the guild-houses and tea-houses of the men and the inner apartments of the women. We see it on all sides, and the disastrous effects of the habit come under our notice every day. Chance is invited more largely into the affairs of men in China, we venture to say, than in any other country in the world, and it is perhaps this constant permeation of the air with the gambling spirit that makes the residents from the West when in China amongst the most insanely speculative species of their race. Association with a nation of gamblers like the Chinese must exercise in the long run an appreciable effect upon the minds and habits and mode of thought of other people who dwell amongst them. Nor is the passion for gambling more encouraged by the laws of China than it was by the laws of Rome in the early days of its decline, or, say, of England in the period immediately preceding the Reformation. Perhaps it is that the effeminacy and want of martial spirit, which are the most distinctive characteristics of the Chinese to-day, are due to their inordinate and universal passion for dice and cards and hazard games of all kinds. HENRY VIII passed an act for "maintaining archery and debarring unlawful games of chance," for he saw in the increasing skill of his people in casting dice a growing clumsiness and falling off in their expertness with the "yew bow," and he directed stringent legislation against the former practice. China's decadence in the martial arts must in some measure be ascribed to the same cause, for in a country where the whole year is one long saturnalia, in which gambling may be indulged in with immunity from legal penalty, the people have no time or inclination for martial or ruder exercises. Not only does the rich man in China strive with dice and cards to add to his wealth, but take a walk through any Chinese city or through any Chinese street in our own Foreign Settlements, and you can see the poor coolie wooing the fickle goddess with equal fevour, but on a smaller scale. Even the toddling children are taught to gamble with a *cash* or two with some itinerant and sporting *restaurateur*, for a few sweetmeats or cakes, instead of making their purchases direct. The sweetmeat merchant has affixed to his paraphernalia a rude and miniature roulette board, with a revolving hand, which his youthful customer tempts to let stand on a lucky number, when he gets twice or thrice the value of his money, or if the fates are adverse, the spindle tops an unluckly figure and he loses his *cash*. Yet he loses it like a little philosopher and accepts the results with the nonchalance and suavity of the most confirmed punter at Monte Carlo or Monaco. The tired workman, instead of buying his evening meal, prefers in the same way to gamble for it with the owner of the travelling cook-shop. He draws a stick from a bundle, and according to its number wins or loses his bread or rice-cake. If gambling were confined to a class of people who do not risk their all in winning or losing stakes, it would be bad enough; but in China, not only the beggars gamble away their few *cash* bestowed on them by charitable people, but the very prisoners in their bamboo cages gamble with the scanty scraps of food or the few rags of clothing they get from the compassionate. In short, all would rather starve than forego the pleasures of the game, and the fact we think is demonstrable that it is only when he has nothing more to lose or stake that the Chinaman ever commits suicide. Outside the Tartar City of Peking, to the south and at the entrance to the Chinese City, is a bridge colloquially called "The Beggars' Bridge," the true "bridge of sighs," for here may be seen the most abject poverty and human misery,—sights pitiful enough to draw tears from the eyes of the gorgeous granite-stone dragons who watch the passing, living stream of wretchedness. The deformed, the leprous, the blind, and the most hideous and disgusting semblance of humanity squat in rows and knots along the sides of this bridge, soliciting, with horrid wails, the charity of the passers-by, and forthwith venturing the scanty results of their begging in gambling. As inevitably as the stakes are lost and won, quarrels between the miserable gamblers make the scene more frightful. No private gaming houses are found in the Celestial capital, but in almost every street or lane there are private resorts open to their habitues all night. In the vicinity of the Foreign Legations and in the street commonly called Taichi-chang, not far from the Customs residences, the high and long walls of a ducal palace may be seen on the east side of the road. The entrance is on the north side, in a street running parallel with Legation Street. This is the residence of one of the great men of Peking; yet even this place is used as a common gambling-house, while the gate-houses of the Foreign Legations are surreptitiously converted by the Native staffs into gambling dens. In the residences and grounds of the high Peking officials and aristocracy gambling is more or less openly carried on, entrance being regulated by the watchmen who admit only the initiated. Sometimes the *gendarmerie* of the city make a half-hearted attempt to catch the denizens of these resorts at their game, but the system of signals is so perfect that, as we know in Shanghai even our own police are seldom able to catch the offenders *in flagrante delicto*. The arm of the law in China is too short and too puny to deal with the evil that is eating the hearts out of the people, and that does more harm than all the opium that was ever imported from Malwa, Patna, and Benares put together. Mandarins, merchants, compradors, shroffs, tradesmen, and domestic servants all alike enjoy a little flutter with the cards or dice, and each province and every district of each province has its own peculiar form of gambling. Even in the everyday experience of the Foreigner in China,—and he hears or knows but little of the domestic or social life of the Natives,—the subject of Chinese gambling is one that is constantly cropping up. One day it is a bank comprador who bolts with a few lakhs of dollars in consequence of a big gamble going wrong, next day it is one's own house-boy or cook who has got caught in the toils, owing to a little miscalculation or misfortune in *fan-tan* or *po-tsze*. Everywhere it is the same story, and of all the evils that China is afflicted with the inveterate attachment of the people, from the highest to the lowest, for games of chance and gambling in all its forms is the worst, and does more to sap the life-blood of the nation and divert their energies from more legitimate and, in the long run, more certain roads to profit than all the drowsy drugs in the world.

THE CELESTIAL "BOULEVARDS" OF SHANGHAI, OR FOOCHOW ROAD BY DAY AND NIGHT.

ESTERN civilization probably never encounters a greater stumbling-block in the Celestial Empire than when it attempts to bear upon the social institutions of the Chinese; and this is not to be wondered at, for all of us know how reluctantly we are persuaded to adopt customs and manners at variance with those to which we have been used from our earliest childhood, and which we have always looked upon as an inheritance from our forefathers. How much the more difficult must it prove to revolutionize—for in the present instance it means nothing less—the inner life of a nation claiming to be the most ancient and populous in the world, and which, by its ineradicable superstitious beliefs, presents so powerful an anti-lever that all attempts of "Western barbarians" to put out of its track the primæval form of its social institutions and inaugurate a reform, appear to be almost a "dream of the sweetly impossible!" The Chinese claim that their usages originated at a date anterior to that assigned to the Deluge, and they are attached to them with a tenacity perhaps greater than that of any other Asiatic nation for its ancient customs.

No other treaty port in China offers such a rich field for research with regard to the gradual adoption of Western social manners by the Chinese as Shanghai, which may be termed the pioneer city in the social reform movement. The reasons are obvious: not only is our port one of those which were opened to foreign trade immediately after the treaty of Nanking in 1842, but Shanghai has also been raised, within less than half a century, from the insignificant rank of a third-class Chinese city to the fame and wealth of one of the chief commercial emporia of the world, in which concentrate all the riches of a province emphatically called the "Garden" of the Middle Kingdom. The wealth which lies accumulated within the boundaries and jurisdiction of our port may be termed enormous; and luxury, the natural offspring of opulence, has found here a homestead which forms an interesting counterpart to the outward splendour of Western "high life" of which our settlements have a right to boast. That the Chinese have adopted some of our social institutions must be evident to even a superficial observer. Slowly but surely the "Heathen Chinee" moves along the high road of progress, and the roar of the mighty wave of civilization, rolling onward from the West, is already distinctly audible in almost every part of the greatest empire that the sun shines upon.

The street which, from a Chinese point of view, forms *the* public thoroughfare of our settlements, is Foochow Road, which may be rightly styled

THE CELESTIAL "BOULEVARDS" OF SHANGHAI.

The surprise and bewilderment of an English country lad who for the first time finds himself in one of the principal thoroughfares of the great British metropolis, cannot be greater than what the Celestial peasant experiences who for the first time visits our settlements and, naturally, is piloted into the fashionable avenue of the Celestial quarter—Foochow Road.

True, there is no more resemblance between the last-named street and the Boulevards of Paris than there is between the "Front Street" of a mushroom city of the Far West and the "Strand" on the Thames, as far, at least, as the buildings are concerned; but then, what the houses lack in outward appearance they make up for in their interior arrangements; at least to a Celestial's way of thinking. Foochow Road possesses but very few fair specimens of semi-Chinese architecture, considering its length. It is as narrow as the average of the roads in Shanghai, being just about wide enough to permit two carriages to pass each other; but, on the other hand, it possesses the great advantage, rarely found in our settlements, of being almost as straight as an arrow. An occasional visitor will be struck by the great number of Chinese hotels, some of which bear, besides their names in Chinese, English designations, such as "Bowling Alley," "Billiard Rooms," &c.; then there are a number of Chinese confectionery shops, displaying in their windows the most "highly praised" dainties of Western *confiseurs;* stores which deal in edibles such as decorate the tables of Western *gente decente;* several livery stables, letting out on hire vehicles of all possible descriptions, and numerous other establishments which will be described later on, and which, could a bird's-eye view be taken of them, would form a most varied and interesting panorama.

London Bridge, with its myriads of people daily crossing, can hardly present a more striking picture than the

TRAFFIC IN FOOCHOW ROAD.

Just post yourself, for about half an hour, between the hours of 5 and 6 in the afternoon, alongside the celebrated "Louen Yuen" Billiard Saloon, and the panorama which unfolds itself before you will copiously repay your trouble. You will stare, and perhaps not get tired of the curious sight. As in the wedding procession of some distinguished nobleman, carriage after carriage comes driving along. The sedan-chair, which at one time monopolised street traffic as a means of personal conveyance, has become conspicuous by its absence during the daytime; however, when the shades of evening are beginning to fall fast, and during the hours of night when the roll of the carriages dies away, you will see innumerable palanquins making their way hither and thither; their occupants are mostly almond-eyed beauties in the gayest and richest attire. Where they are bound to, is one of the mysteries of Foochow Road.

It takes a strong physical constitution to stand, for any length of time, the deafening noise these carriages make. Yet how picturesque are the groups of passengers which they carry! And what

CURIOUS SPECIMENS OF VEHICLES

these avail themselves of! There is, for instance, a species of carriage which I would call the Celestial "droska;" to all appearance it is a morphodite product of Western and Eastern cartwright's work. This "cab," which can accommodate about four persons, has spread over its frame-work a cover made of coloured cotton stuff, shaped much like an umbrella, but of somewhat gigantic dimensions; this can be opened and shut at pleasure. The principal advantage which this vehicle offers is its cheapness; for a few *cash* the Celestial can enjoy a ride of a mile or more. Of course, it will be obvious that only "second-hand gentry" avail themselves of these carriages. The Mongolian chargers yoked to the shafts would form, as to their condition, not a bad counterpart to the lean kine of King Pharaoh. The poor animals move along in a style not unlike that of a wooden horse in a puppet-show. In years gone by these full-bred Mongolians were hopeful candidates for the honours of a Shanghai "Derby" or a "Ladies' Purse;" but, alas! when put to the test they turned out to be "duffers" of the first water, and were sold as discarded griffins at the average figure of Tls. 10 per head. Hark! dost thou not hear the dull and rumbling sound, resembling far off thunder or that of heavy artillery crossing a wooden bridge? Lo! there comes the vehicle which, at a distance, one might easily mistake for a hearse. It turns out, however, to be the "buss" of John Chinaman. As compared with the vehicle at home, the Celestial omnibus is of much smaller dimensions, fitted up to hold about eight persons. It has no top gallery, so Celestial dudes here cannot have the pleasure of staring at all the world passing by, as is the case in Western countries. In other respects the comfort, or—properly speaking—the inconvenience of a Chinese "buss," is almost on a level with that of a home specimen. But here comes the "craft" *par excellence*, as trim as a Chinese tea-clipper in days of yore—we mean the brougham or landau, private property in most instances. Its occupants represent the *crème de la crème* of Celestial *élite*, probably the heads of large silk or tea firms. *Paterfamilias* and *materfamilias*, who take up the back seat, are the very type of Chinese aristocracy—well fed and well dressed. *Paterfamilias* has his eyes screened by a pair of gigantic spectacles, set in tortoise-shell. The rims of these ponderous appliances are about one fourth of an inch wide; the glass almost as thick as plate-glass, giving the goggles a weight of some five ounces. Opposite the "old folk" are seated their offspring, clad in richly embroidered silk dresses. No doubt the young damsels are in their holiday attire; their faces are white-washed, else they have been dipped into a bag containing extra-fine "Golden Gate" flour. Good care, however, is taken that the sweet little labial appendages are dyed as red as Bobby Burns' "red, red rose." We have often pondered over the question, Why do Chinese ladies colour their lips? Certainly it cannot be with the intention of enticing a Celestial *cavaliero amoroso* to bestow a tender kiss thereon, for it is a well-known fact (at least so we are told) that the darling creatures of the heavenly kingdom on earth do not practise this sinful mode of exchanging reciprocal feelings. A kiss is amongst Chinese an unknown momentary deception, if one is credulous enough to believe it. But, how shall we describe the *coiffure* of these Celestial "daisies;" in fact, is it possible? If we should ever be asked to unravel the mysterious knot into which they plait their hair, we should find ourselves in a dilemma much more serious than that in which Alexander the Great found himself in days of old. Their *coiffure* is crowned by such a bountiful and magnificent display of flowers (scented, as a rule), that one fancies oneself entering the Eau de Cologne manufactory of Joahnn Maria Farina, and as to the display, it ought to prove variegated enough to do credit to a flower show on our Bubbling Well Road. There is one weakness, however, which these fair daughters of Han appear to have in common with the fair daughters of Eve in the Far West, namely, the passion for all "that glitters." Their love for gold is apparently as strong as that of the ebony-skinned belles of the Dark Continent, who, for want of the genuine article, deck themselves out with real "Brummagem." Another carriage—a fashionable four-wheeler; it carries two youthful "daisies," who are reclining with aristocratic *nonchalance*. They are, presumably, "hopeful" daughters; their forms are wrapped in silk. A smile, bewitching as that of "Circe," plays around their finely moulded lips, their almond-shaped eyes cast love-sick glances at some dandy-looking passers-by. Two elderly, sedate looking matrons are seated opposite, dressed in plain blue cotton gowns; each is armed with a white-metal pipe. With a most critical eye these two "mentors" view their charge; a hen which for the first time takes her newly hatched brood out for a walk can hardly bestow greater care on her chickens than these matrons do on their "gems." They also serve, so to say, as crotch, whenever the "hopeful" one engages in the difficult task of taking a walk; a feat not unlike the balancing of a tight-rope walker, and bearing much resemblance to the waddling of a duck. Lo! in the rear of this carriage

"Who comes ?
High towers a shape in knightly garb—
Behold the rider and the bard!"

Yes! Behold in him the type of

A CELESTIAL DUDE.

Yet how different, as regards "rig," to his Western *confrère!* If people oftentimes wonder how the occidental masher manages to squeeze his limbs into the tightly fitting clothing, which the least awkward motion threatens to burst, so does the Celestial dude's outer appearance present the very counterpart; his clothing, should a gentle garlic-laden zephyr be blowing cross the street, resembles that of an air-balloon, which expands and contracts as the hydrogen gas heats the air in the silken bag. The Celestial masher is all flowing robe; his *rosinante* a full-bred Mongolian, the beauty—or rather the reverse—of which has not been improved upon by European *technique*. White ponies are generally preferred by them, although a charger of such colour is a *rara avis*, if not something unknown altogether amongst the Chinese. White ponies kept by them have about as much claim to that colour as the pink-coloured sacred elephant of Siam has a right to be called white. Want of cleanness, we presume, makes them look so "colourless." There are two things in which the Celestial dude appears to take equal pride—his queue and the tail of the pony he rides. The queue of the Celestial masher must be long enough to sweep the ground, and the pony's tail must correspond. Of course, the longer the queue the more patrician its wearer; thus, analogous to this notion, the charger will present a more aristocratic aspect. Rather a funny sight to see the animal's and its rider's caudal appendages flying about. The Celestial dude generally fortifies his eyes with a pair of gigantic goggles, the colour of the glass variegating, ostensibly, to match the dress. Whether the different hues of the glass may have an injurious effect on the eyesight appears to be considered a matter of indifference. Put a riding whip in one hand of the equestrian, and a "Manila" in the other, and you will have the portrait of a Celestial masher on horseback.

No less interesting than the traffic abroad on carriage or horseback is

THE STREAM OF PEDESTRIANS

going hither and thither. Amongst these one will be struck with the great number of females who, in the majority of cases, may deserve to be called attractive. China is no exception to the rule that the worm invariably attacks the choicest fruit; we refer to the Celestial "Magdalens." Their number in Foochow Road is legion. The position these soiled doves hold in society, however, is not so degrading as is generally believed; many of them, by becoming concubines, pass afterwards for "honest" women. Here the vociferous cries of cooks recommending their cakes and dishes (though the savour emanating from their frying pans is not quite as odoriferous as the night breeze pregnant with the aroma of a southern clime); there travelling blacksmiths with their shops, tinkers, umbrella-menders, ambulatory barbers, peregrinatory medicine-men, itinerant cobblers, pastry men, fortune-tellers, each of them howling his own peculiar note; coolies of burden, jinrickshas, and the quaint old wheelbarrow—a scene so varied and original as to make one forget for a moment that one is standing on "ground set apart for foreigners."

It is but natural that Foochow Road should be chosen by the bulk of Celestial *chevaliers d'industrie* for their head-quarters. The light-fingered fraternity usually pitch their tents in this vicinity, where they seldom experience any difficulty in duping strangers from the outlying rural districts whom they may happen to come across. Charlatans, such as quacks, conjurers, fortune-tellers, and mountebanks of every imaginable description, make this street their temporary home. Under the last named category come

THE CHINESE "BARNUMS."

Their number is comparatively small, and their exhibitions are insignificant. One would think that in so vast an empire as China there should be no difficulty in getting up a good "show." Monstrosities of the brute creation or of the human species ought to be plentiful; however, John Chinaman, acute as he is in matters of business, apparently never attempts to benefit pecuniarily by exhibiting them. A menagerie, in the sense we understand the term, is a thing unknown to the Chinese; their "shows" are usually confined to a few harmless snakes, armadillos, bears, and occasionally one meets with cured animals, which are said to have existed in pre-Adamite ages. Such specimens never fail to rouse the curiosity of the Celestial, as does everything else that claims to have had its origin in the hoary ages of the globe. The specimens on exhibition, at all events, include no fossil remains of a mastodon or mammoth, but are clever forgeries, modelled after illustrations such as Chinese mythology depicts them. On one occasion we recollect seeing in one of these shows a frog of gigantic dimensions. It measured some five feet long in a resting position. The skin was marked like the shell of a tortoise; the claws were some ten inches in length, and undoubtedly they raised the jealousy of many a "high-toned" Celestial visitor, whose finger nails were put in the shade by the frog's digital extremities. The batrachian's jaw was spiked with four rows of teeth, very much like those of a shark, and altogether it presented a most ferocious appearance. Of course, Celestial charlatans, like their Western brethren, possess the "gift of the gab;" which is a *conditio sine quâ non*. Evidently the showman's gullible audience was being treated to an original yarn with regard to the capture of the defunct "king of frogs." A couple of hundred years ago the creature was said to have committed fearful ravages amongst the inhabitants of the Anhwei province, till, by an Imperial Decree, a small army was ordered to hunt it up. It was secured, but not until a few hundred "braves" had fallen a victim to the monster's attacks. The story reminded me somewhat of Homer's famous Batrochomyomachy.

Foochow Road has several places in which the Celestial dude and the moon-eyed dudess can restore their failing "masticators." The other day we paid a visit to the shop of

A CELESTIAL D.D.S.

His dark and cobwebbed establishment did not impress us greatly; the Doctor himself we found reclining on an opium bench, inhaling the fumes of the noxious drug. On his noticing our entry he got up and addressed us in tolerably good English. In the conversation which followed we learned that he had acquired his knowledge of the profession in the Colonies, having served his apprenticeship to an English D.D.S. From questions we asked him, we came to the conclusion that the would-be representative of the tooth-extracting profession was but a bogus practitioner, who, presumably, had been living as a No. 1 "boy" with some Colonial dentist, in whose service he managed to pick up a superficial knowledge of the profession. We ourselves certainly would not care for his services, should we find ourself in the unpleasant situation of being compelled to have some of our brown "fangs" drawn out. The charge for beautifying one's jaw with a single tooth is $10. Another Celestial D.D.S., living a few doors from the last named operator, made a much more favourable impression on us. The shop-window of his establishment betrayed that the Doctor had some Yankee notions about him. It exhibited, *en miniature*, the lay-figure of a Celestial *gentilhomme*, the mouth opened at an angle calculated to swallow a spring chicken. The labial aperture showed a set of snow-white teeth, whilst the dummy held in his hands a pair of jaw-bones filled with a few specimens of decayed bicuspids; the exhibition of the sound and rotten molars in juxtaposition was certainly not a bad idea of the dentist to puff his art. The D.D.S. received us in a very polite manner, and the "down-easter" accent with which he spoke English, left no doubt as to the country in which he had acquired his professional knowledge. He told us that he had studied dentistry in the United States, and he was only too ready to explain his *modus operandi;* he also showed us his stock of "masticators," imported from the States, some of the specimens being of gigantic dimensions, almost big enough to have fitted into the ass's jaw-bone with which Samson slew thousands of his enemies. His business, he told us, was brisk, and his charges low. Before parting he drew attention to the exorbitant charges made by the Western D.D.S. in the Far East. Whether he did so with the view of getting us to persuade acquaintances of ours to try his skill, we are not quite sure; we must confess, however, that his remarks were pretty correct.

A nation just emerging from semi-barbarism will give up nothing more reluctantly than the food to which it has been accustomed from time immemorial. A striking proof is furnished by our insular neighbours, the Japanese. Though a goodly number of them have readily adopted our mode of dressing, their daily bill of fare is yet composed of the dishes that tickled the palates of their ancestors. Seated at a table steaming with the savoury scents of a Western cuisine, dressed in a "swallow-tail," with the neck tied up with a white "choker," the eyes of the "Jap" will pass cursorily over the various dainties until they meet the dish containing his favourite "swamp-seed," and, as a rule, this comes in for a considerable share of his attention. It is therefore curious to find John Chinaman, who in matters of social reform is so far behind the Japanese, going in for food cooked in European style. The fact that the Chinese are much greater gourmands than the natives of Dai Nipon may partly account for the phenomenon. That the better class of Celestials frequently partake of European food is proved by the

RESTAURANTS IN FOREIGN STYLE,

several of which will be found in Fochow Road. These establishments are carried on very creditably, and are run by Celestials who previously held the much coveted situation of

No. 1 "boys" or cooks in some of our hotels or foreign hongs. Visitors can obtain a substantial meal at $1 per head; they can also be served with wines and liquors of the best brands at a very moderate charge—almost cost price. The drawback, however, is that they are supplied by the bottle only, as these establishments have no licence to retail liquor by the glass. Business is here in full swing between the hours of 6 p.m. and midnight. The dining-room is comfortably fitted up; the tables are neatly covered with cloth, plates, and dishes of European manufacture, and the bill-of-fare, in English and Chinese, is not omitted. "John Bull" can be accommodated with roast beef and plum-pudding, Johnny Crapaud with a dish of excellently curried hind legs of a frog, and "Dutchy" with a plate of bratwurst and sauerkraut. Foreigners who frequent these places invariably do so in company with some of their Chinese friends. The majority of Celestial visitors to these restaurants belong to the compradoric class, and occasionally there are found officers and captains of the Great Emperor's "Navee," who, away from the war-junk, appear anxious to exchange their chop-sticks for a knife and fork. In order to supply the wants of parties who wish to enjoy *sans gêne* an hour or two in company of "wife, wine and song," part of the top storey is partitioned into small apartments, furnished in European fashion. It is a rather funny sight to see those lily-footed Adelina Pattis reclining in an easy-chair, enlivening the Bacchanalia with sweet music, which they elicit from a so-called musical instrument of the genus banjo. The melody of the Anacreontic song is weird enough to make one's hair stand on end, though the Celestial "boss," seated on a lounge, swallows the notes that flow from the lips of these fair sirens with apparent satisfaction, exercising an impression not unlike that of the flute of the Indian snake-charmer over the ophidian reptile.

We think it but natural that the "ubiquitous" "Jap," with a keen eye to business, should put up a ranch in the most frequented street of our native districts. Evidently following the track taken by the Frenchman, who whenever he colonizes a country sets up a *café* as the first indication of Western civilization, the native of Dai Nipon opens commercial relations by setting up

A JAPANESE TEA HOUSE.

There is probably nothing which the visitor to the lovely shores of the Land of the Rising Sun will cherish so keenly in his memory as the pastoral tea-houses which one meets with all over Japan. An indescribable charm hovers around these establishments. What cheerful spots they are, these neat cots. How trim their diminutive gardens, tastefully laid out with beds of choice flowers, dwarf firs, and a miniature *jet d'eau*; and then, last but not least, comes the dark-eyed daughter who acts as *fille d'hôtel*, serving you with the fragrant decoction of the colourless tea. How funny you think them when making curtseys low as the pious pilgrim who stoops down to kiss the big-toe of the Holy Father in Rome. Although the concerts of the *musume* are anything but calculated to cause rapture to a foreign visitor, so are these fair "banjo pickers" probably mindful that "music hath charms," whether produced on a jew's harp or a barrel-organ. What is sauce for the goose is sauce for the gander. The "Jap" being aware how greatly his tea-house is appreciated by European travellers, came to the conclusion that such establishments would prove equally successful in "fetching" the black-haired sons of Ham; hence the numerous Japanese shops in Foochow Road. Yet what a difference there is between a tea-house in Japan and those in Shanghai! The "sign" denotes that the places are "conducted on the Japanese system," but over this "system" we must throw the veil of silence. Suffice it to say that these shops are run by the very outcasts of humanity. Situated in some back-alley, the places are musty hovels, hardly ever penetrated by the rays of the sun. We would not advise any one who through sheer curiosity visits one of these "tea-houses" to be persuaded by the fair (?) maids in waiting to partake of the stuff they offer one as tea. Though they charge *only* twenty cents for a cup (a few cakes *à la Japonaise* included), it is quite possible that one will have to spend a mexican or two at one's druggist's for medicine to remove the pernicious effects of the so-called "pure Japanese tea"—in all probability a mixture of last season's hay and weeds gathered near the Race Course. We wonder why the Japanese authorities, who only a short time ago adopted strict measures to root out the increasing evil at Shanghai, have not yet attempted to break up these haunts of profligacy, and despatch the "unfortunates" to their native country. Difficult as it may be, it is certainly within the reach of possibility to bring these abandoned shop-keepers within the clutches of Japanese law. The sooner this is done the better it will be for the fair fame of a nation which already claims to be recognised as "civilized."

"Who loves not wife, wine, and song
Remains a fool his whole life long."

Thus wrote the great German Reformer several centuries ago, and the "Heathen Chinee" of to-day appears to be equally sensible of the truth of the apophthegm as Martin Luther was in days of yore. Though we have no objection to the way in which a Celestial views the "wife and wine" question, we certainly beg to differ from him with regard to his "sing-song-pidgin," for, as a rule, what he understands by the word music we look upon as a "racket" horrible enough to electrify a dead person. The art of Orpheus is, nevertheless, held in much higher esteem in China than Western folk usually believe. This fact may be partly accounted for by the circumstance that an invention dating back to pre-historic ages invariably enjoys high veneration in the Flowery Kingdom; for, according to the legends of the country, Emperor Fu, a contemporary of Tubal, not only invented the divine art, but he is also credited with having taught his people the rudimentary rules of music. Yet, as with everything else in China, the art since those days (more than 4,000 years ago) has made little, if any, progress; it still stands on the same stage of perfection, or rather imperfection, and is characterised by the same incongruities as it was at the time when Father Noah's crew warbled their adieus on the occasion of their preparing to set out on the first voyage of discovery recorded in the annals of mankind. A place, therefore, which to foreigners visiting the "Boulevards" offers several points of interest is

THE CELESTIAL MUSIC HALL.

These establishments are of comparatively recent date in Foochow Road. Last year, we understand, there were only one or two such places in existence; at present there are more than half a dozen. The number is said to have thus increased within such a short period in consequence of the Taotai's recent proclamation, which prohibits females visiting any of the many opium shops in the settlement. The door leading to these "Free and Easys" is decorated by several sign-boards, each of which bears the name, place of birth, &c., of the fair performers; their talent, also, no doubt, being eulogised. Two "concerts" take place daily, between the hours of 5 p.m. and midnight. The charge of admission for natives is eighty *cash*; foreigners, of course, should they happen to drop in, are "squeezed," and have to pay a trifle more for their inquisitiveness. This payment entitles the visitor to as many cups of tea as he can swallow during a performance; dried melon seeds are passed round to the audience from time to time, and during the summer months there is also a constant supply of steaming sweat-rags,—pieces of flannel, steeped in hot water; a great boon, undoubtedly, to "John," to whom a pocket-handkerchief is as "caviare to the general." Some of these Halls will hold a couple of hundred people; visitors are seated around small tables. The stage is raised a couple of feet from the ground, railed in, the top being set off by coloured curtains. A large gilt-framed mirror is hung up at the end of the stage, presumably for the purpose of showing the audience the admirably done up *coiffures* of the fair performers. The orchestra consists of eight musicians; at least that number is considered necessary to make up a "full band." Usually there are the following instruments: two balloon-shaped guitars (played by girls, who sing at the same time), one three stringed guitar, two violins, one flute, one *yang-chin*, and one small drum to beat time. All these instruments play, or, properly speaking, try to play *unisono*, whilst each performer aims to distinguish herself above her colleagues by making as much noise as possible. The music is mostly ballad music. These Celestial "nightingales" are, without exception, courtesans, and (those of two of the "sing-song" houses excepted, whither Can onese exclusively flock, and where the performers sing in the Cantonese dialect) all natives of Soochow *fu*, considered by Chinese the "Garden of Eden." The district in question certainly enjoys the reputation of producing the handsomest women in the Celestial empire. As the Chinese proverb says: "To be happy on earth one must be born in Soochow, for it has the handsomest people." Now, we do not profess to be connoisseurs in this speciality, but we believe the Chinese are quite right in their taste; there is something aristocratic about these Soochow women, and they are rather fair-skinned. But then there is another thing which renders them irresistibly fascinating creatures in the eyes of "John," though we cannot agree with him in this,—they are all small-footed bipeds. The slender waist of a European belle hardly plays such an important rôle with us as these "golden lilies" do in China. Small feet are an index of gentility in the Middle Kingdom; it is the fashionable form; they are not an index of wealth, but girls with crippled feet stand a considerably better chance of marrying into more respectable families than those whose feet are of the natural size. If there is anything in China which constitutes caste, it is the distinction between the shape of the feet of the women. The genteel shoe of the bandaged foot is about 3 inches long in the sole, and the "lily-footed" belle apparently bestows as much attention on her hoofs as a western *dulcinea* does on her head-gear. Usually they wrap up their feet in flaming red silk or satin, tastefully embroidered, the heels brightly painted. The petticoat or the pantaloons are generally the prettiest part of the dress. Their hair is copiously ornamented with natural or artificial flowers, and with strings of pearls; their arms, and the hand especially which comes into prominent use when playing, are richly adorned with jade-stone and jewellery. The face, of course, is bedaubed with paint, and rouge is added to the lips and cheeks. One advantage, certainly, is derived from their thus beautifying themselves— it saves these sirens their blushes, for they cannot be seen through the paint; the eye thus becomes the only index of emotion. The eyebrows are blackened with charred sticks and are arched and narrowed, resembling the moon when a couple of days old. The foregoing, we believe, is a pretty fair picture of one and all of these Celestial "nightingales," whom the poetical genius of a modern Celestial 'Anacreon' describes as having "cheeks like the almond flower, lips like a peach blossom, eyes bright as dancing ripples in the sun, and footsteps like the lotus flower." Ahem! exactly so. But how shall we describe the impression which the vocal and instrumental efforts of these performers make upon a western ear? Is it possible at all? There are things which one must see or hear to fully appreciate, or the contrary, and I think these so-called concerts belong to this category. If it is difficult to give in print a correct idea about Chinese instrumental music, it is considerably more so with respect to their vocalization. The fact of the matter is, no description can convey a true idea of Chinese vocal music, and very few are able to imitate it when they have heard it. These "Adelinas" of course sing, as all the Celestial race do, in the falsetto key, this feature prevailing throughout. It will readily be understood that such a mode of singing (especially when the *voix de tête* is pitched below the *d*) is anything but an edifying treat to a foreign barbarian. The sounds, moreover, seem to proceed from the nose; the tongue, teeth, and lips, which play such a prominent part with us in singing, have, apparently, very little to do with it, except in the enunciation of words. That this falsetto, with a melody always in unison, always in the same key, without a *forte* or *piano*, equally loud and unchangeable in movement, must soon become very wearisome and monotonous to ears accustomed to complicated airs is obvious. Chinese melodies, furthermore, have no *major* or *minor* key; they are constantly floating between the two; therefore they are neither majestic, martial nor sprightly, as our *major* mode, and, on the other hand, they lack the softness, tenderness, and plaintive sadness of our *minor* airs. Altogether the vocalization of some of the most celebrated Chinese ballads by these Soochow "nightingales" somewhat reminds us of the *soirée musicale* to which we are treated regularly each month when the moon is "as full as full he can be," on which occasion an animal of the genus *canis* sneaks around our quiet domicile and warbles in howling cadenzas " Fair moon to thee I sing," with slight variations *à la* Sir Arthur. Hardly less horrifying is the orchestral accompaniment; seemingly, each of these would-be fair *duennas* plays her own tune. Moreover, their accompaniments sound very harsh, as in Chinese music no such thing is known as "temperament;" hence the notes are either too high or too flat. Notwithstanding all these incongruities, extremely offensive to us, the Celestial audience enjoys the treat, to judge by the strained attention with which they listen to the music; presumably they are mindful of Dryden's lines:—

> "And if even words are sweet, what, what is song
> When lips we love the melody prolong?

Yes, the Chinese, at any rate, show common-sense by not kicking up such a fearful racket as our foreign audiences occasionally do; they believe it unnecessary and, perhaps, against good taste, to show appreciation by clapping of hands, stamping of feet, or by whistling; none of all this shilly-shallying for a Chinaman; like a stoic he listens to the warbling of these Celestial skylarks, but no "encore" or "bravo" comes from him; only a simple smile, and it speaks volumes. We partook of some tea, which at intervals is handed round to the audience, and we deemed its quality not so bad; also of the roasted melon-seeds, provided *gratis*, and of which Celestials are as fond as the Yankee is of his peanuts; but we could not be persuaded to make use of those steaming rags. These "sing-song" girls, we hear, are not paid by the keeper of the establishment. They make a trifle occasionally when a visitor orders a favourite song of his to be sung; the appreciation of such an extra treat must be emphasized by paying one Mexican. The *prima donna* elect receives one-half of the amount, the other half going to the landlord. Visitors are permitted to take these damsels out for an evening, for a drive along the Celestial Esplanade, *alias* Bubbling Well Road, or else to brighten the *assemblée* of a native theatre in Canton or Hupeh Roads. There is never any difficulty in filling up the temporary vacancies, as there are numerous substitutes in readiness to take their places in the orchestra for the evening. Three Mexicans have to be "planted" with the proprietor of the Hall if one of these sirens accepts the offer to accompany you on a drive, or on a visit to a theatre. They also keep private restaurants, where the *noblesse* can be served with an A 1 dinner. However, those who venture into the haunts of these *donnas* must have well-spiced pockets, as a dinner party, we understand, cannot be provided for a less sum than $15. Yet even at that stiff rate there are daily found many who entangle themselves in the toils of these fair "Arachnides."

The Chinese race is emphatically phlegmatic; anything but muscular or corporeal exercise for them. They laugh at us taking our customary morning or evening walk, or when enjoying cricketing or rowing; they prefer sitting still with their sleeves tucked up, staring before them and gaping, the very picture of *ennui*. It is therefore somewhat surprising and paradoxical to find them taking to western games which call for bodily exercise; such, however, is the case. When taking a stroll through Foochow Road (the magnetic pole for the Celestial contingent of our settlement), one is struck with a three-storied building, far-and-away the largest in that locality, having a large signboard over the main entrance with the words in English

"LOUEN-YUEN BILLIARD SALOON."

The house is a good specimen of semi-Chinese architecture; the lower storey is built of brick, whilst the two upper storeys are constructed of wood; in fact, they appear to be one huge pane of glass, the framework of which is handsomely carved in grotesque Chinese fashion. We are at a loss to fathom why the establishment should have been called a "Billiard Saloon," for although several specimens of "tables are to be found therein," the principal revenue, evidently, is derived from supplying customers with an infusion of the fragrant leaf, else the noxious drug. The establishment in question, *de facto*, is a morphodite product of an oriental and occidental "saloon." There are several billiard tables and a bowling alley on the ground floor, whilst the second and third flats accommodate tea-drinkers and opium smokers. The fourth flat is exclusively for the convenience of the latter class of *habitués* to the place, and is handsomely fitted up for the purpose. Each "set" of smokers have their own cabin, where they can enjoy unnoticed the tantalizing pleasures of the drug. The rooms, of course, are set aside for the use of the patrician Celestial, and they are supposed to represent the acme in the way of accommodation. The furniture is neatly carved; the tops of the tables are marble, at least an imitation of the stone (in reality a fissille, crystalized lime-stone, stained with acids); the benches are ornamented with pictures *en bas relief* on a greenish stone, commonly confounded by Europeans with the genuine jadestone; scrolls, bearing famous sayings of the great sages of the Middle Kingdom, are suspended from the walls, probably for the purpose of elevating the thoughts of the "helpless victim" before he drops off into that state of reverie in which imagination, led captive by the drug, takes flights which in loftiness surpass the visions of a religious fanatic. Certainly an egregious irony these quotations, emphazised by the degradation of these body and mind destroying places. The visitors to this establishment form very picturesque groups, and it almost seemed to us as if the spirit of republicanism prevailed amongst the Chinese race. *Fraternité et égalité* appears to reign here; the pot-bellied and chub-cheeked silk or tea merchant partakes of the refreshments face to face with the unpretending and hard-working artisan; the Celestial dude, whose motto is "wife, wine, and song," engages in a confidential conversation with the "bald-headed" ass, as in reproach the followers of Buddah are called. Caste, this mighty lever with us western folks, appears to be unknown here. The part of the establishment which accommodates the

SIPPERS OF THE FRAGRANT LEAF DECOCTION

is not devoid of interest. In point of decorative art the place is not up to much; there are the same small tables, with bizarre embellishment, as are found in all resorts of a similar character, and of a workmanship which allows of their being knocked about for a couple of centuries; there is also the same quaint bamboo stool. That the locality should be crammed with visitors all day is but natural. Tea is the common beverage of China, a decoction of the black sort; Chinese, we are told, never use green tea. Cold water is regarded as unhealthy. This "hydrophobia," which is a characteristic trait of the black-haired race of Han, may probably date back from the Deluge. On the other hand, we believe the constant drinking of tea without any substantial food accompanying it has made the nation so submissive and cowardly as it is, and here the question arises, whether by introducing tea as a beverage into Europe more extensively we could not suppress all thoughts of freedom, annihilate the nihilists, socialists, &c. and thus form an empire of eternal peace? But then it may be questioned whether the almost total abstinence from alcohol, as practised amongst the Chinese, may not have considerably influenced the moral and intellectual development of the nation. Let us survey, for instance, the nations which abstain from alcohol—the vast Mussulman population and the millions of Asia. Everybody will recognize that they are, upon the whole, far inferior to the alcohol drinking nations of the west. The Japanese are the only Asiatic people who for centuries have consumed alcohol largely, and it is curious to note that they exhibit a mental receptivity and love of progress in marked contrast with the stagnation around them. These strange facts, of course, are not wholly due to alcohol; but alcohol may be a contributory factor. But *revenons à nos moutons*. Tea, which is said to have not been introduced generally into China before A.D. 800, has certainly been an important factor, having contributed to bring the East and West into more intimate intercourse. Next to rice, it is considered by "John" the greatest necessity of his existence, and the character of a Chinaman can, perhaps, be studied more accurately when he is sipping his tea than at any other time. That the "cup which cheers but not inebriates" contains a considerable quantity of stimulating ingredients we all know; how loquacious, for instance, a party of old spinsters sitting around their tea-pot become, and how often has their talk and chatter not annoyed us? But, on the other hand, it is evident that the fragrant leaf is equally potent in loosening the tongue of the sterner sex; the noise and chatter going on amongst the *habitués* of this locale generally, are sufficient to have rivalled the famous confusion of languages at the building of the tower of Babel.

In striking contrast to the last named division of the Louen-Yuen Billiard Saloon is the part assigned for the use of

OPIUM SMOKERS.

Silence, aye, oftentimes dead silence, reigns here, notwithstanding the number of guests who assemble to enjoy the bewitching influence of the narcotic. Truly the opium smoking division of the establishment offers a picture which would have formed an excellent subject for the brush of a Doré or the pen of a Dante. A sickening odour pervades the whole vicinity where the unfortunate victims are lying on their platforms. People talk of the nefarious trade carried on by publicans in England, and of the misery that is brought upon the nation by the sale of intoxicating liquors. Just step in here for a minute or two and view the scene, and the question will inevitably present itself, whether those who encourage the importation of the poisonous drug ought to be considered any better. Step in here, and cast a cursory glance at those human beings, some of whom are tottering on the brink of the grave, haggard, blare-eyed, and cadaverous looking, a picture of God's noblest creation on earth in its lowest stage of misery. Look at those features strikingly changed; pallid and death-like is their cast; skeletons still inhaling the fumes of the slow poison. And if it is a disgraceful sight to see males addicted to the use of the drug, how much more painful to see the gentle sex victimized by it. What a loathsome spectacle! Women, oftentimes in the bloom of youth, their cheeks faded, their eyes void of expression. Utter apathy is expressed in the features of these useless members of their nation and of the world at large. Through the exertions of our local government females were prohibited from using these shops. In 1885 Shao issued a proclamation forbiding, under a heavy fine, women from frequenting them. A copy of this proclamation is posted in every opium shop, and though the Taotai's orders were strictly executed for the first month or so, we found that the law had already begun to shut its eyes, and numbers of women flock again to these dens to indulge in the demoralizing and destructive habit of opium-smoking. The amount of money which passes through the hands of the proprietors of these establishments must be enormous. The smallest quantity of opium supplied to a customer is one-tenth of an ounce, for which ten cents have to be paid. This is the cheapest stuff, and is mostly supplied to guests who avail themselves of the No. 2 accommodation. The gentry, who smoke their pipes in the No. 1 section, usually pay two-hundred *cash* for one-tenth of an ounce of the drug. The number of visitors in a single day to the Louen-Yuen Saloon may be said to be legion; like bees in a beehive, people are constantly entering and leaving the premises, and the profits gained by the shareholders in the concern, we understand, put in the shade those of some of our largest foreign mercantile hongs.

Nothing in the Louen-Yuen Billiard Saloon, perhaps, will strike the eye of a foreigner so forcibly, and call to his mind so many sad "memories of the past," as a poster bearing the well-known "Positively no chits taken"—this thunderbolt of Jove to many a "bar-young-man." "John," evidently, does not believe in accumulating waste paper, for such chits are in but too many instances, and we must give him credit for his shrewdness. There is no notice to the same effect in Chinese, and hence one is forced to the conclusion that the "gentle hint" is principally intended for foreigners, who occasionally visit the place. The greater part of these belong to the seafaring class; and the *restaurateur*, having probably had some sad experience of their paying with the proverbial "main-topsail," thought it no doubt the only way to prevent "misunderstandings." We cannot bid farewell to the establishment in question without saying a word or two about the ways of the "heathen Chinee" when playing a game at billiards or ten-pins. Were it possible that Confucius could rise from his grave and be led blindfolded into the Louen-Yuen Saloon, the ancient philosopher, at the sight of the strange spectacle, would rub his eyes in greater astonishment than the more modern Rip Van Winkle is said to have done. No doubt

CELESTIALS AT TEN-PINS

are amusing. As we previously remarked, it seems inconsistent that "John," who exhibits such a marked antipathy for all body exercise, should have taken to this game; nevertheless, the Foochow-Road-Louen-Yuen-Billiard-Saloon-bar-young-man apparently finds a game at ten-pins very entertaining. The double bowling alley is kept in tolerably good condition. So far as my observation goes, a Chinaman makes a very poor "show" at bowling. Like the "brave," who manages to miss a target nine times out of ten shots at the 200 yards range, the Celestial bowler is successful in hitting the pins once in ten throws. "John" handles a ball much after the fashion in which a woman would throw it. In most instances he lets it "fly" with both hands, and this with a force about sufficient to permit its reaching the goal, when he generally succeeds in knocking down all the ten-pins, as they are put up all in a heap. In placing them so close together, "John's" action is analogous to the system adopted in Chinese military tactics, according to which a general crowds as many "braves" in a lump as possible. The bowling is recorded much after our manner. The charge for ten balls, of three throws each, is thirty *cash* (about three cents) per member. Of course, this division of the establishment always enjoys the patronage of a large number of on-lookers, especially from the outlying rural districts, who view the spectacle with as much curiosity as a youngster does the panorama of an itinerant showman. We now come to

THE BILLIARD SALOON.

It is difficult to explain why the Chinese should have so readily adopted the game of billiards; they have, so far as we are aware, no game of their own which is at all related to it. Evidently, however, it has found much favour with them, to judge by the numerous billiard rooms scattered over the various parts of the native district of our settlement, all of which are extensively patronized. There are about half a dozen "tables" in the Louen-Yuen Saloon. They are wretched-looking articles,—second, aye, perhaps tenth hand specimens which had previously done service, probably, in foreign establishments for a dozen years or more. It is difficult to make out the colour of the cloth, as Celestial players are wont to keep tally of their scores by chalking the figures thereon. The patches in it are as numerous as the colours in Joseph's coat. All the tables which came under our observation were American tables; why Chinese should prefer these to English tables we are unable to say. Pool, apparently, is not played at all, the figuring in the game, presumably, being too difficult for them. Our remarks as to the proficiency of a Celestial in a game of ten-pins cannot be applied to his average skill at billiards. We found a good many able players amongst these "knights of the cue," some of whom would stand a fair chance in a contest with our local champions of the green-cloth. The majority of the class which goes in for the game belong to the compradoric and clerk tribes, or the genus dude in general, and their antics when playing are similar to those of Westerners. Conversation is oftentimes carried on in English. Crowds of spectators are always watching the game, partly to kill time, whilst others are evidently interested in it. As we do, they will criticise shots, interrupt the player to explain how he could have made a run, apostrophise the fellow who has just missed a cannon, and often declare that they never saw a game worse played; though if those who criticize handle the wood themselves and miss the ball, they will throw the cue on the floor and blame the wretched table for their bad shots. The charge for a game up to 35 is five cents during the day and ten cents by gas-light, though the illumination somewhat reminded us of the twilight which is said to reign in polar regions during one half of the year.

Respice finem,—a friendly warning strikes our ear. We fear our readers have begun to grow tired of following us any longer in our wanderings through the Celestial "Boulevards" of Shanghai, a designation we consider not inappropriate.

China is unquestionably the most sigular and wonderful country that the sun shines upon. Excellent, rich soil and a poor nation; a teeming population and vast tracts of land lying uncultivated; profound philosophers and yet the most cruel treatment of man. As a recent writer remarks: "China has 3,000 miles of sea coast, indented with numerous harbours, and populous cities. There are no grander or more extensive deserts and plains on the globe than in the Middle Kingdom. One vast fertile plain alone is one half larger than the entire empire of Germany. The rivers of China are not exceeded in extent and number anywhere. The torrid zone and the arctic snows mark her confines. Her area exceeds that of all Europe by more than about a million of square miles. No man ever saw China in its entirety. The nation numbers a hundred million more people than all North and South America, Africa, and Australia. Of every five babies born in the world one is a Chinese. In China every day 35,000 human beings die. Its nation has preserved her independence for over 4,000 years, considerably longer than any other nation which ever existed on our globe. Education is universal. It is said that if all the classics of China were gathered in one immense heap and burned to finest ashes, there are in China a million of men who could reproduce them from memory. True, we are now outstripping in every form of development the people of Asia, but they had the start of us by many, many a century."

The few pictures we have attempted to draw, will show, we think, that reformation is slowly but surely pushing its way. Though the change for the better accomplished thus far appears to be but a "drop in the ocean," we must remember that the bending of the reed oftentimes indicates the direction whence we may expect the coming of the wind.

> "Not in vain the distance beacons;
> Forward, forward, let us range,
> Let the great world spin for ever
> Down the ringing grooves of change.
> Through the shadow of the globe
> We sweep into the younger day;
> Better fifty years of Europe
> Than a cycle of Cathay."

THE JINRICSHA AND ITS COOLIE.

ALMOST everyone who has had any opportunity of writing about Shanghai has expatiated on the 'ricksha, and a great deal more has been written about it by travellers in Japan, where these peculiar vehicles were first used. It is only a few years since they were introduced into Shanghai, as the Municipal Council had to regenerate this swamp and macadamise the roads before the jinricsha could be used on Celestial soil. This vehicle has been compared to dear knows how many different things: it strikes some people as being more like a perambulator than anything else, but perambulators have three, and jinricshas only two wheels; others see in the jinricsha a resemblance to the invalid's Bath-chair, but the number of wheels don't coincide here either. It is a miniature gig more than anything else, and when the hood of canvas on a bamboo frame is put up to shelter the occupant from the drenching rain, or to protect him from the fierce rays of a blazing sun, when the thermometer is over 90° in the shade, then the Japanese " man-carriage " is very much like a London hansom, without any driver's box behind. The coolie takes his place between a narrow and light pair of shafts. A back stay is attached to prevent the vehicle being upset, but it does not always prove an effectual guard, as it is no uncommon thing to see a jinricsha making a backward turn, with the occupant's heels high in the air and the coolie suspended from the shafts or the cross-bar between them.

The average Chinese jinricsha coolie is said to be far inferior to his *confrère* in Japan; the latter is of better physique, and can do his work with great ease, and his speed and endurance are much greater. A few good 'ricksha coolies, however, are to be found amongst the Celestial band, but the great majority are most miserable looking wretches. It depends very much on the fare whether the coolie will go well. If he has a native in his vehicle, from whom he will only get a few *cash*, he jogs along as if in a funeral procession; if he has a foreigner and the foreigner has a stick, the coolie will go at the rate of seven or eight miles an hour; a first rate coolie will run you along, when the roads are dry, almost as rapidly as a pony trotting easily; if the roads are bad, the coolie feeble or broken-winded, and the hirer in a hurry, then one had much better walk. Some coolies are very stupid; they don't know the rules of the road, and if there is a chance of getting run down by a trap they will put you to the peril; others again, who have got some "savee," observe the rules well enough, keep out of danger, and go very fast too. When a passenger wants his coolie to turn to the left he touches him with a stick on the left side, or kicks him with his left foot on the part of his *corpus* nearest to the passenger's foot; and the same signals delivered on the right side by the right foot will make him wheel to the right. But that is only practicable with the coolies that are not stupid; if you try to get a stupid one to turn to the right, he is sure to go in the opposite direction, or stop in front of some door where you don't want to be set down. If you want the coolie to stop, you cry "man, man." There are various simple phrases synonymous with "go on" and other calls in frequent use. It is rather amusing to see and hear a stranger trying to stop his 'ricksha coolie; the passenger shouts "stop," forgetting that the coolie does not understand English; as the coolie still goes on apace, the passenger shouts again and again, kicks the coolie, or strikes him with a stick, which makes the coolie go all the faster; the passenger gets so excited that the coolie thinks there is something very seriously wrong with him, and he is eventually brought to bay; "man, man," would have made him drop the shafts at once. The coolies are great impostors when they can get away with it; if a stranger offers one 20 cents, when that is four times too much, the coolie has the cheek to cry "hap-dallah, mastah;" foreigners resident here are not imposed upon, however, as they soon learn what is a fair charge, and the coolie has to take his five or ten cents as the case may be, and if he makes a "bobbery" he not infrequently gets something more than he wanted, if the foreigner has a cane handy. Jinricsha coolies spot a new arrival at once, and the coolie which the stranger first hires will haunt him for months afterwards; if the coolie brought the new arrival from a wharf to a hotel in the settlement, the coolie watches that foreigner, and rushes at him on the Bund or any other place, shouting "'ricsha wanchee?" The first fare paid by the new arrival was probably an excessive one, and the coolie wants to get good fares as long as he can, before the stranger learns that five cents are quite enough. Jinricsha coolies consider that foreigners have no right to walk on the roads; they think the roads were made for their jinricshas, and that a foreigner is doing them an injustice if he walks along the street; every unengaged coolie rushes over to him, lowering the shafts as he comes up close close to the pedestrian, and shouting "'ricsha wanchee; numbah wan 'ricsha; 'ricsha, mastah, 'ricsha." Or if the foreigner comes out of a hotel, store, or any place where there is a stand for 'ricsha coolies on the opposite side of the street, half-a-dozen or more of them make a rush at him, dragging their 'ricshas with them, and in the charge the wheels get jammed, or some of the coolies get knocked over, or they come so close up to the pedestrian that they often hurt his shins with the shafts of the 'ricshas; and though the foreigner in such a case were as meek as Moses or as harmless as a dove, still he could not help striking a few of them if he had a stick; they will then go off, and the fellows that get chastised are laughed at by all the others.

The jinricsha coolie hires his carriage by the month, and has to pay the owner of the vehicle $2; the coolie has also to pay for two licenses, $1 each, issued by the English and French Municipal Councils. There are a great deal too many of these vehicles in the Foreign Settlements of Shanghai, as the Municipal Council for the English and American Settlements and the French Municipal Council issue a large number of licenses. The vehicles are owned by Chinamen who make their business by letting them out on hire; a great deal of money must be made by them some way, else so many of them would not be kept plying on the roads of the foreign settlements. Some of the coolies are known to make a few dollars profit in two or three days, and then lie back for the rest of the week, living like swells, patronising tea shops and gambling houses, and perhaps opium smoking saloons. Their food is of the commonest Chinese kind—chiefly rice, so that it does not require many cents to satisfy them with chow chow, and the intinerant cooks have the jinricsha coolies as their customers. They don't spend much in dress either. In the height of the summer weather the coolie's full attire consists of an immense straw hat, a pair of hempen sandals, two or three small pieces of cotton round his waist, and a very short pair of pants; some, however, do not wear any covering for the head, and they can run about in the fiercest rays of the sun without any protection, whereas a European would get sunstroke in ten minutes if he did so. In winter they put on an immense quantity of blue cotton, stuffed with cotton padding, and the suit once on is kept on till next summer; the mass of rags and patches is kept together by strings. The better class of coolies in wet weather wear green or yellow oilskins, but the poorer ones put on cloaks made of straw,— a very primitive, thatch-like covering. Some of the smartest of the coolies appear in half-Chinese, half-European, clothes; one may have a pair of tweed trousers and a blue cotton jacket; another has cotton rags for pants, and two or three tweed vests and coats on; while all the imaginable styles in felt hats are worn by these coolies; it seems as if most of the felt hats imported into Shanghai came eventually into the possession of the jinricsha coolies, but by the time they do so they are very dilapidated, and all style or shape knocked out of them.

The introduction of jinricshas into Shanghai some nineteen years ago occurred at a time when there was not much increase in the foreign population, but the influx of the native element from the City into the settlements was very considerable. Means had therefore to be provided to supply the want of a suitable mode of personal conveyance; for previous to that time, with the exception of a small number of private carriages, the only means of locomotion, besides walking, were the clumsy and old-fashioned wheelbarrows, which on rare occasions only were made use of by foreigners. The jinricsha, which was then a novel invention, was considered to have supplied the want. A Frenchman introduced about twenty of these vehicles into Shanghai from Japan, and a natural consequence of the large extent to which they were patronized was their great and rapid augmentation; at the present day the number of jinricshas plying for hire in the different settlements exceeds 3,000.

We do not know who is responsible for the original laying out of the roads of our settlements, but certainly it could never have struck the deviser that Shanghai would become the great emporium of the Far East. Most of the public thoroughfares are nothing but lanes, and they are completely inadequate for the large traffic for which they have to serve. Besides those 3,000 jinricshas, there are plying for hire several hundred wheelbarrows, and a very large number of native carriages, not taking into account the private vehicles belonging to our foreign and native community. The principal cause of the obstruction of our public roads are undoubtedly jinricshas, and measures should be taken to remedy this evil, which from day to day becomes more annoying.

People who defend the use of 'ricshas, and who in some instances advocate not only their maintenance but also their further multiplication, give as a reason that this mode of conveyance is cheaper than any other save "Shanks' mare." This belief, although generally accepted as correct, is nevertheless utterly erroneous, for the human labour which supplies the motive power for the 'ricsha is more expensive than any other mode of traction introduced into a civilized country; and for the amount spent in Shanghai on these vehicles annually, there could be provided a much more convenient, safer, faster, and cheaper mode of conveyance; leaving out of question the semi-barbarous character of the system, which reminds one of the childish pastimes with which youngsters at home wile away their hours of idleness.

As already stated, there are on an average some 3,000 jinricshas plying for hire in Shanghai. Estimating the earnings of a coolie at 25 cents per day only, this would give a sum of $22,500 per month, or $270,000 per annum, which seems an astoundingly large amount to be spent annually on these vehicles. But let us now take also into consideration the large number of carriages and wheelbarrows which ply for hire. We do not think we exaggerate when we put down the amount of money spent on these at about $130,000, making thus a total of about $400,000 which Shanghai spends annually on the various modes of personal conveyance.

What great conveniences we could have for this large sum by, for instance, introducing tramways; a company which started such an enterprise here would be certain to realise good profits. There can be no doubt that foreigners as well as natives would go in largely for the tramway, which would lead to a rapid abatement of the nuisance caused by jinricshas. And then look at the various advantages which would be gained by doing away with such vehicles and introducing tramways in their place. Ragged and filthy coolies would no longer lounge about the streets, blocking up every passage, and endangering our lives and property; pedestrians would not be pestered by the constant touting for fares; a large contingent of our Police Force could be made use of for better purposes than seeing that these coolies keep the rule of the road, which they nevertheless only half succeed in making them do; foreigners would not run the risk of being taken into the country and robbed there of their valuables by these wretches, as is only too often the case; and last but not least, by the introduction of tramcars, people would gain an immense advantage by being able to ride in a clean, comfortable and well-appointed vehicle, adapted for all kinds of weather.

Previous to the introduction of jinricshas into Japan there were in that country, besides "Shanks' mare," two modes of personal conveyance in vogue, viz., riding on horseback and a species of palanquin called a "cango." The former had one great drawback : the Japanese pony being of vicious propensities, was fond of biting and kicking. The second mode offered the great disadvantage that persons not accustomed to the peculiar shape of the "cango" found it very uncomfortable, as it was necessary to sit cross-legged *à la Japonais*, or else let your legs dangle on either side, and both positions were rather trying to a novice. So a missionary, whose vocation necessitated his setting ont on long journeys into the interior of the country, hit upon the idea of constructing a vehicle which would do away with the inconveniences mentioned, and he invented one which he very appropriately termed a *jinricsha*, which means a "man-pulled-car." As is the case with a great number of inventions, it never occurred to the deviser that his would ere long be adopted to a very great extent. Acquainted with the characteristic features of the Japanese people, he could reckon with confidence on the success of applying human power to such a mode of conveyance; he found sufficient proof of the hardly surpassable endurance and suppleness of the people in the astonishing feats of *bettoes*, or hostlers, who keep up on foot with ponies for miles; and in the extraordinary performances of "cango" bearers, who with the greatest ease surmount the difficulties of carrying their fares over the mountainous regions without stopping to take a rest.

It is a great error, however, to suppose that things adapted for one race of people are equally suitable for all. And here it was where the Shanghai resident who first introduced jinricshas into our settlements made the mistake. He was wrong in thinking that what is sauce for the goose must be sauce for the gander; he possibly never had an opportunity of noticing the enormous difference which exists between the natives of Japan and China; for herein we have to look for the cause of the failure of these vehicles in China to give satisfaction.

Every temporary sojourner in the Far East must be struck by the vast difference which exists between the Chinese and Japanese jinricsha coolie and their perambulators. The reasons for this are manifold. In Japan most of these vehicles are owned by the persons who draw them; hence the interest which is taken in keeping them clean and in order, to which may be added the natural propensity of the Japanese people to cleanliness. Travellers in Japan will find these vehicles completely sheltered against the inclemencies of the weather, and amply provided with nice soft cushions to sit and recline on. The coolie is dressed in what we may call a uniform, always neat and tidy; and when receiving his proper fare he will thank you cordially for it, and not grumble or abuse you, as is the case in Shanghai. The rate at which he travels is very fast; he will not obstruct public thoroughfares, as he has a stand pointed out to him which he is bound to keep; and herein Japan is greatly ahead of the "Model Settlement," where the ears and the nerves of pedestrians get strained by the constant touting for fares.

And how stand matters in China? The Chinese have an inveterate dislike to the least physical exertion beyond what is absolutely necessary; and the number of those who do hard work is exceedingly small compared with the immense population of the country. Those who mean to earn their living by hard manual labour prefer a steady engagement to a precarious one, as, for instance, the work of a jinricsha coolie. For to-day the latter may earn twice as much a common day labourer, but the following two or three days he may not be able to make enough to pay the hire of the vehicle to its owner. Hence it happens that coolies engaged in this sort of labour are mostly the lowest class of individuals, who stake their few cents on the hire of a vehicle in the expectation of making a pile; for a couple of days of good "chancee" may earn them money enough to keep them for a week, during which time they hire the 'ricsha out to someone else, and enjoy a *dolce far niente* till their funds are exhausted. It is not therefore likely that under such circumstances a coolie will take any interest in his machine; hence its filthy appearance and his ragged dress, as the surplus of his earnings is spent in opium. And what comfort is there in a Shanghai jinricsha? Its cushions feel about as soft as if stuffed with pebble-sand or small stones. The outer appearance of the coolie is often the very picture of human misery, starvation staring and glaring out of his eyes; besides this there are a number who are complete cripples, and why they should be allowed to ply for hire we are quite at a loss to conceive. Their strength being quite used up by the use of the soothing drug, they are unable to pull their loads, and crawl along our roads objects calculated to excite sympathy, and the sooner something is done to bring about a change the better.

The good people of Shanghai can console themselves with the thought that they are not the only folk who have jinricsha grievances. A cry of indignation comes from the southernmost extremity of Asia. These vehicles were introduced into Singapore some time ago, and according to the *Straits Times* they are anything but giving satisfaction to residents there. "That outcome of Japanese ingenuity, the jinricsha," says our contemporary, "requires the exercise of reforming zeal, in so far as Singapore is concerned. Certainly it does not play such a leading part in passenger conveyance as in Hongkong and Shanghai, yet for all that, the jinricsha is a factor, and an important one, too in our street traffic. We have not a loud word to say as to the men between the shafts, who are sometimes weak-kneed, wheezy, and generally broken down. But the crying complaint which seems to indicate the need of reforming zeal is the total lack of regulation as to stations, and the pullers observing the rule of the road. Now if a station were fixed, these Ishmaels of the road could be cribbed, cabined and confined within reasonable bounds; they would not be hurrying and scurrying hither and thither, aimlessly, and, for aught we know, to create in themselves the gentle stimulant of excitement. We should like to see some steps taken to secure these much-to-be desired ends, for we are assured that if the present confusion is to go on like Tennyson's brook, then farewell all peace of mind; the local cabbies' and the trap drivers' "occupation's gone."

We read that the Japanese government intend ultimately to prohibit jinricsha labour entirely, and as a preliminary a heavy tax will soon be levied on these vehicles. This is a step in the right direction, which our model authorities would do well to follow. By home papers we learn that a few jinricshas have even made their appearance in the streets of Paris and London. But it is not likely that this mode of conveyance will ever come in to vogue at home; we doubt whether any home government would allow such vehicles to ply for hire; for, as a Japan contemporary remarks, "a lower and more degrading form of labour cannot well be conceived; every man performing it sinks into the lowest social depths, and bears the stamp of his vocation in visible marks."

A CURIOSITY STALL AT THE CITY GATE.

AT the Old North Gate of the City of Shanghai, the small wooden bridge which spans the city moat is thronged with natives passing into and out of the city, and a number of old men have old curiosity shops on a very small scale; they take up their position at the approaches to the bridge, and expose for sale all sorts of old articles, generally of very little value. Both sides of the short winding-path from the bridge to the gate is occupied by these men, and on the bridge itself old-clothes dealers exhibit native garments of every description, stretched out on bamboo canes and leaning up against the parapet rails. Others have most extraordinary collections of old and worthless curiosities. The articles are laid on mats on the ground, on trays, or in small boxes and baskets, and the vendors sit beside their lots, squatting on a mat, smoking long pipes, reading a native newspaper or book, or perhaps more actively engaged in pursuit of a flea. The articles in some lots are really a curious mixture of native and foreign goods; here are a pair of thick-soled pipe-clayed Chinese shoes, a pair of hempen sandals, an old white hat of London make, a box of nails, Chinese type and carved blocks, an opium pipe, a basket full of old corks, and a smaller lot in a box, selected as being of more than ordinary value, as they still retain patches of yellow, red, or black sealing wax, with vintners' names and trade marks; shirt studs, watch keys, ear-rings, jade-stone amulets, screw nails, old knives, small mirrors, miniature wooden gods, Chinese *cash* of various dynasties, miscellaneous coins, and a bronze halfpenny bearing the image and superscription of Victoria, D.G., F.D., Reg. Brit., &c., of 1861. The halfpenny, and all the *other* valuable articles, might have been purchased for a few cents.

THE CHINESE WHEELBARROW AND ITS COOLIE.

HE primitive Chinese wheelbarrow, first of all the types of wheelbarrows, is that used from time immemorial and at the present day as the chief means of overland locomotion in the central part of the Celestial Empire, or in the provinces which are in the valley of the great Yangtsze River. In the more northern regions, pack-mules and camels are used as beasts of burden, and the rude Pekingese cart is the chief vehicle. In the southern provinces, the coolies and their bamboo carrying-poles are the only available means for transport of goods, and, as one writer said, the Chinese coolie competes successfully with the beasts of burden. Wheelbarrows were only introduced into the Shanghai district some 28 or 30 years ago. There are no roads, beyond the limits of those made by the foreign municipalities, and the wheelbarrow is the only machine that can be used on the narrow footpaths through the fields. The Chinese wheelbarrow, to look at it, is more clumsy than any agricultural vehicle of the same kind to be seen anywhere; but still its peculiar construction possesses advantages for the varied purposes for which it can be used; it is good for passenger traffic, or for conveyance of live stock, or dead meat, or cotton bales; a Chinaman can put almost anything on his wheelbarrow. It is constructed with a broad horizontal frame of flat bars, the wheel is placed in the middle of the frame, and the upper half of the wheel is covered with a small box frame; this leaves room for a person to sit at each side of the wheel, and the small frame serves as a support for his side, or something to hold on by; in the open space at the front bar of the horizontal frame the passenger clenches one foot, and the other foot hangs down by the side, on a stirrup or piece of hemp rope. The wheel is of wood, the rim three or four inches in depth, and the spokes of proportionate clumsiness. The shafts come out behind the horizontal frame, and at their extremities they are about three feet apart, leaving plenty of room for the coolie to stagger under his heavy load; the coolie has a shoulder-strap twisted under his arms and attached to knobs on the shafts, to keep the strap from shifting; when on the move, and loaded, the weight is mainly upon his shoulders, his arms are used in balancing the vehicle, and he can exercise every muscle of his body in pushing it before him. When he has got a couple of passengers, and the passengers have as many bundles and boxes and baskets as they can keep hold of, the coolie can still manage quite easily; the frame is cushioned, and the passengers may possibly have a tolerably comfortable seat; time is no consideration with them, and three miles an hour, or even less, is quite sufficient to overtake their most pressing business appointments, or to hasten on their journeys of pleasure. If the coolie has only one passenger he can hitch his shoulder-strap a bit, and balance the wheelbarrow; but if possible he will get hold of some piece of furniture, or a bale, box, or anything handy, as he doesn't care to go without full cargo; he seems best pleased when he has a gorgeously painted female on one side, and a live black pig on the other, the pig being laid on its back, without a cushion, its feet tied fore and aft, and securely lashed to the frame. When in the crowded streets of the foreign settlements, the wheelbarrow coolies have to keep close to the side of the road, and they are much in the way of the more

advanced jinricsha coolies, with whom they have frequent disputes as to who is in the way of the other. The wheelbarrow coolie occasionally comes in the way of a pony and trap at a street corner, and then if his cargo is human, he hitches the shafts and sends his passengers sprawling on the road if there is the slightest danger of his valuable, though not ornamental, vehicle being smashed ; how he settles this rudeness with his fares is a mystery. Wheelbarrow coolies are very stupid at times, more especially when they hear a pony and trap coming up behind them ; it is almost certain that the coolie will put himself in the way, by turning round to see where the trap is, and in doing so he may neglect his first duty, that of maintaining the equilibrium of his ancient vehicle ; the result is that the barrow is capsized just right in front of the trap, whereas if the coolie had tried to get as near to the side of the road as he could, and never thought of turning round, he would have been all right. His curiosity to see what is coming behind him is in inverse ratio to his ability to control his vehicle ; for when he has three or four large bales lashed on the sides and top of his barrow, or when he has several long planks, trees, or perhaps a load of bar iron,—then he is certain to turn round every now and then, and not infrequently comes to grief and blocks up the road. When his barrow is capsized the first thing he does is to take a quiet walk round it, and then a rest, occupying his leisure time by lighting his tobacco pipe ; he may require assistance from some other coolies before he gets his vehicle and load righted again, and a native policeman finds some harmless amusement in looking on, but never thinks of hurrying the coolies to make them get out of the way ; the native policeman has the same idea as the coolies, that the roads were made for them, and that it doesn't matter though they obstruct the traffic, as they are not in a hurry, and nobody else has a right to be. The wheelbarrows used in the foreign settlements are licensed by the Municipal Councils, and hired by the coolies from owners the same as jinricshas. The most of them are used in conveying cargo from wharves to godowns, and it is matter of surprise to see the tremendous loads the wheelbarrow coolie can take ; he will put two bales of piece goods, four half-chests of tea, or two bales of hides on his wheelbarrow, and struggle along under the heavy load, not infrequently capsizing on the Garden Bridge or the side of the Bund. The conveyance of treasure from the mail steamers to the banks, and *vice versa*, is a job for wheelbarrow coolies, and then you will see a procession of two or three dozen of them, —on each barrow two boxes of shoes of silver sycee, Mexicans, or gold bars, perhaps $250,000 of treasure in that procession ; but the boxes are reckoned carefully, and several Chinese servants of the bank compradores are in charge, so that there is no fear of any coolie running off with a big haul.

About 3,000 of these vehicles apply for licenses in Shanghai monthly, and the sum of about Tls. 10,000 per annum is collected by the Municipal Council; each wheelbarrow pays 400 cash per month.

CHINESE PRINTERS.

ABOUT the best thing missionaries have done in China is the establishment of mission printing offices, where Chinese have learnt to be compositors and pressmen; these have been nurseries for the newspaper offices, and of the large number of Chinese who are now engaged in the latter you will find that nearly all of them have been in mission offices. Some of the Chinese compositors also have learned English at mission schools, and the slight knowledge of English they have, is to a certain extent advantageous in their trade. Besides the newspaper offices in Shanghai there is a large number of small jobbing offices; most of the latter are owned and managed solely by Chinese, and they ruin the other offices by their cheap labour, as they do jobs under what is reckoned cost price in any other place. The Portuguese form a large proportion of those engaged in the printing trade, and there are none of the newspaper offices we know of where there are not more Portuguese than Chinese; but of the former we do not propose to say anything further than that some of them know English as well, and do their work almost efficiently, as if they had served an apprenticeship in an office in England; others do not know much English, and canont work so well as some of the Chinese. But this is a very delicate part of the subject, for if we go beyond the fair mark the printers will strike, and throw the type on the floor.

Chinese compositors learn first to set type off print "copy," and knowing where all the letters are to be found in the case, they can put them together without having the slightest idea of what the words mean; but even off print copy they can't make a clean proof, because if they pick up a wrong letter they let it pass. Then in adjusting the lines it is occasionally necessary that a word must be "divided;" here they take the simplest plan—without regard to consonants, vowels, or syllables,—and just put as many letters of the word in the first line as there is room for, and run the remainder over to the next line; no word is too small for them to split up; they would divide "small" with "sm" in one line, and "all" in the next; or if they have to divide "notwithstanding," they may put it "notwit-," "anding," or "notwi-" "thstanding," or any way except by the syllables. When manuscript copy is carefully written, the Chinese compositors can set from it fairly well; or even if the handwriting is not very good, if it is that which they have every day, and are accustomed to, they can make it out. The copy of occasional contributors,—who may think they have written very plainly, and which would certainly pass for good copy in the hands of an English printer,—has often to be re-written; if it were given in as it came, the proof-sheet would be intolerably bad. Some of the more intelligent Chinese compositors make well-intentioned but desperate efforts to decipher a word which is not clearly written; we know one who always keeps a sixpenny English dictionary on his frame, and if he sticks at a word he tries to fix the first three letters and then looks up the dictionary for the remainder, an expedient which is successful only sometimes, and by chance. The Chinese compositors come to know a great many words in common use, and if another word having a similarity to a more common one is used, they don't follow their copy, but put in the other word they have learned before. Printers' errors are very often amusing, and the errors of Chinese compositors are sometimes laughable though annoying; but proof-reading for them will soon make a man grayhaired. The other day we noticed a ridiculous error, but which didn't pass the proofs;—in the report of a military ball, there was a phrase about the ladies being adorned with their husband's "sashes;" and the compositor dropped the first "s," because he knew "ashes" was an English word, and he had never seen the word "sashes" before. We knew one Chinese compositor, who evidently must have served his apprenticeship in a mission office, for he always in setting up the name of Lord so-and-so, puts it "the Lord." In an article the other day, the phrase "Land of the Leal" occurred, but the compositor made it "Land of the Lead,"—he had evidently thought it was commercial news. In setting up this page, a compositor made it "hand of the head. We were told that one fellow in setting up the usual weekly local paragraph of the Cathedral Services, made a very curious and original blunder (but we scarcely believe it, as we did not see it). The anthem for evening service was entitled, "From the rising of the Sun," and the compositor is said to have put it "from the *Rising Sun and Nagasaki Express!*" At any rate we know this for a fact, that the compositors on newspapers here take note of the names of river and coast steamers, and they seldom fail to observe the custom of putting these names in italics; but although this is all very well as far as it goes, it leads them into a trap sometimes. For instance, we remember a phrase occurring in an article where China was referred to as an El Dorado; the Chinese compositor knew that was the name of a steamer running between Shanghai and the Northern Ports, and therefore he put it *El Dorado.* Again, there was in some article a reference to the *Great Eastern,* and though the name of the steamer was underlined on the copy, the compositor *thought* that was a mistake, as he knew well enough the *Great Eastern* did not trade on this coast, so he set it up in Roman type, and did not even give it big initials. We will give a few specimens of premeditated mistakes in words of similarity, as discovered in proof sheets within a few days:—

Words in Copy.	Words in Proof Sheet.	Words in Copy.	Words in Proof Sheet.
Answered.	Assured.	Mr. So & So.	The So & So.
Approach.	Approval.	Obvious.	Glorious.
Artiste.	Article.	Opinion.	Opium.
Attacked.	Stacked.	Overture.	Overturn.
Author.	Another.	Quiet.	Quite.
Blunder.	Blinder.	Quietly.	Guilty.
Chairman.	Chinaman.	Quite.	Quiet.
Chater, (Mr.)	Charter, (Mr.)	Retain.	Return.
Comic Annual.	Comic Animal.	Reviling.	Railing.
Conservatism.	Conversation.	Roars.	Wars.
Counsel.	Council.	Ruining.	Running.
Expect.	Except.	Satow (Mr.)	Swatow (Mr.)
First Lord of the Admiralty.	Fire Board of the Admiralty.	Sums.	Guns.
		Snug.	Sung.
Handy.	Hardly.	Title rôle.	Little rôle.
Leal.	Lead.	Soft.	Spot.
Line.	Time.	Supplies.	Applies,
Lunacy.	Sunday.	Tame Duck.	Lame Duck.
Martial.	Material.	Then.	Their.
Mild Hindoo.	Wild Hindoo.	Tardy.	Thirdly.

Chinese compositors would do very well to set up Welsh, as nobody could ever detect a mistake in it. They have a curious upside-down way of doing their work, which they can't get out of. In correcting a column, they begin at the bottom instead of the top; in "running over" a line or two, they do it in the column, without taking the lines into a composing stick; we once ventured to give a Chinese compositor some hints about the way to correct a proof and run over lines, but he told us he had been a compositor for ten years, that he learned at a mission press, and he knew better; though we had learned how to do it fifteen years ago, he would not be persuaded, and he had to be left to do it his own way.

The pressmen, however, are more amusing than the compositors. There is scarcely a Chinese pressman that will venture to lift up a large page of type; they always perfer shoving it on a board, and carrying it that way; and it is perhaps just as well that they do, for their "locking up" of a form is not to be depended on; the most extraordinary thing in this way we ever saw was in a Hongkong newspaper office, where the large pages of seven very long columns were made up on brass galleys, and carried to the press on them. In working a hand press, such as a double-demy Columbian or Albion, the Chinese pressmen have some curious ways. "No. 1" pressman puts the sheet of paper on the "tympan," and rolls in the bed of the press, but he does not, as he ought, pull over the bar or lever by which the impression is produced. No, he's No. 1, and he only does the skilful work of putting on the paper, and rolling in and out the bed. "No. 2" works the hand ink roller, and a coolie on the off-side does the heavy work by shoving over the lever with both hands, and he has to take off the printed sheet too. They can print about 300 copies an hour this way. In working a very small hand press, the first pressman pulls the handle to himself. In the *Mercury* office, a "proof galley press" lay in a corner unused for some time, because the Chinese pressmen said they couldn't work it. We had it taken out from its obscurity, and found there was nothing wrong with it, but still the pressmen said they could not cast a proof on that thing,—a longitudinal iron tray, and an iron cylinder, and nothing in the world simpler than to cast a proof on it, only to run the cylinder over the column of type. We got one or two of the pressmen to use it, but one old man tried to avoid it as long as he could; he would rather put himself to any amount of trouble in getting a proof on a hand press, waiting till it was disengaged, before he would touch that cylindrical proof galley press; in fact, he seemed to to think that this newfangled machine disturbed the Celestial ghosts; but by and bye he got over it, when he had seen it used day after day, without anything serious happening; still when he uses it, he does so with great caution, and looks as if he were afraid of it.

When a Wharfedale machine came to be fitted up at the *Mercury* office, several Chinese mechanics were engaged to put it in working order; they had taken it down at another place, and the number one man said he could "savee all what b'long that ting;" he could put it together again as easily as he could make a bowl of rice disappear. After they got all the pieces brought to the office by coolies carrying them suspended from bamboo poles, the Celestial engineers set to work cleaning, and they put up the frame on the second day; they took another day to put in the driving wheel and cog wheels, by means of which the bed of the machine travels; on the next day they put on the bed and inking-table, and also the cylinder. On the sixth day they fixed up all the gear round the machine, and put on the feeding board. The latter article was viewed by them as the most important part of the whole machine, and one of the men had spent nearly his whole time in polishing the brass gratings. They thought they had at last got everything right, when they managed to make the cylinder turn round, but they found the grippers did not work; and more than that, the cylinder reversed when the bed travelled backwards under it. However, the number one engineer thought that was all right, for when he got the grippers to take round a sheet of paper with them, he called on his men to gather up their tools, they put all their screw keys, wrenches, screw drivers, and hammers into a bag, and the number one man reported "that ting all b'long ploper." "You b'long too muchee foolo," was the reply he got when it was discovered that he had not altered some things he was told about, for he had put some eccentric wheels upside down, and the cylinder was not fixed properly at all. We ultimately got the machine put right, and then a Chinese pressman tried to improve on it, and set it all wrong again. Another Chinese pressman came and said he could make it all proper; he walked round the machine and then sat down on a small box, and lighted his tobacco-pipe, but at the same time leisurely unscrewed a nut on one of the minor parts of the gear; then he fastened it again, leaving it just as he had found it; he next turned the driving wheel slowly, and gave the cylinder one revolution; another seat and a smoke; and so on, he wasted a whole forenoon without doing anything. But another man came from a native daily newspaper office and set the machine all right, so that it worked first rate; he took an afternoon to fix it, and the other old man sat watching him the whole time; not only that, he came back next day, and crawled round the machine for hours, without anybody saying anything to him, except asking what he wanted, and he said he was trying to see how the other man made it all right. He was anxious to get a job to work this new machine, but he didn't.

CHINESE LEGERDEMAIN: THE SHOWMEN ON HONGKEW WHARF.

ONE of the most amusing sight in Shanghai is the jugglers, wizard, or Celestial professor of legerdemain who is almost every day to be seen performing alongside of the steamers lying at the Hongkew Wharf. We have seen several different performers there, and some of their tricks are certainly very clever,—equal to anything that can be done by professionals in that line at home, and there is a grotesqueness in the performers which adds greatly to the fun. We remember last summer seeing one fellow coming along the wharf, while we were on board one of the steamers there paying a visit to the captain. It was in the hottest days of August, and the Celestial attire at that season is very scant; the fellow we had noticed was a long, lean, skin and bone Celestial of not very tender years, but to guess his age to a nicety would be beyond any one's power. He was arrayed in a piece of dirty blue cotton, tied round his waist, and a pair of short pants; not another stitch about him, and not even a covering for his head nor sandals for his feet. Under his arm he carried a small suspicious looking bundle; and if it had been dark a policeman would have been warranted in arresting him on a charge of stealing it, for the manner in which he skipped along the wharf, and the cautious looks which he gave along the decks, excited a feeling of mystery as to what he was after. He stopped opposite the quarter deck of the steamer we were on, and then immediately commenced business by unfolding his parcel on the wharf planks, and taking out some articles which at once showed that he was a Celestial showman in the sleight of hand line. He began by placing three or four large beads and marbles on the planks, and shifted them about mysteriously so that you could never know exactly where any of them were, and he kept talking to himself all the time, or using incantations, occasionally interspersed with "pidgin" English to interest the crowd of sailors who had soon gathered round him, and the "pidgin" English was not of a very refined or polite nature; there was a good deal of forecastle slang about it. In manipulating the beads and marbles, he showed great dexterity, and occasionally repeated the trick of pretending to let one fall accidentally and roll through between the planking—here he brought "pidgin" English quotations to his service—and then he picked the lost bead out of his left eye! Or he might follow up this bit of legerdemain by putting the bead under the eye-lid, holding one fist over the eye and striking it with the other fist, then showing his eye as if it were swollen by the bead being under the skin; the next second he held up both arms to show there was nothing under his armpits, while the next move would be to take the crystal bead and several others like it out under his armpits, pretend to swallow them, and then take them one by one from his nostrils. Then he went through some genuine swallowing feats. He had a small brass bell, the same as those attached to the collar of a mandarin's pony, the bell being of exactly the size and shape of a large walnut shell; this he swallowed, and no cheating, about it; you could see the big lump as it went down his throat, and more than that, when it was down he danced "the perfect cure" on the wharf, to the music of the bell inside his body. This was the point when he made his most clamorous appeals for "cumshaw." "Hap dallah cumshaw, captain," he shouted over and over again till he had actually convinced himself that he was to get it; "hap dallah cumshaw" took the place of all his chin-chinning invocations, and he got so excited over it that, like an auctioneer, he thought he was receiving higher bids, for he soon changed the cry to "Wan dallah cumshaw, captain; wan dallah, cumshaw!" After convulsive coughings and evident pain in making severe efforts, he drew his breath, wheezed, coughed, twisted his body and contorted his features, and almost turned himself upside down and inside out, till he brought the bell out of his mouth again, and then he went on the walk round to receive contributions, of which he had a full share. His performance was only about half through, and this was the way he spent the "usual interval." His next feats were remarkable but not very pleasant to witness. He slapped his bony hands on his bare chest, and shouted "No hab got chow chow," and at the same instant he drew a long breath, and all his intestines seemed to be drawn up under his chest, for under the lower ribs there was nothing but skin, close to his back bone. A walk round in this skeleton-like condition was made, shouting "no hab got chow chow; wan dallah cumshaw hab got;" and then he changed his state by inhaling as much wind as almost made him a balloon, and his rotundity was as extraordinary as his previous extreme as a skeleton. Among other tricks of this fellow, he showed wonderful cleverness in juggling, twirling a stick on the points of other two, turning a plate on the point of a stick balanced on the point of his nose, and in the latter performance he rendered his appearance most grotesque by taking his queue,—a very short and spare one,—doubling it up, and tieing it round with the extremity of the silk thread till it stood erect six inches from the crown of his head. So much for what we remember of a performance witnessed more than six months ago.

The other day we happened to be on board the same steamer, at the same wharf, and the showmen were on the boards again; there were two or three of them, but the "no hab got chow chow" fellow did not put in an appearance. One of them was quite a young man, who could not do much in the showman "pidgin"; he was too much like the old fellow we once saw in the City, walking backwards and forwards, striking attitudes, and throwing about his arms in a promiscuous manner; but he afterwards did some feats in tumbling which were rather good for the clumsy looking Chinaman that he was. He tumbled a series of somersaults, first putting both hands on the ground, then only one hand, then three fingers, next two fingers, next only the fore-finger, and then he went round and round without ever touching the ground at all. His greatest feat, however, was to take nine porcelain bowls, holding one under each armpit, one in his teeth, and three in each hand, and then turn somersaults, placing his forehead on the ground, without ever dropping one of the bowls. He soon gave place to another, who was more like the lanky fellow first described; but it was winter now, and the costume is much different, for this fellow was loaded with blue cottons and dirty rags, and it was a constant trouble to him to pull up his bulky sleeves to show there was "no deception" there, and that it was "all done by the turn of the wrist." He went down on his knees on the wharf, laid down a small box which he had carried under his arm, and a group of Celestials gathered round him, while he had about half a dozen foreign spectators on the steamer. He went in largely for incantations, for his tongue never halted,—always jabbering away, at times quietly and anon very excitedly, while his peculiar gestures and the varying expressions on his brazen countenance were evidently essential to the working of his miracles. One of his first tricks was to show a pair of small teacups, place one, inverted over the other, get a little boy to puff his breath in between the cups, and then he shook them, when there was heard the noise of a metallic substance inside; he exposed the interior of both cups, and there was nothing to be seen; separated them again, and found " two piecee *cash*" in one of them; then he manipulated these *cash* for a time, changing them from one cup to another, covering one cup with the other, and shaking them, producing the tinkling sound at will; but he did not make anyone believe that there was much in this trick, for inside one of the cups we could see some pitch, and he evidently got the *cash* stuck on it when he did not want them to make a noise. And when he showed the interior of the cups, pretending there was nothing in them, we noticed he was always careful to have two fingers on the inside of the cup, and just where the pitch or other black substance was. His next performance was to cover a walnut shell with an inverted teacup, use incantations for a few minutes, and draw his fingers mysteriously round the cup; he lifted it, and the walnut shell was gone, and in its place was a hen's egg; this he rolled about and showed it was genuine. He next placed the egg inside a small bowl, inverted another bowl on the top of it, and held up one, two, three, and four fingers successively, to show he was going to produce a miraculous multiplication of hen's eggs. Sure enough, when he moved the uppermost cup a little aside, there were three eggs seen lying in the bottom of the other, and when he lifted the covering cup altogether, there were four eggs in the lower cup. This genius was certainly a porcelain wizard, for in nearly all his tricks pieces of old China were used. He took a pair of small cups, held them upside down to show they were empty, closed them together, and then the lower one was immediately afterwards found to be full of water; he divided the water between the two cups and drank up both their contents, squirting the water from his mouth again; but still the cups remained full; he tried to empty them again, held them one by one over his mouth while his head was held backwards, so that it seemed certain that the water must have gone down his throat; but whether it did or not, we don't know; at any rate there seemed to be an inexhaustible fullness in the cups; he tried for two or three minutes to drink them empty but could not do it, and then pitched the water on the wharf; with what he threw from the cups and squirted from his mouth, he had drenched quite a large portion of the planking. In his next performance he produced a piece of stoneware—not of native manufacture, and nothing more mysterious than one of Day & Martin's brown-coloured blacking-bottles. The bottle was shown to be quite empty, and the wizard placed it on the plank before him where he sat. He next took a small bag from the box he had at his left hand. This box, by the way, contained all his paraphernalia in bowls, cups, saucers, eggs, and walnuts, but he kept a dirty rag covering the top of the small box, and this covering was essential in the trick about to be performed. In the small bag he took from the box, there were two or three handfuls of rice,—chow chow rice, or as the showman called it, " chow chow lice,"—as the Chinese cannot pronounce " r," and substitute "l" for it. He exhibited the rice, put back the bag into the box, but left the open mouth of a bag lying over the side of the box; the covering mentioned obscured the rest of it. Then he put his hand into the mouth of the bag and took out " one piecee lice," dropped it into the blacking-bottle, covered the mouth of the bottle with a small piece of paper, and then threw over it a piece of cloth, and worked himself into fits by his manœuvres in calling spirits to his aid for this great miracle he was about to accomplish. He succeeded, and triumphantly unveiled the blacking-bottle, showing that it was full to overflowing with rice, and, catching hold of the projecting part of the bag in the box, he pulled it out and showed it was quite empty. He was not to stop here either, for he proceeded with the parallel feat of conveying all the enchanted rice from the blacking-bottle into the bag again, and then turned up the bottle, when only " one piecee lice " was found to be in it! This trick, although it at first seems marvellous, is easily explained. The manipulation was certainly very cleverly done, and it was only on the double trick being repeated a second time that, in watching more closely, we discovered how it was managed. When he placed the full bag of rice in the box, he did not, as he pretended, leave its mouth exposed, but the mouth of another empty bag; and the bottle was never really filled with rice at all, but when covering it up he had his hands under the cloth, stuck a cork in the bottle, and the cork had some layers of rice glued on the top of it. The trick was, nevertheless, a very clever one. He next proceeded to swallow nine needles,—each about an inch long, rather clumsy and evidently of native manufacture; he pretended to put them all down his throat, and on being told they were all in the side of his gums, he showed that they were not there. After swallowing, or pretending to swallow, the needles—in which he had great difficulty, and either real or pretended pain—he took a white cotton thread, about three feet in length, and commenced to gobble up one end of it; when he had about ten or twelves inches of it in his mouth, he drew in his breath and the rest of the thread went straight into his jaws in the twinkling of an eye, and was out of sight even when he held his mouth open. He did not seem very comfortable for the next minute or two, and then he began to writhe as if in agony in attempting to bring up the needles again ; after severe efforts he spat out a small piece of cotton thread which proved to be the end of the yard of thread he had swallowed, and he pulled it slowly from his throat, with nine needles threaded upon it! This may seem incredible, but we saw it, and can prove it was seen by several other people. We don't pretend to explain how this was done, but if anyone doesn't believe it, he can see it done, and perhaps he will be able to find out that there was some "dark trick" about it which we could not discover. We suppose he never swallowed the needles at all, but he appeared to do so, and the deception was exceedingly clever. This showman got plenty cumshaw that afternoon, and seemed to be proud of the result of his performances, which would enable him to get "chow chow lice" for a few days to come.

ANGLO-CHINESE SIGNBOARDS.

SIGNBOARD painting is an art the progress of which would form a very interesting and amusing study. There are many primitive signboards to be seen in towns at home, where there is not only something strange in the words, but the way they have been spelled by the painter and the zig-zag formation of some of the letters give the signboard a comicality all its own. The bad arrangement of the words often leads to curious interpretations. There is one in London where a tradesman of the Italian name of Smith puts the street number of his shop in the middle of the name of his firm, which would make one believe that he had a very large family, for the signboard reads:

J. SMITH 108 SONS & Co.

But we will not endeavour to recall from memory curious signboards to be seen at home, our object being to give a few specimens of what are to be seen in the Foreign Settlements here; and as they are the English signboards put up over Chinese shops, the letters painted by Chinese, it is not surprising that some of them are fearfully and wonderfully made. Foreigners in Shanghai even have some curious signboards, as, for instance, one, which has certainly the name of a foreigner on it, to be seen in the Rue du Consulat, French Concession. Of course at all the Chinese shops, there are the usual oblong tablets with Chinese inscriptions, but we must leave them out of consideration, as we can't read Chinese and don't want to. The signboards bearing words in English have generally also some Chinese characters spattered about in a miscellaneous manner to fill up odd corners. The greatest variety of curious signboards is to be found in Broadway, Hongkew (American Settlement), and in some of the by-streets off that main thoroughfare. As with the Chinese tablets, which are hung so that characters can be seen on both sides, so it is with most of the other signboards; some shopkeepers have their names and occupations emblazoned on the front of their wooden shanties, but most of them have also an English signboard stretching outwards at right angles, and painted on both sides. The extent to which they go in English signboards, the size of the boards, and the amount of labour spent on them, is proportionate to the extent of the business; as, for example, a barber generally has only about two square feet of boarding, and a big hong may have a very substantial signboard. We will now give some specimens, making the reproduction as near the original as we can by using ordinary type. We will take a few of the barbers first. None of them have yet adopted the red and white striped pole and brass plate. Here is one, who seems to consider it a special recommendation that he comes from Canton:—

BAR BAR
HAIR CUTTING
AH FOO
FROM CANTON.

Another barber has got his name awfully jumbled, for on his signboard it appears as one word, whereas there are three words in it:—

LEAUYUENWOO
SHAVING SHOP
AND
HAIR CUTTER

The next one we give has an eye to catching sailors on shore, for on the knight of the razor's small wooden board, right under his name, he has the English and American ensigns rudely painted, but we haven't blocks to reproduce them. The flags are such wretched imitations that it is a wonder some sailor does not knock down the signboard:—

FE WO TANG
NATIVE BARBER
SHAVING AND
HAIR CUTTER

The next one we give as a specimen of the genius of the painter in forming the word "and":—

CHING KEE
NATIVE BARBER

a ⋍𝒩ᵈ d

Hair Cutter

The barbers have little to put on their signboards; but when we come to the blacksmith and general tinker man, he has an awful yarn,—a catalogue of his stock in trade, and he says he makes "blacksmiths" as well as pistols and locks. The best one of this kind is in a road running parallel with Broadway:—

ZEY CHONG.
DEALER IN
OLD.NEW.COPPER.BRASS
LOCK.AND.REAP.HOOK.BEST
PISTOL.GAS.BURNER.STOVE
BLACKSMITH.MAKER

Another genius in the "brass-lock-hook-gas-stove-line" has his shop away down the road, and his signboard contains almost exactly the same words as the above, but whereas Zey Chong is content to have his in plain letters and even lines, his rival, Sun Chong, has secured a painter who has scattered about the words, in yellow letters, on blue ground, in a terrible manner, twisting them in grand flourishes that defy reproduction with type; but as a signboard it is not a success, it is too difficult to read; you would almost have to stand on your head to do it, and it looks as if it had been painted in a typhoon. Another blacksmith is less ostentatious, and merely has a small board with this on it:—

YEE SHUNG
BLACKSMITH COPPER
AND
TIN SMLTH

But the painter must have got stupid when his work was nearly done, for he puts an "L" instead of an "I" in "Smith":

The furniture-storekeepers of Hongkew go in for big signboards with a great deal of reading on them, as for example:—

SING KEE HONG
OLD AND NEW FURNITURE STORE ALL KINDS
OF FURNITURE AND OF BEST QUALITY
ARE MADE TO ORDER HERE.

And besides the large signboard as above, this hong has a small black tablet, with gilt letters, on the wall, a repetition of the words on the large signboard, but the artist makes a sad bungle of the word "furniture" as he spells it "Eorhiture," thus:—

NEW AND SECOND HAND EORIIIT
URE.STORE

There is another one down the road, next door to Sun Chong's artistic work, in blue and yellow; and the two seem to have been done by the same hand. This storekeeper is named Yung-Tai,—the name being painted in large "old English" letters; he is a jack-of-all-trades, if we may judge from his signboard (which has too many flourishes for exact reproduction), for he calls himself "Carpenter, Cabinet Maker, Rattan Maker, Painter, Mason, Stone Cutter, Contractor." Another curious board is the small one over the premises of Yung-kee, who is very particular in giving his address in full; and though there is a large block between his shop and the Old Dock, he stretches a point, and says his shop is next door to it, in order to have some good distinguishing mark to indicate his locality:—

YUNG KEE
CARPENTER
CAULKER AND CONTRACTOR
A445 BROAOMAY
H O NGKEW NEXT DOOR TO OLD DOCK.

In the above, the painter must have little experience, else he would not have made such a mess of "Broadway." We will take the shoemakers next, and amongst their signboards we find one in which there is the same idea as Yung Kee had in regard to the fixing of the locality:—

JIM
BOOT AND SHOEMAKER
OPPOSITE HUNT'S WHARF

The small board is ornamented with English and American flags, and pictures of boots and shoes; but "Jim" is not quite correct when he says his shop is opposite the wharf, for he is on the west side of Broadway, and there's several ranges of building between him and the wharf; he might as well have said his shop was opposite the river. The next one is rather curious in the wording, although the letters have been all well formed:—

YA SING
BOOT SHOE AND CARTRIDGE BOX
LEATHER BELTING MAKER
LEATHER WARE OF ALL KINDS.

In the next there is something in the name, if the cobbler had only dropped out the final "g," which would have been appropriate for that of a shoemaker, especially as his signboard displays a picture of a "Wellington" boot :—

LONG SHING

BOOT AND SHOEMAKER

REPAIRSNEATLYEXECUTED.

Long Shing's board is in three spars, which are open from each other, and it is time he had some "repairs neatly executed" on it. The last line is put all in one word, and looks like Welsh. The knights of the needle, Celestial as well as barbarian, are of course not behind their neighbours in eccentricities on their signboards. Here is one, over a small shop in Broadway :—

TUNG FOONG

TAILORS

AND GENTS. OUTFITTERS.

The Celestial tailors may do work for gents, but not much, and Tung-fong's place does not look very fashionable. Another knight has a singular name :—

A. KOW

TAILOR AND OUTFITTER

Mark Twain said he liked to see a man who could spell cow with a big "K," as it gave an idea of a new kind of cow; the above is a Celestial one. The next we take notice of is a regular cosmopolitan outfitter, and he has a new and original way of spelling "outfitter" :—

SING TAYE

FRENCH AND ENGLISH

AMERICAN TAILOR

AND OUTFITAR.

He ought to be proud of his professional ability if he can supply French, English and American fashions in his little shanty. Of all the odd names Chinese tradesmen have adopted, "James" is one we have never met with before. This is how it appears :—

JAMES

TAILOR

ENTRANCE

JAMES

TAILOR AND

OUTFITTER

The first board is at the end of an alley, and the second is up the alley on a gateway. We have heard of "Jim," "Sam," "Jack," and other names being adopted by "John" Chinaman, but "James" is a new one—and James a tailor too! There must be something wrong with him. But there is even a more curious Celestial tailor than "James," for we find a signboard in another road :—

MOSES

TAILOR AND

OUTFITTER

In the Maloo, opposite the Racquet Court, a "knight of the scissors" has the following over his door :—

W SING CHONG & Co
TAILOR & OUTFITTER
AND
MAKE HAT AND LADYS GOWN
Opposite of the RAQUET COURT

Anyone can see that he lives opposite the Racquet Court, and considering a Chinaman is so "close on the dollar," it is a wonder he should have incurred the expense of these extra words. He is evidently a ladies' dressmaker and milliner as well as a tailor and outfitter.

There is another shop in the Maloo, the proprietor of which who must have handed in a bill-head to the sign painter, for it commences :

Bought of

And then follows his name, profession and address.

One of the worst attempts at signboard painting we have come across is the original of the following :—

SAM YUEN
STEVITORE
FROM
SMATAW

This stevedore thinks it important to let people know he comes from Swatow; but he ought to have made his painter do his work better, and not have allowed him to spell it "Smataw." The painters themselves have generally pretty fair signboards, although they are not particular as to the arrangement of the words :—

YE SHING
SHIPS PORTRAIT AND
PAINTER

The next one is an instance of the shopkeeper getting as much as he can crowded on two square feet of boarding. It is difficult to understand whether Shun Kee or the soda-water comes from Canton :—

SHUN KEE
LEMONADE
SODAWATERAND
ALLKINDSFROMCANTON

There are many appropriate names adopted by Chinese tradesmen and shopkeepers. The following is not a Chinese name, it isn't proper English, and must have been adopted because it has something of appropriateness for a carpenter :—

A. CUTM
SHIP CARPENTER
AND
BOAT BUILDER.

The next one is not a bad name for a Celestial photographer:—

LIGHT.MOON
PHOTOGRAPHER AND PAINTER

Perhaps he means it to read, like Chinese, from right to left, so that the name would be "Moon Light." The best name we have seen yet for a Chinese storekeeper is that adopted by a native hong in the Broadway:—

SMILER & CO
SHIPS COMPRADORES AND
GENERAL STOREKEEPERS.

The "smile that was child-like and bland" is upon the face of every Celestial storekeeper when he asks "wan dallah-hap" for an article he is ready to part with at fifty cents when he sees he can't get any more. One of the best known Chinese shops in Hongkew is that of the firm known as "Cheap Jack & Co."—a very good name. They have a bold emblazonment of their name on the front of the building, but some time since, part of it had been obliterated, and it appeared thus:—

CHEAP JACK & CO
HIP CHANDLEr
STORE KEEr

The most extraordinary of all the Anglo-Chinese signboards we have seen is not in Hongkew, but in the Canton Road, English Settlement. It is in black letters of two inches in depth, and looks as if it was printed on paper and stuck on the board. The words are as follows:—

WE HAVE ON HAND WITH SEVERAL
KINDS OF DIFFERENT PACK ALL FIRST
QUALITIES TEA FOR SALE, ANYONE WHO
WOULD FAVOUR US WITH KIND ORDER
WILL APPLY TO

WING CHUNG WO
CANTON ROAD No. 523
SHANGHAI.

As in Hongkew the curious signboards are nearly all to be found on the main thoroughfare, Broadway, and are thickly crowded, we were led to suppose that the best of them were in that district; but a stroll through some of the Chinese streets of the English Settlement and the French Concession convinced us that we were under a misapprehension in writing the first part of this sketch, for although the curious signboards are more widely scattered, still there is a very large number of them, and the eccentricities displayed in them are also very amusing. We thought at first that Zey Chong, the Hongkew tinker man, was entitled to the first prize for his miscellaneous signboard, but there is one in Honan Road, English Settlement, which puts Zey Chong in the shade:—

TAY WOO
FROM HONGKONG BELLHANGER COPPERSMITH
BLACKSMITH FITTER AND PLUMBER
GAS FITTINGS OF ALL DESCRIPTION RELACQUERED OR
REBRONZEDANDMADEASGOODASNEWATTHEMOSTMODERATE
PRICEBRASSOLDIRONANDLEADPIPE,OFALLSZE,INSTOCK

And another tinker man is also entitled to notice :—

SUNG TAI
BLACKSMITH AND GASFITTER
COPPERSMITH CHANDELIERS
AND BRONZE BURNISHED
AND MADE EQUAL TO NEW.

The barbers, too, are even more comical than their brethren in Hongkew, for we find this Irish one in Rue du Consulat, French Concession :—

RORYOMORE
BARBER
AND
HAIRDRESSER

The idea of a Celestial barber adopting an Italian name of that kind is quite laughable. Another tonsorial professor in Hankow Road, English Settlement, has his small signboard embellished with English and American flags and something original in the way of scissors and razors painted on it; his name is a curious one :—

JUHNNIHR
HAIRDRESSING
SALOON

There are a great number of signboards with the shopkeeper's name, and these words added :—

MANILA LOTTERY
SOLD HERE.

But one shopkeeper puts it this way :—

YAK KEE
MANILA LOTTERY TICKETS
FOR SALE HERE
AND
PRIZED TICKETS CASHED

The general storekeepers must give up the palm to one in the French Concession for having selected a good name. In one of the streets there, on a pole stretching from side to side of the road, in Chinese fashion, this storekeeper has a board painted with very large plain letters thus :—

SHANGHAI JIM
GENERAL STOREKEEPER

In the Rue du Consulat there is the following :—

YUE CHONG & COSTOREKEEPER
SHIP COMPRADORE AND BAKERYS

The carpenters and cabinetmakers are heavy on signboards; and here are two or three specimens.

LOONG CHAN
CARPENTER PAINTER
BUILDER AND UPHOLSTERAR

YONG CHONG
CARPENTER UPHOLSTERER
DEALERS FURNITURE RENOVATED

SING CHONG & Co
FURNITURE STORE
AND BRONZE

The tailors have a few curious boards worth reproducing; here is a small one, but there is only one mistake in it:—

TUNG CHEONG
TAILOR
DRAPER
FROM HONGKONG

In the Maloo, there is a board with this name on it:—

ARMAGH TAILOR

Is it Irish? or what?

Then there is the number one name adopted by the tailor in the Maloo:—"Fitall." On the board stretching outwards from his shop he has this on it:

FITALL
TAILOR AND OUTFITTER

And on the wall of his shanty he advertises other branches of his trade:—

FIT ALL
MILLINER AND DRESSMAKER

He is not the only native merchant who has set himself up as a milliner and dressmaker, for on the opposite side of the street he has a rival:—

SHIN LOONG
TAILOR AND GENERAL OUTFITTER
ALSO
LADIES DRESSMAKER

While on this class of signboards, we will give one in Hongkew, omitted from the earlier list:—

SHUN TOW
TAILOR AND OUTFITTER
HOSIERY STRAW HATS
STOCKING SAND 9 CT.

The last line is a curious jumble; the painter had been told to make it "stockings, &c." but he puts it "stocking sand 9 ct.;" the "9 ct." is certainly an original "&c." A Celestial tailor in the Hankow Road has the British coat of arms on his signboard, and beneath it the words:—

SMALL PAGE
TAILOR
BY APPOINTMENT TO
THE ROYAL NAVY

Another similar one is to be found in the Rue du Consulat:—

CHING LING
TAILOR TO THE
ROYAL NAVY

We doubt if the Royal Navy have ever had anything to do with these people. We will conclude by giving some specimens of the signboards adopted by watch and clock-makers. They all have an approximately circular board, painted with the chapters as on the dial of a clock, and in the centre they crowd their designation in cramped letters. Here is one instance where the painter spells watch-maker this way:—

MAT9HMAKER

In another, a Celestial, desiring to tell the public that he can repair New York clocks puts this on his wooden dial:—

WATCH MACKER
REPAIR 1. NY CLOCKS.

The last, and perhaps the richest specimen of all is the following mode of inviting inspection:—

SOEY SUEN
WATCH AND CLOCK
MAKER
Come into the store very justful.

Another queer signboard is to be seen just after passing the small bridge at the top of the Rue du Consulat. The proprietor of the business is evidently not very well up in English. On a board placed over a small dirty creek ditch, appears in large letters:—

KUNG WOO HUH KEE
YUNG HON
SHEEI AND LAMB

"Sheei" is intended for "Sheep." It does not mean that Mr. Kee is either a sheep or a lamb, but simply that he sells these meek creatures. The signboard is painted on both sides; on the reverse side he spells Sheep thus: "Shee."

THE CHINESE POLICEMAN.

THE Municipal Council of Shanghai employ about 300 Chinamen as policemen for the Settlements North of the Yang-king-pang, otherwise called the English and American Settlements. These policemen are to be seen with unfailing regularity at the police stations when the hour for "chow" is at hand; it is only now and again during daytime, and very seldom at night, that one can be seen on the streets. They are dressed in a uniform which is half Chinese, half European. In winter they wear top-boots, thick black cloth trousers, fitting more tightly than the ordinary Chinese style, and a loose blue jacket, with an embroidered number in Arabic numerals on the right breast, and a similar embroidery of the Chinese number on the left breast; their tail hangs down the back of the blue jacket as a temptation for little boys to catch hold of. When it is rainy weather the Chinese policeman covers himself with a big overcoat, of regular policeman style, even to the big buttons and leather waistband; he keeps his tail inside of it; his cap is covered with oilskin or other waterproof covering; big boots, greatcoat, waterproof cloak, and glazed cap are all that is to be seen of him, so that he loses his Celestial appearance; but he also carries an umbrella when it is wet; the umbrella is generally of the three-and-six-penny alpaca order, but sometimes he lowers his dignity so far as to carry an ordinary Chinese umbrella of bamboo and oiled paper. In summer, when we have very warm weather, the native policeman wears a light suit, with a pith helmet, shaped like an inverted soup-plate, and he invariably carries an umbrella when on parade. An umbrella is not a very handy thing for a policeman to carry when he has to run in a prisoner; but then the native policeman so very seldom makes an arrest that he does not find the umbrella in the way.

The Chinese policemen are paid about ten dollars a month, and they consider their occupation a splendid one. They are sent out in squads from the police stations, taking turns on duty extending over four hours. The sergeant in charge at the station calls the roll, the native constables being drawn up in front of him, while a foreign constable is in charge of the squad and standing at their right flank. The constables answer to their names and are told the beats they are to take. They are spoken to in "pidgin" English by the sergeant, and the policeman-interpreter or native constable of the first rank attached to each station also communicates the instructions to them in their own dialect. When asked where they have to go, scarcely anyone of them can tell, so that they have often to be told two or three times over; the one who was told to go to the Bridge "can savee;" he likes that beat because he has nothing to do on it, and has not far to walk, but only to loiter about the end of the Bridge; those who have to go to out-of-the-way corners and back streets, where there is a chance of getting into a row with natives, don't understand where they are told to go to, and often go just anywhere that suits them. When the procession starts, the foreign constable leads the way, a good distance in advance, walking in a dignified manner as if he had no connection with the straggling native constables behind him; they come to crossroads, where some break off to the right, some to the left, till they get scattered over the settlement somewhere or other; but if anyone went all round, ten minutes afterwards, following the routes they had taken, there would not be a single one of them to be seen. The best duty for the Chinese policeman is to look after the Public Garden, where he can study botany and watch the children playing, or make love to the amahs. No Celestials are admitted to the Garden, so there are none of the native riff-raff on his beat, and by no possible chance can he have anything to do in the way of taking a prisoner in charge. But there is one part of the duty he must feel very irksome, annoying, and sometimes dangerous. Dogs are prohibited from entering the Public Garden, and when they stray into it, it is the policeman's duty to put them out. If he sees a small lapdog, poodle, or terrier, he gets into close quarters with it, holding out his baton to try and frighten it; if, however, the dog shows any pluck, as most of them do, and barks at the native policeman, then the dog is master of the situation; if the dog does not run away the policeman will not go a step nearer, and if the animal assumes the offensive, the policeman gives in and skulks away behind the shrubbery. A Chinese policeman when going home to dinner can walk about four miles an hour; when on duty he walks about a mile in three hours. When he sees a row going on between some natives on the street, he goes off in the opposite direction, and turns the first corner. When he gets a good, easy chance to take a quiet, helpless coolie in charge, he seizes him by the queue, and runs him in bravely; but if the coolie had shown any resistance, the policeman most probably would have cleared out at once, and then there would have been a race, with the coolie a bad second. A Chinese policeman was never seen running except when some one was chasing him, or had frightened him in the dark.

CHINESE BOYS.

THE house servants and personal servants employed by foreigners in China are chiefly Cantonese; they range in years from fifteen to fifty, but are all designated "boys." There are, of course, other servants than those known as "boys," such as the cooks and the coolies; but the "boy" takes the place of maid-of-all-work, house-maid, chamber-maid, butler, and valet; he is, in fact, a factotum, and some foreigners who have only one "boy" make him rather too much of a factotum, by using him as house-servant, valet, jinricsha coolie, cook, head bottle-washer, and everything else, which the Celestial will cheerfully do for a few dollars a month, until he gets qualified for, and has a chance of obtaining, a better situation. In a house where there are several boys there is one who is over all and is known as "number-one boy:" then the junior is always called "small boy." Number one has a great air of dignity when he contemptuously refers to "small boy," who is only learning "pidgin," but the "small boy" may still be the sharpest of the lot. The ordinary "boy" servant gets generally about $8 a month; he attends his master at table at all meals, brings coffee or tea to his bedside in the morning, has all his clothes carefully brushed; those required are at hand, and those not required are carefully put away. When his master is at home, the "boy" is always within call of the bell, and is always called if there is anything wanted, provided it is not less trouble for his master to do the thing himself than to pull the bell for the "boy." The Chinese "boy" has many good qualities; most of them are attentive to their duties, but the great complaint is that an honest one is very seldom met with, if indeed an honest one ever existed. Some of them have been with their present masters for many years, but the longer a foreigner stays in China the stronger conviction he will have of Chinese dishonesty; it is the newcomers only who have any faith in the honesty of Chinese "boys," and though the writer has not been here long, he has not got much of that faith left. It all depends upon the style in which it is done; and some "boys" continue pilfering for years without their masters ever discovering it; others go in so heavy all at once that they are soon found out. Not long ago there was a case where a "boy" was caught in the act of breaking open a lock-fast desk; a lot of money had been going astray, which caused suspicion and led to the watching of the "boy's" movements. When caught he was told his master was aware that he stole two dollars six weeks before that, and the young rascal coolly said his master was "too muchee foolo" for not having told him that before, because if he had stopped him six weeks ago he would not have been able to go on stealing from him all that time. The foreigner in that case had been making a collection of all the various silver and gold coins to be got in "change" here, and he discovered it was hard work to bring his collection up to any great size, as the "boy" was abstracting from it, regardless of what coins they were. He has now given up the study of numismatics. Another foreigner got his faith in Chinese "boys" shaken by discovering one wet day that his new silk umbrella had gone the way of all umbrellas, an old one being placed in the cover. That was meant to be a cunning trick, but the Celestial was out of it there, for he could scarcely palm off an old umbrella on his master for a new one; he had not been aware of the troubles that afflict the just in the way of losing umbrellas at church and other public places or he would have abstracted the umbrella, cover and all, and left nothing in its place. The foreigner having had his suspicions aroused, looked round all his locked drawers and desks, but saw that everything was, as he thought, all right; he did not miss anything at the time, but a day or two afterwards, on making a second search, he missed a loaded revolver, a gold watch, chain, and various other articles, and a small pile of money, and discovered, too, that the locks had been tampered with. He called for the "boy" with a vengeance, but the "boy" was off into the country to see his grandmother. The Chinese "boy" has more relations than any other member of the human family; he is always going away to the funeral of some of them, and when leaving he generally takes something with him,—picks up a few dollars and forgets to lay them down. The "boy" is of an inquisitive nature and knows everything about his master, and will tell everything about him if any other "boy" wants to know; these "boys" spread scandals over the place as well as any old women could. They are the chief exponents of "pidgin" English, as their intercourse with foreigners is greater than that of any other class of natives. They can generally speak it very well, but there are exceptions to this rule. We once knew a "boy" who, when waiting at a table where a good number of gentleman sat, used to create some fun by his attempts to speak to a stranger when there happened to be one at the festive board. "Wanchee lice cully," was his usual question when he brought round the rice curry; "blandy flittahs" for "banana fritters;" and various other almost unintelligible phrases. The same fellow used to call corn flour "starch pudding" because he heard a boarder call it that! He couldn't say "custard" for his life, and when he asked a stranger "wanchee cuss!" that stranger was almost tempted to swear at him. The "boys" are good servants when they are well watched, and they are worth watching.

CHINESE AMAHS.

"QUOD SERVII—TOT HOSTES."

H! those were happy, happy times, when a Philemon and Baucis managed their household by themselves; *tota domus duo sunt, eidem parentque jubentque*—as Ovidius puts it. Alas! alas! the lump of mud we are living on has changed since yon rosy days; it has been and is still visited by most variegated plagues and natural evils, such as clouds of locusts and patent corsets, mothers-in-law and pawnshops, parsons and broom-handles, the "chit" system, and cod-liver oil, high-heel Parisian boots and rinderpest, dentists and medical practitioners in general, and an endless list of other sundry plagues, not excluding domestic servants. Yes, gentle reader, believe me or believe me not—it matters little to me and it remains true nevertheless—God made angels, but the D—l servants; and, moreover, the truth of this axiom becomes as much apparent in the Far East as it does in home countries. This wonderful idea struck us when a continually yelping Cerberus, in the shape of a full-bred Mongolian mongrel, was haunting our residence from sunset to sunrise, and we could not get our "boy" to risk an attack on the canine intruder, which he declared to be possessed of the D—l, or else madly in love with the full moon. In our despair we sat down and wrote an epistle on domestics, treating the male portion, of course, first; but soon found, as the thoughts relating to the subject of "boys" flashed quicker and quicker through the mind, that, by placing the thermometer under the arm it had risen to 144°; so fearing a delirious fever as a consequence, we concluded to relax the nervous system by treating the weaker sex first, and so we fell to penning the following—a chapter, gentle reader, which we trust will not cause your hair to stand on end, as it is somewhat less terrifying than Madame Tussaud's Chamber of Horrors. So here she goes, my "Jeremiad" about the fair, fat and forty, almond-eyed Dulcineas of the Far East—"Chinese Amahs."

The reciprocal position in which male and female servants stand to each other possibly finds no more striking contrast than in China. If in the West the female domestic must be considered the *factotum* of a *mater familias*, here in the East the very reverse takes place, for she may rightly be termed the "facnil;" a peculiarity which but stands in conformity with the assertion that in China we find everything *vice-versa* to European customs and manners. Chinese amahs are the very "antipode" to Chinese "boys." The only point probably common to both is the origin of their appellation. It is wrapped in mystery, as occult as esoteric Buddhism; for the word "boy," though so often commented upon, has never yet found a satisfactory interpretation, albeit the probability of its being introduced from India. The word "amah," ostensibly, can be derived from the Indian term "ayah," a female servant; at least there is no sufficient proof for the assertion that the word is a corruption of a Chinese expression.

Chinese amahs, without exaggeration, may be called the most fortunate representatives of their class of servants under the sun. They appear to be born to live for ever in a fool's paradise; for all the woes and miseries, incorporated with the management of a household, are in the Far East placed on the shoulders of the male servant, who, it often must be surprising, does not break down under his burden (not unlike that of Hercules when bearing the heavens on his shoulders during the absence of Atlas). Here is a brief *résumé* of a "boy's" principal occupation: shroff, house-boy in general, cook, scullion, mafoo, jinricksha coolie, office-boy, sampan-man, house coolie, yachtsman, punkah coolie, lackey, chit-coolie, &c., &c. The above-mentioned fact naturally indicates that the responsibility of an amah in a household is of most trifling importance. Their services, in fact, are restricted to those of nurse-maid; and even this "pidgin" does not invoke all the inconveniences connected with similar positions at home. They are tabooed from the precincts of a kitchen, and thus evade those innumerable mortifications connected therewith; in fact, their knowledge in culinary science appears to be confined to the task of dissolving condensed-milk for the use of their little cherubs. Even the broom, this terrifying sceptre in the hands of a white servant, is taken out of their hands. Dressing and feeding babies makes up their day's labour.

Chinese amahs, however, offer the drawback that they do not supply the want of a "confidential person," as white servants do in the West. They cannot be entrusted with any of those secrets, which always hover about the threshold; nor can you disclose to them your petty grievances, on account of their apathy; nor can you engage with them in any gossip. On the other hand, amahs have points in which they are preferable to their European sisters. They are not ladies in their own estimation, nor do they claim partnership in your fancy silk ribbons, or scent-bottles, or pomatum, or other toilet requisites. A stranger in the Far East, on paying an introductory visit, runs also no risk of a possible confounding between servant and "mississee."

Amahs consider their "pidgin" one of considerable importance—in fact, much greater than that of the "boy's." And why should they not? For, don't they enjoy the full confidence of a *mater familias*, as regards the safety of their tender offspring, while "boys" are but given charge of the master's ponies or his pack of hounds? And must they not feel themselves flattered by being put in an elegant "turn-out" and enjoying a ride? The features of a religious fanatic, who in his ecstasies beholds the sunny regions of his future paradise, cannot look more radiant than the full-moon face of an amah who is seated in a carriage with glass-panes all round (thus virtually placed in a glass-box), which permits their being seen by all the world passing by. An amah's "pidgin" is certainly lucrative. Their monthly pay is exceedingly high, as compared with that of a "boy," considering the work she does for it. It ranges from $5 to $15 (about the same amount as paid for a male servant); the difference in the pay presumably depending on the number of children under their care, and their "efficiency," if there is any at all wanted! Now, taking $10 as the average monthly pay, this sum would be equal to about £24 per year; certainly an exorbitant pay, as compared with that which domestics get at home; even if compared with the wages given to amahs in Japan, where a first-class servant can be got for $4 per month. But there wavers an enigmatical point around these *domestiques* —namely, what do they with all the money they earn? They certainly do not spend it on dress, for silk and satin are unknown to them, cotton stuff being only in use. They also do not seem to be extravagant in showing a great display of jewellery; jadestone mostly taking the place of gold. So where

CHINESE AMAHS.

goes their money? We notice that many of these Dulcineas have a "plopa" Romeo, and almost invariably one or two more as "reserve," in case of the first-named jilting her, an accident which often happens, whenever the "selected" finds a better "chancee." So it is not impossible that these hangers-on get away with the better part of their purse.

Chinese amahs have apparently inherited from their western sisters the characteristic trait of garrulity. Just watch them in the Public Garden, when the conversazione is in full swing! And there it becomes most forcibly obvious what important factors they must fancy themselves. We all know what an abiding nuisance these blue-cotton-gowned mentors in charge of a heap of squealing and romping "cherubs" are; with what majesty they sweep the Garden grounds, their eyes refulging with self-consciousness of their magnitude, not unlike that of the lion moving over the boundless deserts of Lybia. Just let them once settle down on a chair and your cry—

"A chair, a chair! A kingdom for a chair!"

will be left unanswered; and sooner, certainly, will you be able to entice a half-starved donkey to leave his bundle of fresh-cut carrots, than persuade an amah to give up the seat once occupied. Amahs have fair opportunities of acquiring the "pidgin" talk, and if their stock of English words is not so large as that of a "boy's," this is to be accounted for by the fact that their sphere of life confines them more indoors, and excludes them from mixing up with the bustle of the town. Some of them, however, succeed in learning "pidgin" English to a creditable degree; and we noticed those especially experts who had served for a number of years in the houses of missionaries; and if the latter happened to hail from the States they even somehow managed to acquire the nasal twang, and some of their Americanisms. As for the rest, an amah's vocabulary is restricted to the "pidgin" equivalents regarding babies' clothing, babies' food, and odds and ends making up the boudoir or sleeping apartment of her "mississee."

China cannot boast of any particular district which is famed for supplying foreigners with female domestics *en masse* who have the reputation of being possessed of special "grit" for adapting themselves to their duties. The necessary contingent is drawn from all the various coast ports, and the interior at times. In Shanghai, the neighbouring districts, and Soochow especially, furnish a large supply, and those from the last-mentioned city are also credited with being of a more handsome and aristocratic appearance than the generality of amahs; however, not being judges of "horse flesh," it would be difficult to vouch for the accuracy of this statement. Canton also sends up a goodly number, and so does Ningpo. In one point, however—and it is the principal—they all appear to resemble each other—namely, they are all alike *stupide;* excuse, gentle reader, the using of a French word, as we fear they might understand us, and———.

Amahs mostly keep on good terms with "boys," though there sometimes arise trifling disputes between them, when they too frequently come to the kitchen and ask for hot water. They are as a rule honest; in fact, unusually honest, as compared with "boys." On very rare occasions have we met with cases of dishonesty, and whenever such a case came before the Mixed Court, so far as our observation goes, it finally transpired that some "boy" was at the root of the evil. Though we are not very edified with the general cleanliness of Celestials, we must confess that amahs, almost invariably, are scrupulously adroit in their dress. Finally, they may be automata, to a certain extent, but then, they have the laudable characteristic of doing what they are told; they never talk one to death, as white servants do; nor do they carry stories out of the house (?), nor do they put impertinent questions; and last, but not least, you can dismiss them without ceremony at any time.

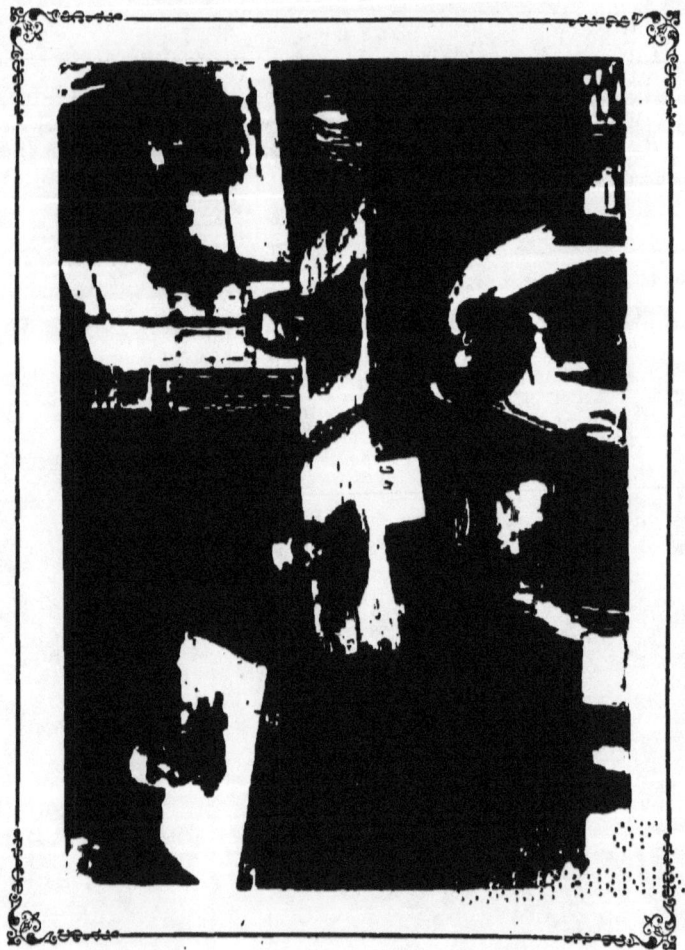

THE CANGUE.

THE CANGUE AND THE CHAIN-GANG.

THE prisoners sentenced at the Mixed Court receive a wide variety of punishments. The Magistrate either imposes a fine, orders a flagellation with bamboo sticks, the cangue, imprisonment in the court goal, in the police cells, or hard labour in the chain-gang; and either of these punishments, or a good many of them combined, may be awarded to the prisoner. The punishment of the cangue is the wearing of a wooden collar by the prisoner for a certain number of days, generally only a few days, but in some cases extending over a month. That wooden board is the most awkward and uncomfortable thing—at least it looks like it—that a fellow could have round his neck. It measures about two feet square, and is divided in two parts which are separated when the collar is to be put on or taken off; but when on, the pieces are securely dove-tailed and the prisoner cannot remove it himself. The board is attached to a chain, which is also wound round the prisoner's waist, and perhaps half a dozen of the fellows may be linked together when sitting in the cages at the entrance to the Mixed Court, or when they are taking exercise in the yards of any of the police stations. It is a very common mode of punishing a thief to place him in the vicinity of the place where he committed the theft; he will have to stand there all day, for he is chained so that he cannot sit down without strangling himself, and a native emissary of the police force will keep an eye on him and bring a supply of "chow-chow" rice to him. Thieves are often chained up this way in the settlements or in the outskirts, and have to remain at their post as a terror to evil-doers for eight or ten hours a day, being taken home to the police stations at night. An incorrigible thief who was once chained up at a garden on the Bubbling Well Road got hold of something which enabled him to file through the link of his long chain, although, like all the thieves which are put out by themselves this way, he was handcuffed. He made his escape across country with the wooden collar still on and two or three yards of chain hanging about him, and being thus heavily handicapped he was easily caught by some natives, who thought they would make a good thing of it by capturing him. The wooden collar is covered with strips of paper, bearing in Chinese characters the name of the prisoner and the offence for which he is being punished, which is meant to be a part of the punishment, and a warning to others; but most of the professional thieves who wear the wooden collar look as if they were quite reconciled to it. The prisoners who are sentenced to long terms generally go through the mill by getting flogged, exposed in the cangue, and then drafted into the chain-gang. Some of the prisoners are sent to the chain-gang for two or three months and others for longer periods, some for two years. There are incorrigibles that are hardly ever out of the gang and are disposed to spend the whole of their lives in it. The majority of the gang are of the coolie class, and habitual and reputed thieves; but we have seen cases where native merchants, and natives who held comparatively good situations, were sent to the chain-gang for serious offences, such as embezzlement, fraud, and theft of large sums. The chain-gang is so called from the fact that the Municipal Council utilize convict labour by making the prisoners do most of the road work in the settlement; the prisoners are yoked together in large teams, and attached to huge street rollers. The Council also employ a large number of coolies for road work, as the prisoners in the chain-gang are so closely chained to each other that they have not sufficient freedom to do all the necessary work. The chain-gang therefore is chiefly employed is dragging street rollers, and while so engaged they are under the charge of a foreign constable and two or three native constables. The filling up of the foreshore of the Bund was a big job for the Municipal Council's coolies and the chain-gang, and there the squads of prisoners had plenty of work for their huge iron rollers. The chain-gang fellows are all dressed uniformly in drab-coloured drill cloth, and the trousers and jackets are all marked with a Chinese character, which means that the wearer is a prisoner. In regard to boots and hats the widest varieties are allowed, and some of the convicts show their pride by wearing polished foreign boots, while others wear hempen sandals, others felt shoes, and others go barefooted. The hats are of all sorts and sizes, both native and foreign styles. On a wet day, nearly everyone in the chain-gang has an umbrella, and as the street roller is dragged slowly along by the team of celestial convicts covered with straw-thatch water-proof coats, and tattered and torn paper-umbrellas or demoralized cotton ones, the whole team presents a very strange sight. These fellows in the chain-gang are as happy as the day is long; their work is light, and infinitely better than coolie labour; they have plentiful supplies of "chow-chow" rice, are well housed, they need have no thought of the morrow, and as they jog along in their chains, watching all the sights on the Bund, they must feel that they are better off than jinricsha or wheelbarrow coolies; many of the latter may envy their countrymen in the chain-gang, and take steps to secure an appointment in it; while those already in the gang will resolve to return to it when their present term expires.

The chain-gang was abolished in 1890, upon the introduction of the steam-roller.

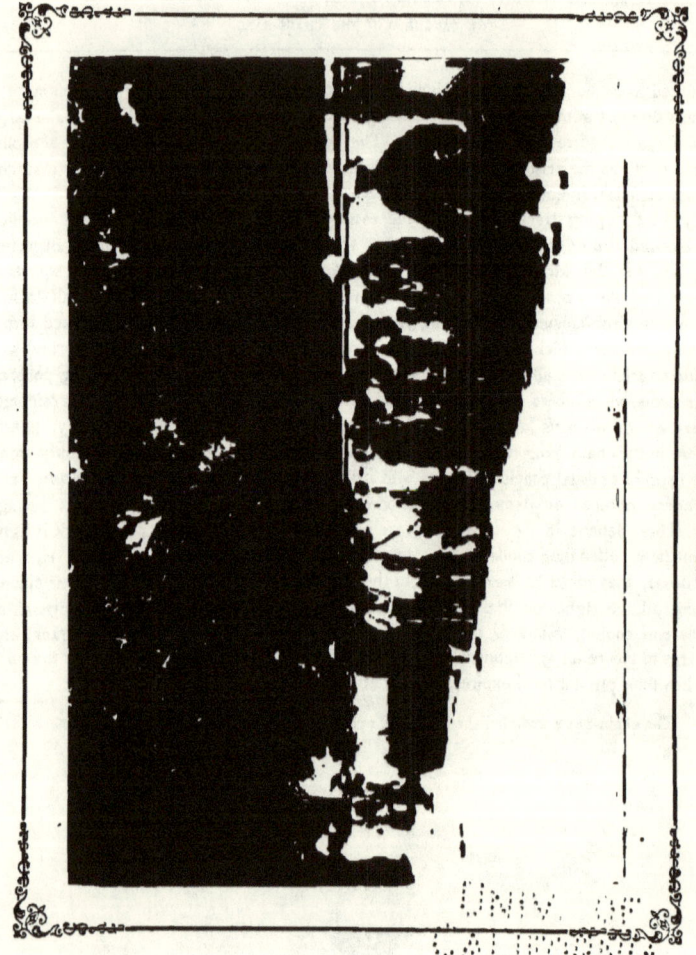

THE CHAIN-GANG.

CHINESE NOISES.

WE have enjoyed the hospitality of the Esquimaux and Patagonian, we have roamed over the vast savannas of the Red Indian and over trackless deserts on the "Dark Continent," we have mixed with the aborigines inhabiting the primeval forests along the banks of the Amazon and La Plata, and we have glared into the camp-fire around which were seated the nomadic tribes who roam the rugged valleys of the snow-capped Cordilleros de los Andes —in fact, the number of queer nooks and corners on this lump of mud which we have visited is almost legion, but, without exaggerating, during all our travels we have never met with a nation that showed such a preponderant propensity for being a "noisy lot" as the "heathen Chinee." Yes, gentle reader, the almond-eyed children of the "Heavenly Kingdom" on earth are the jackdaws and magpies of the human race. From the moment a Celestial makes his entry into this world to the moment he closes his eyes in eternal rest, he is constantly surrounded by an indescribable combination of squeaks and screeches, bangs and clashes, and he never feels more comfortable than when he is able to gather around him a host of people who carry on a conversation to which the Babylonian confusion of languages would have appeared a mere baby's tattle; or else he gratifies his mighty longing for "noise" by hiring a band of musical "roosters," who, by their demoniacal rumbling and scratching on so-called musical instruments, kick up a row, wild and infuriated enough to cause a European to jump out of his skin and sit down alongside of it. Of course, each to his own particular fancy; the Chinese, as far as we are concerned, are quite welcome to their unique intellectual amusements, supposing they keep beyond "reach of shot;" but if they come within "range," then we think it high time to avenge ourselves, and we intend to do so by "slinging ink" by the fathom.

Perusing our daily papers, we met, in a report of a Municipal Council Meeting, with a letter from H.I. German Majesty's Consul-General to the Municipal Council, complaining of the "noise made by the loading and unloading of steamers, which goes on by night as well as by day, and frequently on Sundays, and of the shouting of coolies employed in carrying goods, and which are a constant annoyance and inconvenience." Now, this letter has given us food for meditation, as it reminded us of own suffering. Yes, not only do we suffer from similar "annoyances," but our list of complaints is considerably longer. We certainly trust that our *graphic* (note the word) description of the "metamorphoses" of those hideous "Chinese noises"—whether they appear in the shape of a Celestial Paganini or a Sims Reeves, or in the coolie carrying his load along the street, or in the peacock-feathered official who, with powder and smoke, gongs, and a host of raggamuffins unnecessarily invading our streets, or in any other shape or figure—will somewhat contribute to alleviate the nuisance. Having now exhausted the train of our introductory thoughts, we are ready to proceed with our epistle.

"When you are in Rome you must do as Rome does" is a western phrase, which, however, does not appear to be regarded by Orientals, the Celestial race especially sinning against this commandment. Chinese, nevertheless, would do well to bear in mind the above cited phrase, and there is certainly no reason why foreigners, living on soil which by treaty rights has become their temporary property, should allow those Chinese, whom we graciously allowed to settle amongst us, to infringe rules and regulations which are in direct opposition to western customs and to our byelaws. Chinese ought to know by this time that those hideous noises, which delight their hearts and strike their ears as pleasantly as the music of the spheres, are anything but agreeable to our taste and nervous systems. We can hardly understand whence the difference in conception between us and Celestials arises, though we cannot help thinking that the tympanum of a Chinaman must somewhat resemble, as to its thickness, the hide of a hippopotamus or an elephant. The anatomical dissection of a Celestial's ear ought to prove an interesting study, as its nature, presumably, forms the most characteristic differenee between the Caucasian and Mongolian races.

No better proof that a Chinaman, notwithstanding his boasted hoary civilization, is still in his infancy, could be found than in the taste which he shows with regard to music—be it vocal or instrumental. Gentle reader, should you have a relation who, you fear, may come in for a share of the inheritance of a rich uncle of yours, just put this relative into a room, for about twenty-four hours, in which half a dozen of Celestial virtuosos keep on playing a sonata composed in B.C. 2252 by the great Emperor Fu Hsi (the father of Chinese music), and, we can assure you, you will have no trouble in procuring a legal and medical adviser who will give it to you, in black and white, that your relative, on account of sudden mental derangement, is unfit to share the fortune. Now, we don't blame these Celestial Paganinis for scratching their cat-gut like madmen and thinking the infernal music superior to ours—*de gustibus non est disputandum*; but we cannot see the reason why foreign residents should be compelled to go through the punishment of listening to it. Such, however, is the case, and at present, especially during the warm season, these almond-eyed "Romeos" are keeping up their serenading till dawn of day. Yes, not satisfied with the squeaking of their cat-guts, they accompany their musical soirées with what we suppose they call singing, but what we are inclined to term a *mixtum compositum* of a hyena's howling and the hooting of a horned owl. Some years ago we witnessed the burning of a large menagerie; the frantic howling of the poor beasts that became victims to the flames still rings in our ears, and we always get vividly reminded of the scene whenever we are condemned to listen to Chinese vocal and instrumental music. Now, in the name of commonsense, we ask—Is there any reason why we should allow Celestials to kick up such a diabolical hullaballoo? None, that we are aware of. It is a public nuisance of the gravest character, and as such the local authorities should put a stop to it; for the peace and comfort of foreign residents ought, we submit, to be considered of greater importance than the fanciful intellectual gratification which a Celestial derives from his howling and bawling and screaming, and which, alas! Chinese *civilization* calls music!

There is another "hideous noise" which, perhaps, deserves the attention of our authorities to a still greater extent than the nuisance just described; we refer to the annoyance which native artisans, living in the most frequented parts of our Settlements, cause by working at all hours of the day and night. We know, for instance, one who is so fortunate as to have for neigh-

bours two blacksmiths, a tinker, and a carpenter. They are a rather industrious lot, commencing work some time before daybreak, and seldom knocking off till some time after midnight. Can you imagine, gentle reader, the feelings of a man who, for twenty hours out of twenty-four, must listen to
" their bellows roar,
Must hear them swing their mighty sledge
In measure long and slow ?"
and besides this, to the excruciating tinkling of the tinker's hammer, and to a "duet" of saws which unmercifully try to cut their way through some knotty logs? Sleep, so long as the happy quartette are at work, belongs to the "sweetly impossible." Demonstrations as to the unlawfulness of such doings appear to be superfluous, for these fellows won't listen to you. On a few occasions this friend has called the attention of the police to the nuisance, but their answer invariably was that they had received no instructions on the subject from their superior officers. These "superiors" ought to look into the matter, and instructions ought to be given to the police constables to suppress such hideous noises during the night-time.

Amongst the numerous shocking musical instruments of a celestial, there is none which causes more annoyance than the gong. This plague, which plays such a prominent part in the life of Chinese officials as its deafening sound accompanies the mandarin whenever he leaves his threshold, draws considerably on the nervous systems of Europeans. Why should these peacock-feathered gentlemen be permitted, when parading through our Settlements, which is ground set apart for foreigners, to kick up such a horrifying row? Why should their host of ragamuffins be allowed to emit, at intervals, shouts which would drown the war-cries of Soudanese savages? If such "glorification" is necessary, from a Chinese point of view, to give more emphasis to the majesty of a celestial dignitary, well and good, let them do so, but such ostentation is quite out of place in our Settlements, where it certainly does not tend to inspire foreigners with awe of celestial dignity. The gong, however, now-a-days, appears not to be sufficient to satisfy a Chinaman's insatiable thirst for noise; no; on the arrival or departure of a high mandarin, he orders a thousand "braves" and a dozen war-junks, and they must disturb the peace of the Settlements by unmercifully blazing away, to the great annoyance of everybody. We are even reluctant to allow a foreign prince the honour of a salute; why should we, therefore, grant the honour to the semi-civilized " heathen Chinee?" The local authorities ought to pass a bye-law doing away, once and for ever, with such ridiculous outward shows in our Settlements.

Finally, we come to the nuisance to which His Imperial German Majesty's Consul-General ately referred, adding to it the noises caused by street hawkers and Chinese pedestrians in general. As to the first-named annoyance, everybody will agree as to the justification of the complaint, though, perhaps, those residing in the immediate vicinity of the "river side" are the most affected by it. However, coolies employed in carrying goods along the public streets are a nuisance which concerns us all. Their shouting is hardly less annoying than the noise made by the nine hundred and ninety-nine circular saws of a Michigan lumber mill. Why Chinese labourers, when carrying anything, no matter what its weight, should not be able to do so without accompanying each of their steps with a shout not unlike that of a swarm of bull-frogs chanting their monotonous air *unisono*, is an enigma; this may be an old custom, but it is quite unnecessary, and the police ought to see that " olo custom " is promptly abolished.

CHINESE NOISES.

There is no nation on the earth that loves so much to hear themselves talk as the Chinese. They make night hideous by their talking, and in summer, when we are forced to keep open our windows, their voices frequently awaken one from sweet dreams, leaving one in doubt whether there is a heavy thunderstorm passing over head, or whether four-score-and-five affectionate mothers-in-law are arguing the point; when we come to look for the cause of the noise, however, we find a pair of Celestials, leisurely swaggering along the street, *only* engaged in a gentle conversation. Hawkers, also, in the small hours of the morn, contribute their share to multiply our execrations, by the manner in which they praise up their goods.

The annoyance caused by all those "hideous Chinese noises," not excluding their numerous "chin-chin joss pidgin," by their horrible cries and musical demonstrations in funeral or wedding processions, is one which deserves the special attention of our local authorities. We have partly suppressed the diabolical row caused by firing off crackers, &c., during Chinese New Year, and why should we not be able to put a stop to noises such as those enumerated? China, in its steady though slow advance towards civilisation, will anyhow have to regard them as things of the past in the no distant future, and we think it only becoming and our duty that we should assist the Celestial race and put them on the way to what is but a matter of time and patience.

THE MIXED COURT.

THE circumstances which necessitate the constitution of the tribunal known as the "Mixed Court;" the daily proceedings in that "hall of justice;" the interior of the "hall;" its exterior and surroundings; everthing about it, and everything connected with it; the Chinese Magistrate, the Foreign Assessors, the public prosecutors, the magistrate's runners, the plaintiffs and defendants, prisoners and complainants, all combine to make it the most unique institution ever dedicated to Justice. The Mixed Court for the Foreign Settlements North of the Yang-king-pang Creek is constituted for the administration of "justice" in all civil cases where the plaintiffs are foreigners and the defendants Chinese, and for the trial of natives for criminal offences or contraventions of the Municipal Bye-laws founded on the Land Regulations of these Settlements. The Chinese Magistrate of this Court is a mandarin of the seventh order, subordinate to the Che-Hsien or District Magistrate of Shanghai. The Foreign Assessors sit on the bench with the Chinese Magistrate; they have judicial powers, and their special duty is to look after the interests of the foreign plaintiffs, and to ensure the bye-laws of the Settlements being enforced upon the natives, by the adequate punishment of those who violate them. The Court sits six days every week, except at the Chinese New Year holidays, and on some special festivals during the year. On three days of the week Her Britannic Majesty's Vice-Consul sits as Assessor; two days of the week, the United States Assessor; and the sixth day is taken by the Austro-Hungarian Assessor, or in his absence the German Assessor.

The Court is located in the Maloo, the "hall of justice" forming part of the Mandarin's yamên. A terror to evildoers is witnessed at the entrance to the yamên; close to the street pavement, and flanking the gateway, are two enclosures or huge cages, formed by strong wooden bars, extending from the ground nearly to the first roof of the porch. They look something like John Bunyan's idea of the cage in which Faithful was imprisoned at Vanity Fair; they are for the same purpose as the "stocks" were used in England many years ago; and here these Celestial cages are filled with prisoners, as part of their punishment, and to make others fear and tremble. The bars are almost wide enough for a lean fellow to wriggle through; but the awkward thing against such an attempt is that all the prisoners are so well taken care of, lest anybody should steal them, that each fellow is adorned with a huge wooden collar, about two feet square, the frame-work firmly secured, and an ornamental chain of quarter-inch malleable iron links attached both to the collar and to its wearer, to the one next him, and so round them all, joining in one inseparable heap half a dozen Celestial vagabonds and all their decorations in woodwork and iron. Their hands are free so that they can use the chop-sticks, their supply of rice is plentiful, and they are happy enough, as they sit there with one peak of the wooden collar resting on the breast, corners covering each shoulder, and the other peak away up from the back of the head. Their position is rendered more lively, too, from the presence of friends moving about on the pavement; cooks and other itinerant street merchants have their stalls close to the bars, and the prisoners are evidently comforted at times with more than prisoner's fare, and most of them are able to get hold of a pipe and tobacco.

We pass through the portals, emblazoned with demoniacal pictures of mighty Chinamen in red, blue, green, and all colours in confusion, making flaming combinations that would be worth money to a travelling penny show. We enter a spacious court-yard, having on the right and left small houses occupied by retainers of the yamên; in front of us is the huge picture of a nondescript monster. Is it a dragon? Well, it looks wild enough, hideous enough, and as far as paint goes, extravagant enough to make half a dozen good-sized, decent-looking dragons. This monster is said to be an emblem of "avarice," and it is painted there on a screen, in the open entrance to the mandarin's official residence, as a remembrancer that avarice is a sin which officials are to guard against, and never—hardly ever—do such a thing as squeeze. In and about the front of the official residence are sedan chairs—the mandarin's distinguished from those in which his subordinates are carried by as much difference as there is between the silk dress of a merchant and the rags of a coolie,—the great red umbrella and the gold-lettered tablets, which are used in procession when the mandarin goes forth with all his greasy retinue, and the gong which is sounded to herald the approach of the mighty.

From this court-yard, a narrow passage at the left side leads to another and much smaller yard—surrounded by brick walls on three sides, and the great "hall of justice" forms the north side of the square. The court-yard is exceedingly small; the ground is covered with all sorts of rubbish. When a case of great interest to the natives is before the Court, this small yard is completely crowded with people; when the Maloo murder was being investigated, not only this small yard, but the passage leading to it, in the large court-yard, and out to the street, there was a dense and eager throng of natives; just as at the Central Criminal Court, London, when a sensational trial is about to be finished, the crowds throng Old Bailey from Ludgate Hill to Newgate, waiting for news of the verdict. But the natives here did not have the excitement of a trial and verdict in that Maloo case; the prisoners were taken to the City, kept there a long time, after which they were taken on a grand tour round the province, regulated in a manner that would have done credit to the greatest circumlocutionist that ever handled red tape.

The Court opens every morning at 10 o'clock, and its proceedings always attract attention of a good number of natives; a few of them may chance to get accommodation inside, although only there out of curiosity, but the "general public" have, as a rule, to content themselves with standing in the small courtyard outside. The "hall of justice" is entirely composed of windows and doors of glass, and the outsiders form themselves in rows close against the windows, along the whole front of the building. To force our way through this crowd is sometimes not very easy; some of the idlers have to be pushed out of the way,—a queue pulled or a shin kicked clears the way very well. Once having reached the door, we open it, and step right into the arena of the great "hall of justice." The first time we went there, some years ago, we instinctively and with due reverence took off our hat; but soon discovered that this was a superfluous bit of etiquette while in a "Mixed" Court, and the free and easy manner of the proceedings became more apparent when we observed a friend smoking a cigar. Our notions of the Court were upset; we had just thrown away a cigar after a few puffs; we had come into Court reverentially, with uncovered head; we were out of it in both cases. "Is smoking allowed?" we asked our friend, in a whisper, which the Assessor heard, and made reply, "Oh, yes, smoke away; smoking is the rule here." At this time, old Chên was taking a cheroot from his cigar-case; he lighted it with a match that "light only on the box"; and then handed a cheroot to the Assessor. Four or five cigars were all going like so many houses on fire in a minute after that; and we never think of dropping a cigar amongst the Celestials at the door, or taking off our hat when we go to Court again.

The Court-room is a very small, wooden erection; the roof is a ridged one, the bare rafters are seen, and the whole building has a ramshackle appearance. The bench at which the Magistrate and the Assessor sit is a huge wooden table, very shaky on the legs; it stands on a platform a few inches from the floor, and its position is approximately in the centre of the room; for behind the seats on this platform, there is a screen extending between two pillars, whose primary use is to support the roof; behind that screen is a pretty broad passage, and in it the punkah coolie takes his seat. From the front of the bench to the glass door at which we enter, is the arena, where prisoners are made to kneel and *kow-tow*; and on the right and left sides the arena is marked off by wooden railings. The space to the right side from the bench is divided by another railing at right angles; at the end of the bench, the space there is reserved for the Superintendent and Inspectors of Municipal Police, who conduct the prosecutions; and the other open space at that side of the building is for foreign plaintiffs or others. At the left side of the Court, the arena is hemmed in by a cordon of the Magistrate's runners, who stand shoulder to shoulder, and sometimes in double ranks. At that side of the bench, the Magistrate's secretary takes notes; and all round about there are Chinese of whom it would be difficult to say whether they have any duty there or not. One noticeable figure in the group is the tall, lanky Celestial, of about forty years of age, whose peculiar features put one in mind of a popular print purporting to be a likeness of Judas Iscariot; this Celestial is the Magistrate's "boy," and he stands close at the back of his master, looking over his shoulder at every document Chên may have in his hand. Another character often seen about the Court is Chên's boy in the real sense,—young Chên, his son. He is a bright little cuss, who takes evident pleasure in running about up and down on the bench; now behind his father, then behind the Assessor or by his side, playing with the Assessor's silver-mounted walking-stick; or, in winter time, poking up the fire in the stove at the right hand corner of the bench. His greatest glee is manifested when there is a seizure of counterfeit dollars, and he gets the brass dollars from his father and goes to the stove fire and tries to melt them.

The Magistrate sits near the centre of the bench, with the Assessor on his right hand;—there is room for three or four seats on the bench, and sometimes there are, when a Foreign Consul may be specially interested in any case. In his winter costume,—with great fur-lined silk coat, embroidered in mandarin style; and his up-turned hat, with peacock feather, Chên presents a more dignified appearance than in his thin summer costume. The old man—for he is over sixty, and looks like seventy—seems oppressed with the heat, and overcome with fatigue. He often sits bareheaded and is seen to be very bald; there is barely enough natural hair on his scalp to form a queue, the tail which hangs thereby being nearly all of silk.

There is nothing very remarkable about his features; his expression is rather pleasant; eyes small, dark, and keen; his nose small but not too broad; his upper lip rather large, only a few gray hairs at each side, and a long distance between these two remnants of a moustache; his cheek bones high, and cheeks fallen in slightly; he is not so sleek as he might have been some years ago; and the wrinkles of age are upon his forehead. To see him sit quietly amid all the squabbling of prisoners and runners before him, one would not think he had so much vigour left in him as he sometimes displays when he scolds a prisoner. On the bench before him he keeps a huge leaden inkstand, with tablets of Chinese ink; and there is a curious-looking article in lead, which is on the table behind this stand. It is in the shape of a human hand, cut at the wrist, and is said to be a representation of Buddha's hand; it stands on the wrist as the base, and the fingers are wide apart; it is much larger than the biggest hand of flesh and blood ever seen; if it was stuck on a broom handle it would make a good back-scratcher for the greatest Celestial giant ever heard of. This peculiar article is the simple device which serves as a pen or pencil rack, to prevent the bench being dirtied by the official red ink used in writing on the documents which comes to Chên's hands. Besides these articles mentioned, there are of course the small teapot and smaller teacups always at his left hand; his cigar-case and a box of matches that "light only on the box," always directly before him; and there are still other two things worth mentioning,—these are of simple construction, frequent in use, and yet the use of them is very hard to see. They are two pieces of hardwood, about twelve inches long, and about an inch in thickness and breadth. When Chên is in a rage,—when he shouts as loudly as he can, and uses up all the strong expletives in his vocabulary, hurling his wild thunders at an unfortunate prisoner,—the grand climax of his invective is reached when he seizes one of these pieces of hardwood, and strikes the other piece, making a tremendous noise that almost drowns his voice, and which, we suppose, he considers an effectual means of striking terror into the heart of the person who is thus so forcibly and violently admonished. When he is beating these sticks, he looks as if he were going to shy one of them at the prisoner's head, and some of the prisoners look as if they expected it too, and were preparing to dodge it.

The prisoners who are brought before this Court every morning are generally of the lower class of the native community, and they are a motley crew. Sometimes there may be more than twenty separate cases before the Court; two or three prisoners in most of these cases; and, not unfrequently, there may be more than a dozen prisoners all brought up on one charge. It therefore often happens that nearly a hundred prisoners are dealt with in one morning. It is also a fact that as a general rule the offences or crimes investigated at this Court are of a paltry nature; the large majority of cases are very trivial, and only on rare occasions do we hear of a serious case; so that the records of this Court show that for such a large and mixed population,—including all the different kinds of Chinese, the natives of this province, of course, greatly preponderating, but mixed largely with Cantonese, Fukienese, and many from the northern provinces,—the crime perpetrated in this large centre of native as well as foreign commerce,—Shanghai being a rendezvous for all sorts of waifs and bad characters—is exceedingly small, in proportion to the population, and taking into consideration the conglomeration of different classes found here. The majority of cases are petty larcenies; and we believe the most of them are thefts from natives. True, it is not an uncommon thing to hear of a case where a foreigner prosecutes his house "boy" or servant for the theft of a few dollars, an article of wearing apparel, or some trinket or valuable jewellery;—many Celestial "boys" are like the Irishman's donkey, which was good-natured for a long time just to get all the better a chance of kicking his master; but the more common cases of larceny are where a native has stolen a pipe, a few cash, a coat, or something of little value from some other native—from an opium shop, a lodging-house, or a tea-shop.

The jinricsha and wheelbarrow coolies are not very honest, and they figure prominently in the criminal class; the cargo-boatmen and sampanmen are also represented occasionally; the mafoos are not guiltless; nor are the small shopmen and servants of merchants without guile; but the thieving is for the most part done by those who are by habit and repute thieves. There are many natives who make thieving and imprisonment their only pastimes; and many of them are known as "trainers of young thieves." No sooner are they liberated from gaol than they turn up at their old haunts, steal some trifling thing, are soon caught, and consigned to the gaol again, or they may receive an appointment on the "chain-gang" for a longer term than they had before; which term they cheerfully work out—if they do not get a good chance to escape—and once more free, they steal again, and are again secured.

Another class of criminals are the street gamblers; they practise their games in by-streets, with a dozen or two of idlers round them, while someone keeps a look-out to report the approach of a policeman coming round the corner at the rate of half-a-mile an hour, and the gamblers then scatter till the majesty of the law passes by in procession, and the coast being once more clear, they resume the game. Gangs of these fellows are not unfrequently caught, and they get off with light sentences, as their small game is not a very serious offence The keepers and also the patrons of gambling houses, however, are severely punished sometimes, but it is very seldom that they are caught; before the police can get near the house, the watchmen have given an alarm, the gamblers make their escape, and by the time the police get in, all traces of gambling have disappeared. In 1879, a notorious gambling den was raided by the police, and over 40 Chinamen were arrested; that was a pretty nice crowd to bring before a Court—there was scarcely room for them. The amount of fines paid was $900; many of the prisoners could not avail themselves of the alternative of a fine, and had therefore to undergo a short term of imprisonment; one of the chief offenders, a merchant, bolted to Canton, but the Court compelled the man who was left in charge of his shop to pay a fine of $200; the merchant came back some months afterwards, and was at once brought to Court and sentenced to one year's servitude in the "chain-gang."

Tea-shop fights, and destruction of property in them are most common offences; as the tea-shop is the "public house" of the Chinaman, where he goes to refresh himself, so also is it the place where many meet, either by accident or preconcerted purpose, and settle disputes, which are not always amicably arranged, but which may often end in blows, and the furnishings of the tea-shop are thrown about in a promiscuous manner the bill for damages generally being the most serious matter for the party held responsible for the row.

Of robberies by violence there are very few,—either violent robberies from Chinese or foreigners. Of burglaries, there are many small cases, such as breaking into native houses; and the residences of foreigners have also been visited,—the wine cellars in general being the chief attraction.

Many of the most peculiar cases are those which could only occur amongst Chinese, such as malicious cases of squeezing, kidnapping; disputes as to the selling of wives and mortgaging of concubines; the desertion of wives from husbands and prosecutions to enforce return; and such like cases, many of them being more civil than criminal in their nature according to Western ideas, but the party prosecuted in such cases is a criminal under the Chinese law.

The prisoners are, as a rule, brought to Court in custody of the Municipal Police; in many cases they appear in answer to a warrant or summons, or having been liberated on bail, they surrender themselves; but in the ordinary case, the prisoner is brought in custody, his guardian angel holding a firm hold of him by the queue, or two or three of them may be tied together by that appendage. They are ushered into Court in an unceremonious manner, —crushing through the crowd outside, the glass door hurrredly opened and with much clattering, and the custodian of the prisoners pushes them right into the arena, where they drop down on their knees, and perform the *kow-tow* before the bench. They must remain on their knees all the time during the hearing of the cases, and in a long and tedious hearing, they get rather tired sometimes, but the court runners—who take charge of them when they are in Court—are relentless in pulling the prisoners by the queue and making them sit erect, whenever they show any dispositon to squat down in a more comfortable attitude than on their marrow bones. Some of the prisoners make a tremendous demonstration in kow-towing; they beat their head, not only nine times,—which is the regulation number,—but continue dashing their forehead on the floor with such violence and so rapidly that they raise clouds of dust, and look as if they meant either to fracture their skull or knock a hole in the floor. And while this goes on, such yelling, such shouting, such weeping, such wailing, such gnashing of teeth, was never witnessed in any other place this side of "that bourne." If the prisoner is likely to take fits and never cease his hullabaloo, he is brought to his senses by that useful appendage his queue; a runner takes hold of it, and pulls and jerks away until he makes the prisoner keep quiet, the latter being pretty well played out by yelling before this is accomplished; and then he will drop into silence and present a calmness and composure which at once show that all his excitement and trouble was put on. The runners interrogate him,—not one of them at a time, but a half-dozen or more shouting at him,—for his name, which is given by the exhausted prisoner, is shouted in volumes to the Chinese secretary of the Court; and further interrogatories are put in wholesale fashion to the prisoner, and the replies delivered in the same voluminous manner to the Magistrate. Then the prisoner tells his story in defence, and the complainant may at the same be getting quite as much excited, and goes down on his knees too; and the proceedings are carried on in the most noisy and turbulent manner. The Superintendent or Inspector of the Police will have told the Assessor all about the case while these demonstrations have been going on; the Assessor tells the Magistrate the facts; if witnesses are present, they are questioned; and then the Magistrate cross-examines the prisoner. If the case is likely to go against him, the prisoner spares neither his tongue, nor his tears, nor his forehead, for by yelling, crying, and beating the floor, he protests his innocence, or implores mercy; a heavy fine of twenty cents, with the alternative of two or three days' imprisonment, overwhelms the prisoner with grief; his kow-towing is more violent than ever; but the runner pulls him up by the queue and drags him outside the Court, where of course he at once reconciles himself to his fate, and chuckles over his good luck in getting off so easy.

There is another class of prisoners who are just the very opposite to those excited and sensational ones who try to knock holes in the floor when they are kow-towing; this class are more calm and unconcerned, even though their situation may be serious enough; they perform just enough of the kow-towing as will pass for due obeisance; they make their statements in defence without any apparent excitement; and they look as pleasant as they can, under the circumstance, when they hear their sentence. Relatives are very useful for anyone unfortunate enough to have to appear before the Court. If the prisoner can bring his relatives for two or three generations back, he is almost certain to get off; if he has no relatives, the best thing he can do is to get some old man to appear as his grandfather; for the presence of a grandfather or a grandmother is better than proof of extenuating circumstances, it is strong proof of exemplary character, and the professions of filial piety may often have great weight with the Magistrate although there may be no proof that the father, grandfather, or great-grandfather is a genuine one; but their weeping and wailing may save the culprit's back from stripes, or ensure a shorter term of imprisonment. If a prisoner is charged with assault, or has been in any row, the next best thing to bringing his grandfather to Court, is to have his face covered with blood, two or three bruises on his arms, and a huge plaster on his chest. Then he must pretend to be in great pain, hold his hand on the plaster, breathe as if he could only do so with difficulty, shed a few tears, and if possible let drops of blood fall from his nose to the palm of his hand, and then smear his face with it,—and if that man's pitiable, but at the same time counterfeit, aspect does not win the compassion of the Magistrate his case must be a very bad one; his imposture will tell in his favour to a certain extent, if he does not get free altogether by making the Magistrate believe that he (the prisoner) has suffered more than the complainant. A Celestial who has been assaulted would not on any account wash the blood off his face until he appeared in Court to complain against the one who had struck him; he would rather have the blood on his face than six witnesses who could declare they saw him struck; and of course the prisoner manages to get blood on his face too, and tries to make out that he came off worst. Then they have a handicap lying match; but if the true circumstances are known to the police, the lies on either side may be wasted.

In this Court there is no such thing as perjury, for the Chinese "swear not at all." Lying therefore is unrestrained; the biggest liar has most chance of winning his case against a neighbour who is conscientious, or another who tells lies but not 'cute enough in the invention of them; the criminal who has the best chance of getting off is the one who tells most lies himself, or who can hire other better liars than himself to speak on his behalf. And though the lies are found out, as they often are, being too glaring or not cunningly devised, the prisoner is none the less thought of because he did his level best as a liar; he will only lose his case because he did not do it well enough. If a Chinaman is in a fix, either civil or criminal offences bringing trouble on his head, he can for a slight consideration, in the shape of a few hundred cash, or a few dollars if the case is worth it, get any number of his guileless brethren to declare that black is white, or white black, – either way as the dollars go.

Not long ago a Celestial of bad repute as a thief, vagabond, and general dodger, contrived to make use of this tribunal for the purpose of getting a relative into trouble—a relative who had given him money times and ways without number, but had offended him because he refused to do so any more. The vagabond gave himself up to the police, and made a solemn and penitential confession that he had stolen ten dollars,—which was a lie, as it afterwards turned out;—and another man who was hand in hand with him, appeared as the accuser, declaring that his dollars had been stolen,—which was another lie. The penitent thief said he had given the money to his relative, - the one who used to befriend him, but had now cast him off; this was the way he wanted to get at him,—to have him prosecuted for receiving stolen money. When the case came before the Court, the biggest rogue pretended that his hands had been injured by torture to induce confession of the theft; he declared that his thumbs had been squeezed between bamboos, and had his body suspended with all the weight on the thumbs, till he was compelled to confess the theft and tell what he had done with the money; but the injury to his hands, if real, must have been from another cause, for he concocted the story of the theft and torture to induce confession, and was only an invention to strengthen his false accusation. However, this part of the story was believed by the Magistrate and he got off, because he had already suffered, or was supposed to have suffered; the other party to the malicious prosecution, who pretended to have lost the ten dollars, got off with a hundred blows; and the abused friend had his character cleared, as it was found that he had not received any money, and he got off free. There was not quite enough lying in the case, else the result might have been different for him.

One of the smartest tricks we have heard of being done by a prisoner at this Court, was when three or four men were convicted of some paltry offence, and each of them fined 20 cents, with the alternative of three days' imprisonment. All the prisoners, except one, made great lamentations, and tried to excite compassion by their cries and tears; but one got up from his knees at once, as soon as he heard the sentence, boldly stepped forward to the Magistrate's bench, tabled his wealth in payment of the fine, and hurried out of Court. A few minutes afterwards, but when it was too late, his 20 cent piece was found to be a brass one.

The sentences inflicted on offenders vary in severity from fines of 20 cents to 250 dollars or more; imprisonment of from 24 hours to two years, and some for "an indefinite time;" flogging, from 20 to 400 or 500 blows with bamboo sticks; wearing the cangue in public street corners, for part of the term of imprisonment; and the most of the time, called imprisonment, is spent in working at the repair of roads in the Settlement, in the "chain-gang," so called from the gangs of prisoners yoked to the street-roller by long chains. The flogging takes place in the small yard in front of the Court, the culprit being laid on the ground face downwards; his hands, head, and feet held down by Court runners, while the flagellation is administered on his bare thighs; the bamboo sticks,—which are long thin pieces, of an inch in breadth—being wielded by a lictor; and it all depends upon whether the prisoner has succeeded in obtaining the lictor's good graces whether the flogging be severe or not. Some of the poor fellows will have their skin severely cut by fifty blows, others may have a hundred blows without nearly so much suffering,—as the lictor can give the blows hard, or just merely let the stick fall, as he is inclined,—and of course the inclination on his part is regulated by the most upright motives in obeying the Celestial injunction never to take bribes, for dollars are filthy lucre, and money is the root of all evil. The flogging causes great excitement in Court amongst the spectators; the punishment may be, and sometimes is, given immediately after sentence; but as a general rule the flogging takes place in the afternoon after the Court sitting is over. A hundred blows are said to make a prisoner feel very uncomfortable for a few days; and after 400 he won't be able to sit down for a fortnight.

The relations between the Magistrate and the Foreign Assessors who sit on the bench with him form an interesting chapter in the history of foreign intercourse with China. The protection of the interests of foreigners, the enforcement of the regulations for the good government of these Settlements, the suppression of crime amongst the natives who enjoy the benefit of that good government, and the adequate punishment of offenders, depend in a great measure upon the attitude taken by the Foreign Assessors, and the firmness with which they maintain their position. In many a case, injustice would be done to foreign plaintiffs or complainants, or native defendants, or prisoners would get off, were it not that the Foreign Assessor opposes the view taken by the Magistrate and convinces him against his will that the decision of the case must be different to his first intention. The Assessors also many a time prevent injustice being done to a native, where the case is purely of native concern. And yet we must say that cases frequently occur where it appears that the Assessors had not been firm enough, for we often hear of anomalous sentences — sometimes very heavy punishment for an offence which was not an aggravated one, and light sentences imposed on vagabonds that deserved much more severe sentences; the mistake generally being in the latter respect. The police inspectors, who conduct the prosecutions, stand up boldly for proper punishment being given to such characters as have distinguished themselves by being "well-known to the police;" they lay the facts of the case before the Assessor, and request him to see that the punishment which is deserved shall be given; and the Assessor may have a debate with the Magistrate for five, ten, or fifteen minutes before he will consent to the foreign measure of flogging, imprisonment, or fine; a compromise may have to be made; or perhaps the Magistrate will refuse to yield, and, telling them he is Magistrate of the Court, he will have his own way.

A case occurred some years ago, which gave rise to an amusing episode, and the particulars, as related to us by one who witnessed the scene, are worth producing here,—and this is perhaps the first time they have been made public. A prisoner had been sentenced to a short term of imprisonment; there was no difficulty about the sentence of itself; but from some cause, not very clearly understood,—it appeared only to be due to the supplications of the prisoner's grandmother, who was in Court, and doing her best at weeping and wailing,— Chên, who was the Magistrate at the time, said that the prisoner would be allowed to put in the whole term of imprisonment at the Court gaol, instead of being sent to the Municipal cells at any of the police stations. The police officers protested against this; the Assessor strongly opposed Chên's idea; and excited argument followed. And then there was a "scene" in the great "hall of justice,"—a "scene" that could be paralleled nowhere on the face of the globe. Chên completely lost his temper; he was in a terrible rage to think that his compassion on the prisoner and his grandmother,—who was most likely the prisoner's *only support!* should be thwarted by the Foreign Assessor, who refused to yield to his proposal. He rose from the bench, came round to the arena in front of the big wooden table, and addressing himself to the Assessor, used words to this effect, "You seem to be judge here, and I am nobody; if you are judge, punish me; send me to gaol!" The Assessor asked the old man to come up to his seat on the bench and not make a fool of himself; but seeing things were coming to a pass, he at the same time ordered the police to remove the prisoner. In the twinkling of an eye, three or four native policemen pulled the prisoner up from his knees, some dragging him by the queue and others taking hold of him by his coat; and they lugged him out of Court in a tremendous hurry. Chên followed after them, but the police inspectors were a rear guard to the squad of native policemen, and Chên could not do anything to effect the rescue of the prisoner, although he pulled at the inspectors' coat sleeves, and shouted and yelled for the prisoner to be brought back. As soon as the native police got outside the yamên, they put their charge on a native wheelbarrow, and made the coolie run off with him as fast as he could to the Central Police Station, the native policemen forming a guard on each side of the antiquated vehicle that was made to do duty for the prison van of the West. The Assessor left the bench, and the proceedings of that day were thus hurriedly closed. Old Chên had summoned his runners, and before the Assessor was out of Court, the enraged mandarin was off in procession, in his great sedan chair, preceded by the red umbrella bearer, gong-beater, and attended by all his retinue. The Assessor went straight home to his Consulate,—and drove too, if we are correctly informed,—but Chên was there before him and was setting off a long story to the Consul about the way he had been abused! The dispute was settled all right, and there was no word of it afterwards at Court; but Chên was baffled for once, for he had to give in; and the prisoner had to put in his time at the Municipal cells.

In giving a full account of the Mixed Court of Shanghai, our task would be incomplete did we not make special reference to the work which the officers of the Municipal Police perform—and perform very efficiently,—in investigating all the cases reported to them by foreigners or natives, or cases coming under the notice of the police in their ordinary duty in watching the Settlements. As we have stated before, the police officers act as public prosecutors at this Court. The greatest part of the work of the police in investigating any case is to disprove all the lies told by the natives who are implicated. What appears to be a good clue, according to the first statements of parties concerned, may be easily found out; but then the police officer finds he is on the wrong track, because he discovers they have been telling a parcel of lies. The police here have a wonderful power, which could not be exercised over people at home. If they can't get hold of a man they want, it will help them greatly to take his brother, or his father, or any of his relations into custody; if any of these relations of the "wanted" individual have a jinricsha or a wheelbarrow, or anything that can be got hold of, the police will retain that, and tell the owner he won't get it back till he assists the native detective in finding out where the relative has gone. The details of a case which has occurred furnish a good example of what an investigation into a Chinese case frequently amounts to:—Some time ago, a British sailor reported at the Hongkew Police Station that two jinricsha men had taken him at night to the open country opposite the Old Ningpo Wharf, and that they threw dust in his eyes, knocked him down, and robbed him of ten sovereigns. The Inspector of Hongkew Station, being indisposed, the case was taken up by the Inspector of the Louza Station. For a day or two nothing could be found out about the robbery; and doubts as to the truth of the story had from the first been entertained; but it subsequently all came out, and that in a peculiar way. The first that the police heard of the gold was this: a jinricsha coolie told a friend, who told a friend of one of the native detectives, who told that detective, that another jinricsha coolie had been seen changing a gold coin at a cash or exchange shop in the French Concession. The jinricsha coolie reported against was soon arrested, and when questioned about having had gold in his possession he set off with the first good square lie in the case. He said he took a naval officer on a certain evening from the Astor House to the Club, and received from him two coins, which he afterwards found to be gold—a sovereign and a half sovereign. He declared this to be true; it had to be proved or disproved. After sending on board all the men-of-war in port, and to the Hotel and the Club, it was found out that the story was false. The coolie was told it was so, and then he coolly said he knew it was. Where did he get the gold? His next explanation was on first thought even more improbable than the naval officer yarn; he said he was sitting in the Canton Road with his jinricsha; he left it a short time, and on returning found a small bag on the seat, and in the bag were two gold pieces. That would not go down at first; but his additional statement had a sting in it. He said he believed the money was placed there to get him into trouble, and that it was placed there by another jinricsha coolie, who had been dogging him about—who was dogging him when he changed the gold at the cash-shop, had dogged him to the police station when he was arrested; and had been round at the station several times, and was even then just outside of it. This coolie was arrested, and the case took a new turn, for it was discovered that this was the man who reported through his friends to the detective that the gold had been changed. He was a consummate fool for his own sake; there must have been something strange which kept him hovering about that police station to see how the fellow he had a spite at was getting on when he was in danger himself. He was accused of having put the gold in the other fellow's jinricsha, and, after many lies, he admitted that he did so out of spite and to get the other one into trouble. He was next accused of robbing the sailor, which he first denied, and told lies right and left, and then admitted that he was one of the two coolies who perpetrated the robbery. He was prepared to tell all about it, but he thought he had just better put out his spite on two or three people as long as he had a chance. He said three sovereigns were changed in a shop in the city, and that they were changed by a woman who kept a lodging-house at Sinza, and also that two men lodging there were implicated in the robbery. The police found out the cash-shop in the city, and, sure enough, three sovereigns had been changed there; then they went for that lodging-house at Sinza, and arrested a woman and two men, all of whom protested that they knew nothing of the gold, and they also said the accuser had a spite at them because he was put away from the house two months before. This champion liar had blamed these people only from spite! His next story was that the woman and two men he ought to have informed about lived on the Yang-king-pang, but one of the men was away into the interior, past Soochow, and had three sovereigns with him; and the woman and the other man had just started a day or two before on a wheelbarrow, and were to camp the first night at a small village a little south and west of Shanghai city. He was again mixing lies and truth together: it was found that a woman and two men lived on the Yang-king-pang, at a certain house he named, and they had all cleared out, and two had gone on a wheelbarrow; the other might have gone to Jericho if he liked, for it was found he had not three sovereigns with him. The police could not find the wheelbarrow coolie who took the couple into the country; but they found his brother; a jinricsha belonging to him was seized, and he was told he would have to assist in finding his brother; he did this gladly. The wheelbarrow coolie was found, his barrow seized, and he was enlisted into the detective staff for the nonce, and sent out into the country in pursuit of his late fare, who was soon discovered and brought back; one sovereign was found on him, and he actually turned out to be the second jinricsha coolie who took part in the robbery. The police even succeeded in finding all the ten sovereigns—one and a half from the first coolie, who had only spent thirty *cash* of the change; one and a half which the chief prisoner changed; three which he "planked" under the doorstep of the house on the Yang-king-pang, but had said the man who had gone to Soochow had taken; one from the second prisoner; and three which the woman had changed. The case was disposed of at Court some days after the sailor who lost the money had left the port; so that the presence of the complainant is not always necessary at this Court. The two jinricsha coolies were each sentenced to nine months' imprisonment; and the jinricsha proprietor, who let his vehicles on hire to these villains, was also brought under the arm of the law—which stretches wonderfully here—for he was ordered to pay some fifteen dollars and odd cents,—with which the three sovereigns changed by the woman were redeemed. All the identical gold pieces stolen from the sailor were thus recovered, and were given to the agents of the vessel, who remitted the money to him.

THE MALOO BRIDEWELL.

OW many of the European residents of Shanghai ever think of visiting the strange scenes by which they are surrounded, or feel a passing curiosity about the daily lives of the peculiar people in whose midst they have settled? The jealous reservation of this most ancient and conservative of empires has hitherto to a certain extent baffled the researches of the most diligent, and rendered difficult every effort made to communicate its inner history and usages to the outer world. A people so interesting, and a condition of society in such striking contrast to that of Western nations, would naturally be expected to awaken the keenest interest in those to whom a higher order of civilization has always been familiar; and the apathy of Europeans here to the state of things around them is all the more to be wondered at, when it is remembered that they have comparatively many facilities of observing native life in China. Perhaps it is that foreigners coming here are satiated with wonders, and lose their relish for the marvellous, or it may be that the pursuit of business absorbs all their thoughts and renders them unmindful of everything passing around them, except the state of trade, the fluctuations of the shares and exchange, or the prospects of promotion in the various departments of the public service. Whatever the cause may be, the fact remains that, out of the large number of Europeans here, only a few are conversant with the manners, or are even aware of many things of real interest that happen in the Settlement every day. Take the Mixed Court for instance. How many Europeans ever think of going to see how justice is administered there, or how the inmates of the prison attached are housed and provided for in their confinement? and yet the subject is one calculated to excite a keen curiosity in those who have been accustomed to the procedure of the law in European countries. It it just opposite the Maloo Market, and one cannot well pass without noticing it for the crowds of voluble coolies that gather outside its white walls when the hearing of cases is in progress inside. You enter either of the two wide wooden gates, and find yourself in a small courtyard. The walls are high and whitewashed, and on them are painted grotesque frescoes—dragons, winged lions, and other monsters, to strike terror into the hearts of malefactors. Facing the Nanking Road is another wooden doorway, leading into a larger courtyard, and on each side of this doorway is a large wooden cage, in which the prisoners undergoing the punishment of the cangue are confined. Two or three wretches may be crouching inside the bars, with this contrivance: a heavy frame of wood, with a hole in the centre for the head to come through, resting on their shoulders; and slips of paper, telling the crime for which they are suffering, are pasted on the apparatus; and criminals are condemned to wear this for one, two, three, or four days, or weeks, or months, according to the nature of their offence. Passing through the inner courtyard, around which are ranged the offices connected with the Court, and at the further end, a large and brilliantly painted door leading to the native Magistrate's house ; then, turning up a narrow passage to the left, you reach the Court itself. It is a good-sized square room, with whitewashed walls, a table at which the Mixed Court Magistrate and the European Assesors sit, and a few chairs. A space is railed off in front of the Magistrate's table, inside of which, the prosecutor, witnesses, interpreters, and prisoners take their places, the latter kneeling. The body of the court-room is usually filled with a crowd of natives—idlers, petitioners, or friends of the persons to be charged. It is seldom a European appears, except the Assessors, the Police, or persons interested in a case. When a case is called the prisoners are led in at a double quick trot by one of the runners, of whom a goodly number are always at hand, and dumped down in a kneeling position before the Magistrates. The prosecutor then makes his statement, then the witnesses, and then the prisoner. If his dialect is unintelligible to the Court, the services of an interpreter are brought into requisition. Perhaps the prisoner is convicted; and sentenced to imprisonment and flogging with the bamboo; if so, the bamboo is frequently applied there and then; he is seized and held firmly by two or three of the lictors, while another delivers the blows, on the face, hands or feet, as the case may be. This is sometimes a very revolting sight, the poor wretch writhing and screaming whilst his flesh is being pounded into a jelly by the official flagellators, who, with the most merciless deliberation and apathy, tell out the blows as if they were threshing corn. When the full number has been delivered, the prisoner is seized by the pigtail and led off to his place of confinement. These blows can be made to fall much lighter if the prisoner only " tips " the lictor : the more he pays the lighter the blows.

The prison for men is on the right-hand side of the outer courtyard as you enter from the Nanking Road; that for women is on the other side. Sometimes as many as a hundred men are crowded into this squalid den, which is about 30 feet long by 20 feet wide.

To go through it, all that is necessary is to ask permission of one of the Court attendants. Entrance is effected by raising one of the wooden bars that shut off the inmates from the outer world, and passing through the aperture thus made. This may seem a very loose method of caging in criminals, but it is really as secure as any other, because half-a-dozen jailors are always on the watch outside. As a matter of fact it is generally one of the prisoners themselves that admits you; your guide comes up to the bars, and calls to someone inside to let you and him enter. Once within, nothing can be conceived more abject than the scenes of squalor that arrest your attention on every side. The stench is sickening, the dirt revolting; and everything calculated to debase and brutalise a human being is to be found within those reeking walls. Vice and misery are huddled together here, and vie with each other to render the place a pest-house, and a forcing-house of crime. In one corner a group of hardened ruffians are endeavouring to lighten their incarceration by gambling for cash, or clothes, or anything that the rapacity of their jailor may have left them ; even scraps of food are played for, and the daily sustenance of the gamblers depends as often as not upon the issue of the dice-box. But all the inmates are not so callous to their condition; some of them are still quite young, and suffering for their first offence. These are to be found huddled up in odd corners or crouching on their wretched pallets, shrinking from intercourse with their older brethren, past-masters in villainy, or trying to forget their miseries in sleep. However, if their sojourn amongst the abandoned criminals, whom they now shudder at, be long, they will themselves become as bad in time, and young minds that may be almost prepared to turn to better things will be poisoned with the contact, and so far will their imprisonment be from having any beneficial effect on them that they will leave that jail more determined thieves and villains, and more cunning in the ways of vice than they were before imprisonment. The practice of herding criminals of all grades and ages in one room has for many years been condemned and abandoned in European countries, and a modern Chinese prison amply exemplifies the wisdom of our prison reformers. Verily some imitator of the great Howard is wanted in China, where there are more abuses connected with prison administration than in any country basting of civilization.

THE CHINA INLAND MISSION.

MANY of our readers will have observed new and handsome premises on the Woosung Road, just beyond Garden Villas, in the American Settlement, or Hongkew, erected for the China Inland Mission. These buildings, as every one now knows, have been built mainly through the munificence of one donor, a member of the C. I. M., and they furnish a magnificent monument of liberality to a good cause. Without having much claim to architectural beauty, the buildings are substantial, effective looking, and admirably suited for the purpose for which they were built—namely, the head-quarters of this Mission in China, and, for the future, members of the Mission visiting Shanghai will have no occasion to want for accommodation, the new premises being amply sufficient for any strain that is likely to be put upon its resources for many a year. The premises, which stand within their own grounds, also donated to the Mission, are in two blocks, one, three storeys high, facing the Woosung Road, and the other a very long two-storey building running at right angles to this for a distance of $256\frac{1}{2}$ feet. In the centre of the front range of buildings is a very fine, lofty, and commodious Prayer Hall, the dimensions of which are 43 feet by 36 feet, the height being probably about 20 feet. The ceiling is supported by massive pillars of Oregon pine, and the general aspect of the hall, if somewhat plain, is cheerful, and very well lighted by large windows during the day and well-placed gas jets at night. At one end is a platform and reading-desk. The hall will easily accommodate a couple of hundred persons. In this block, which is divided up into four separate houses, are situated the offices and apartments of the four permanent officers of the Mission, and excellent servants' accommodation. The rooms throughout are somewhat small and plainly finished, but very comfortable and well designed. The ceilings are lofty, and the ventilation has been well attended to. A long corridor runs along the back of the block, from which a spiral iron staircase, outside the building, descends into the spacious grounds at the back, which would serve admirably as a means of escape if a fire should unfortunately break out in the building. Here it may be mentioned that all the buildings have fire-proof walls. Underneath the three-storey building, a long colonade, supported by brick arches, runs along the back and gives access to the premises. The Mission-house proper, where the members of the Mission find accommodation, is a very long, two-storey building, and is divided into east, centre, and west sections. In the centre of the building, on the ground-floor, is situated the large well-fitted dining-room, neatly furnished and very cheerful, with tables and seats for sixty or seventy persons; opposite the dining-room are a couple of tastefully arranged sitting-rooms. In the east section on the ground-floor are found box-rooms, store-rooms, with well packed shelves of provisions of all kinds, piles of stationery, which indicate voluminous correspondence and other literary activity; and a post-office, with boxes for the various stations. The west section of the ground-floor is devoted to offices for the directors of the Mission and secretary's office. The whole of the upper portion of all three sections is ocupied by redrooms, each section having one large room upstairs and five small ones, all facing on the lawn, except five at the back. Each room has its own verandah shut off from the others and looking out upon the trim-looking lawn. There are in all 36 bed-rooms in the building, with six more in the front building; so that there is plenty of room, even at the periodic busy times, for the missionaries gathered from all parts of the country for the Conferences. A long gallery runs along the three sections at the back, where kitchens, pantrys, etc., are situated. On the other side of the lawn, on the left-hand side of the high building, are situated the quarters for natives attached to the Mission, etc. The back of these quarters, a high brick wall without windows forms the boundary of the lhwn on one side. Fourteen sleeping-rooms, with two guest-rooms are provided, with cook-houses, etc., with a verandah running along the entire range. The whole of the buildings are of grey brick, faced with red; the windows have the usual venetian shutters, and the premises are all well raised from the ground and ventilated by a through current of air underneath. The buildings are well supplied with water and gas. The roofs of all the buildings are of corrugated iron. The lawn, which is as yet quite plain, has a fanciful Chinese pavilion of brick in the centre, and comprises several *mow* of land. The entire site occupied by the Mission is 12 *mow*. There are several entrances to the premises—one from the Boone Road and two or three from the Woosung Road. The centre of the building facing the latter thoroughfare bears the plain legend "China Inland Mission, A.D. 1890," cut on a slab of granite over the Prayer Hall. The Mission is certainly to be congratulated upon the excellent premises which they have acquired, and upon the great generosity of the donor, who has thus provided one of the most deserving and thorough-going of the Missions working in China with suitable head-quarters. In closing this article we will add a very brief extract from *China's Millions*, of May 1893, where, at the May meeting of the Mission in London, the worthy organizer and director of the Mission, Dr. Hudson Taylor, refers to their new premises in Shanghai as follows:—" In those premises, I believe lives have been spared, sick ones restored, and weary ones refreshed not a few, who otherwise might have been lost to the work, or who might have had to come here at considerable loss of time as well as expense."

THE THOMAS HANBURY SCHOOL AND CHILDREN'S HOME.

HE fine new building at the junction of Boone and Miller Roads, which has grown out of the amalgamation of the old Eurasian School, which stood on the same site, and the Children's Home, Markham Road, has now fairly entered upon its career of charity and rescue, and henceforward will be looked upon with pride by Shanghai people as one of their most imposing edifices, and one of the most truly philanthropic institutions in the Far East. The new amalgamated institution was opened in September 1891. The following description of the house will serve to show what a large scheme of charity the founders contemplated, and the energetic way the work has been carried on since its inception. Built entirely of red and grey brick, it is the most striking edifice in Hongkew, with a noble frontage along Boone Road, and an altitude which commands one of the most comprehensive views in the Settlement; of a plain, bold, architectural style, none of the funds have been wasted in unnecessary exterior ornamentation, but everything about the building has been carried out with a view to securing the greatest possible amount of space and comfort for the little inmates on the alloted space, and as the completed structure stands, it bids fair to endure for generations as a solid evidence of the noble generosity of its founders and endowers. There are four stories in the edifice, exclusive of the lofty attic, and the gables tower 73 feet above the roadway. The frontage is 92 feet and the depth 55, and as the ground-plan is an unbroken parallelogram, some idea can be gathered of the immense amount of accommodation there is within its walls. There are, of course, the usual out-offices, wash-houses, kitchens, etc., in a separate block in the rear. The principal entrance is from Boone Road, under a 7-feet porch, while a smaller entrance on each side of the main one gives admittance to boys, on the left, and girls, on the right. The main entrance opens into a spacious hall, floored with polished teak, and measuring 10 feet in breadth, with the wide main staircase opening off the end, and a sitting-room, 17 feet by 3 inches by 19 feet, on each side. Each sitting-room adjoins a school-room, that on the left being assigned to boys and that on the right to girls. In fact the whole building is thus divided, all to the right of the main staircase in all the storeys being occupied by girls, and all on the left by boys, and as both sides correspond exactly in plan, a description of one side of the house will suffice for both. Taking the girls' side, which is exactly similar to the boys,—except that perhaps it is kept a little tidier by the youthful occupants,—we will commence with the school-room, and ascend to the attic. We find the school-room a spacious and well-ventilated apartment, measuring 45 feet by 25 feet, lighted from the right side and front by 7 long windows Every school-boy knows what the furniture of such a temple of instruction is, so we will not describe all the desks, maps, blackboards, and forms in this apartment, but, remarking only *en passant* that the pupils are an orderly and attentive swarm of happy-looking juveniles, we will proceed to the class-rooms on the same floor, which has (like the school-room) its fellow on the other side of the house. This apartment is 19 feet by 17 feet, and is at present used as a dining-room, want of funds having hitherto forbade the building of the large dining-rooms at the rear originally contemplated. The first, second, and third floors are divided off into dormitories, superintendent's and teachers' rooms, lavatories, bath-rooms, etc., and are more or less counterparts of one another. The dormitories are beautifully kept,—clean, cool and comfortable, and intended to contain 14 beds each. Off each is a lavatory, with five tin basins, towel-rails, toilet tables, etc., and everything in them is kept as spick and shining as possible. The teachers' rooms, which are in front and open out on the verandah, adjoin the dormitories, so that an eye can be kept on the youngsters, and their slightest move heard by the teachers during the night. Each teacher's room is provided with a separate bath-room and lavatory, and each of these rooms corresponds in dimensions with the sitting-rooms on the ground floor. The eerie attic up among the tiles and rafters is given up to the boxes and the bats, but the climb up among the dust and cob-webs, of which after all there are not so many, is well repaid by the magnificent view to be obtained from this elevation, one of the highest in Shanghai. A considerable section of the river, and that section the busiest, is taken in, and the country around lies like a map before the spectator, the hills even being visible on a clear day. Up in the attic there is a self-supplying hot water tank, from which hot water is distributed throughout the building. The furniture throughout corresponds well with the general air of solid comfort reigning here, and the building is roofed with patent French tiles sent by Mr. Hanbury. The institution is designed for the accommodation of 84 pupils, and even when quite full, there will still be plenty of air space for the inmates. The kitchens, store-rooms, and wash-houses on the right side of the building are administered entirely by the girls, and as a picture of cleanliness are not to be surpassed. This side of the house is, at the time of writing this article, under the superintendence of Mrs. Vale, who we believe is immensely popular with her little charges, while the boys cannot find encomiums high enough for Mrs. Youngson and Miss Deighton. The play-ground, like everything else within the outside railings (which by the way, are for want of funds nothing more than a totally inadequate bamboo fencing), is divided between the boys and girls, the former being relegated to the left and the latter to the right. Here is the bell which summons the youngsters to their different duties. Mr. Cory, the architect, is on the whole, to be congratulated on his achievement. The history of the institution, for though, as the inscription above the main doorway informs the visitor, dates only from this year, it has a history, is well known in Shanghai, where the names of Thomas Hanbury, and the disinterested ladies and gentlemen who have borne the brunt of the work of making the noble charity an accomplished fact, will long be remembered as generous and kindly-hearted philanthropists.

ST. FRANCIS XAVIER'S SCHOOL.

I.—The Building.

HIS institution, conducted by the Jesuit Fathers, was originally started in 1874, in the French Concession, within the enclosure in which St. Joseph's Church stands. Commencing with only four pupils, amongst whom were represented the four nationalities—English, American, French, and German, the school, gathering strength as time went on, has expanded into its present proportions. In 1884 it was removed to the new building in Nanzing Road, nearly opposite the Hongkew Roman Catholic Church. This fine, spacious structure, designed by a Brother of the order and erected under his supervision, occupied nearly two years in building, and cost some $40,000, the expense being borne by the Mission. The foundation-stone was laid in November 1882. It is a four-storied brick building, of a plain style of French architecture, its dimensions being 190 feet by 60. Thirteen large windows in each flat afford ample light and ventilation, the latter especially being excellent, as the building, being in an open space, receives the benefit of the breezes from whatever quarter they may blow. There is a spacious playground, shaded by a row of trees at one end, for the use of the pupils. It is 191 feet by 190, and is enclosed by a substantial brick wall, some 15 feet high. A shed of ample dimensions, zinc-roofed, running down one side of the playground affords space for recreation for the boys when the weather will not admit of the playground itself being used. There are another smaller playground and shed in rear of the building for the use of the charity boys. On the first flat are the parlours, the three class rooms for charity boys, the infant class room, a class room for Chinese pupils, dining room for the boarders, and tiffin room for the day scholars. On the second flat there are 4 class rooms for the respective standards, each capable of accommodating 50 pupils, general study room, and a drawing class room. The third flat is appropriated as teachers' rooms, and as an infirmary, &c.; there are four rooms for sick boarders. On this flat there is also a library containing some 1,500 volumes of ancient and modern literature, &c., to which the pupils have access. The fourth flat contains the sleeping room for boarders, one for the charity boys, music room, and clothes and boots rooms. The sleeping rooms are spacious and airy, and command a splendid view of the Settlements on the one side, and of the open country on the other. They are capable of accommodating a much larger number than at present occupies it. Here also are to be seen, within a protecting structure with glass sides, the works of the big clock which ornaments the front of the building and solemnly announces the hour of the day and night to the wearied, business-engrossed denizens of Hongkew. This clock, which cost some $800, including the fixing of it in position, was presented to the school by the then Taotai of Shanghai. It was obtained from Mayet, in the department of Sarthe, France; the maker's name is Gourdin. The usual accessories are, of course, attached to the building,—kitchen, out-houses, &c.; and five bath-rooms, where cold or hot water can be obtained at pleasure, supply all that is needful for the boarders in this direction.

II.—Composition of the School.

During the last scholastic year,—1st September 1893 to 1st July 1894—there were in the institution 7 members of the Society of Jesus, and 5 Marist Brothers. As the latter are especially qualified for Commercial Schools, and have succeeded so well in England, France, America, Australia, and South Africa, it is contemplated to send for more of them to take charge of all the classes. This measure will place St. Francis Xavier's School on the best footing.

In the same period, 210 pupils, of all creeds and nationalities, attended the school, showing an increase of 30 against the preceding year. The greater part are of Shanghai; still, several pupils came from various ports on the coast or on the Yangtze. The pupils were classed as follows:—

<pre>
        4th, or highest standard .... 10 pupils.
        3rd, ... 20   „
        2nd, in two sections 31   „
        1st,   „   „   32   „
        Infant class 28   „
        Special classes for Chinese 38   „
        2nd division, 1st elementary class 22   „
          „   „   2nd   „   „   29   „
</pre>

Of these 210 pupils, 60 were boarders.

III.—The Course of Studies.

The curriculum, which is gradually completed in accordance with the progressive development of the students and the special requirements of China, is made to follow as nearly as possible the plan adopted in the Grammar Schools in England. The ordinary course for all comprises,—English:—reading, writing, grammar, composition, &c.; history and geography; arithmetic and book-keeping, algebra, geometry and surveying; natural history, chemistry, physics, mechanics; French,—translation, composition, conversation; rudiments of music, singing, gymnastics. Extra lessons are given in Latin, Chinese (Mandarin dialect), drawing, and piano. Examinations are held three times a year,—at Christmas, Easter, and end of June. The scholastic year comprises 10 months, beginning in September and ending with the solemn distribution of prizes, which takes place in the last days of June or in the beginning of July. The months of July and August are summer vacations. However, parents can make arrangements with the Director to leave their children at the school during these months. A holidays' task is given to the pupils of the various standards. During the scholastic year, no student will be permitted to leave the school on visits of any length, except from Christmas to the 2nd January; and from Easter to the next Sunday inclusively, if such be the wish of his parents or guardians. Once a month,—viz., on the 1st Thursday or Sunday—boarders, if sent for, are allowed to pass the day with their parents or guardians. All Thursdays in the year are holidays; but, should an extraordinary holiday fall on Tuesday, Wednesday, or Friday, classes may be continued on Thursday. The school hours are from 8 a.m. to 4 p.m., there being an intermission from 11.45 to 1 p.m. for tiffin.

IV.—Conditions of Admission.

No-one is admitted or kept at the institution unless he has a good moral character. Members of any religious denomination are received as pupils, provided they be willing, for the sake of order, to be present with propriety at all the common exercises of the school No undue influence has ever been or will ever be used to make a pupil depart from his religious belief. The terms are as below, stationery and extras not included :—

Boarders, 1st division...............	25 dollars per month.		
„ 2nd „	12	„ „	„
Half-boarders, 1st division...........	15	„ „	„
„ 2nd „	7	„ „	„
Day scholars, 1st division............	6	„ „	„
„ „ 2nd „	2	„ „	„

However, the Directors are always willing to make special conditions according to the circumstances of the families,—in fact, among the 980 pupils who were at the school since it was opened, by far the greater part have been received with reductions; over 300 were received as charity pupils, and even a third part of the latter were boarded and lodged *gratis*.

THE SHANGHAI LIBRARY.

HIS institution, established in 1849, is now situated in the Nanking Road. A subscription library; its affairs are managed by a Committee of Subscribers, who of late years have thrown open the institution as a reading room to the general public, which has the privilege of using it from 9 a.m. to 12, and from 4 to 7 p.m., daily. It may not be out of place if we here give a list of the books, grouped under their respective classes, of which there are seven. The library contains at the time we write:—

A.—Religion, Philosophy, Science, and Art...	945
B.—Poetry and the Drama	315
C.—History and Biography	1,640
D.—Geography, Voyages, and Travels	1,265
E.—Prose Fiction	3,500
F.—Miscellaneous	810
G.—Works of Reference	120
Total...	8,595

As new books are received, lists thereof are printed and sent round to Subscribers. The library receives a monthly supply of books from its London agent, amounting to between three and four hundred works annually. These are carefully selected by the Committee, and a "Suggestion Book" is kept, in which subscribers note the works they would like to be ordered. This book goes before the Committee, who decide what works of those suggested shall be obtained. As a general rule, however, the wishes of Subscribers are met, so long as the outlay is within the means of the institution. The following periodicals are also regularly received :—

Contemporary	Review.	Asiatic Quarterly Review.
Fortnightly	Do.	All the Year Round.
Edinburgh	Do.	Belgravia.
Quarterly	Do.	Chamber's Journal.
British Quarterly	Do.	Cornhill Magazine.
Westminster	Do.	Longman's Magazine (formerly Frazer's).
North American	Do.	London Society.
Review of Reviews.		Harpers'.
Outing.		Nature.
Revue des deux Mondes.		Scribner's Magazine.
Nineteenth Century.		Temple Bar.
Century Magazine (formerly The Scribner).		Athenæum. Notes and Queries.
Blackwood's Magazine.		Proceedings of Royal Geographical.
Macmillan's	Do.	Society, &c., &c.

The catalogue of the books in the library, recently printed, is divided into two parts— subjects and authors—which greatly facilitates the finding of any particular work. Those treating of a great variety of subjects can always be found in the portion devoted to authors. The new catalogue is very well arranged indeed; and although we are told in the introduction that, "being the work of amateurs, it contains many blemishes which it is to be hoped will be treated leniently by Subscribers," yet we are not disposed to accept the statement as a candid expression of the feelings of the "amateurs" who got it up. No doubt, as Colman the younger said, "on their own merits modest men are dumb," but then again, as another writer says, "self-depreciation is not humility."

The subscription is Tls. 12 per annum, Tls. 7 being charged for half a year, and Tls. 4 for three months. The number of Subscribers ranges from 130 to 140 annually. Some four years ago a grant to the library of Tls. 590 was included in the Municipal Budget, in consideration of the institution being thrown open to the general public—free, as a reading room; but in consequence, we understand, of its not being availed of to the extent anticipated by the Committee, the latter body did not feel justified in receiving so large a grant, and so it was reduced to Tls. 100 per annum, at which it now stands. On the removal of the library to its present location in the Nanking Road, the grant by the Municipal Council was increased to Tls. 600 per annum, in consideration for which the Committee furnished the Free Reading Room with the principal reviews and a full supply of English and American illustrated papers, and supplied all the principal Police Stations with books—free. The general feeling amongst the Committee, we learn, is, that the institution should be self-supporting, and that when it ceases to be so it ceases to be a want; but, of course, they are perfectly justified in accepting some *quid pro quo* for throwing it open as a reading room to the public. Our only wonder is that the latter does not avail itself of the reading room to a much greater extent.

There is one direction in which the Municipality could, with propriety, lend valuable aid to the institution, which aid, we consider, could be properly accepted by the Committee without impairing those praiseworthy feelings of independence with which they are animated. As will be readily admitted, it is very important that a library like that which forms the subject of this report should have a good supply of the most recent works of reference, accessible to all. Many of those now in the institution are very ancient. A similar remark applies to modern dictionaries of foreign languages, of which there are very few in the library. It will thus be seen that the Council could, by a liberal grant for these purposes, confer a great boon on the institution and on the public at large. By doing so, it would be aiding, in fact, the cause of public education. Many knotty points also could then be solved. It is only with the greatest care and economy on the part of the Committee that the library can pay its way, and its financial condition will not admit of its purchasing the various works to which we have alluded.

Within the last few years the Shanghai Club has allowed its library books to be taken out of the institution by Members. As a natural consequence, this has militated against the Shanghai Library, by taking away some of its Subscribers. What is really wanted to make the latter institution a success is that, at least, 175 to 200 subscribers should be obtained. This would place it at once on a sound financial footing. It was suggested some eight years ago by Mr. Vice-Consul Allen, that the library should be made a public institution, under the control of the Municipal Council. It would seem, however, that the suggestion did not meet with favour, as nothing would appear to have been done since to invest it with an official character. If the Council took over the institution, it would, of course, be at the request of the Committee.

THE SHANGHAI MUSEUM.

THE Museum is located in the Museum Road, close to the British Post Office. Started in 1874, this valuable and instructive institution, an adjunct of the North China Branch of the Royal Asiatic Society, is under the direction of a curator, who is assisted by a taxidermist. An annual grant to the institution of Tls. 500 is included in the Municipal Budget. The Museum has grown largely during the last few years, and in the natural course of things may be expected to continue the process, but it is at present somewhat cramped for want of space.

The Museum contains a very interesting collection of specimens. In the mammalian section there is a very fine spotted female panther from the Ningpo district. It is a sly, treacherous-looking brute, with grinders capable of doing effective execution on the *corpus* of any unfortunate Celestial whom, when in life, it may have selected for its victim. In the same compartment we recognized an old defunct acquaintance,—a young tiger, 17 months old, which some rears ago graced Chiarini's Circus. A black bear, from Korea, is a very good specimen of the genus Ursus, and a white-moustached wild boar, of 200 catties, from the hills around Tahu Lake, presents an interesting spectacle; there is also a young one. Nor is the "fretful porcupine" unrepresented. There are also some good specimens of the Chinese wild-cat. Amongst the specimens of the deer, there is a fine one of a young animal from the Emperor's park at Peking. It is named "David's deer;" and another specimen called "Michie's deer"—also a young animal—has very pretty glossy hair of a dark brown hue. There are also specimens of the hornless river deer, one, an albino, being perfectly white. The Mongolian hare is a fine, handsome specimen, in every respect superior to its Chinese congener. The Chinese sand-badger and its three young ones are also very nice specimens. The seal, unwieldy, submissive creature as it looks, is an interesting specimen of the family *Phocidæ*. The oviparous alligator, with its rugged, muddy-hued, loathsome body, is calculated to inspire feelings of disgust. The red-faced monkey with the stumpy tail in the Museum should be mounted on the saurian's back.

> "There at his ease he could sit and smile.
> Like Waterton on his crocodile."

There is also two massive jaw-bones of the whale found floating dead at Woosung. They are each nearly nine feet in length and close on two feet at the widest part.

The collection of birds in the Museum is really splendid and would alone amply repay a visit to the institution. We counted over 600 specimens, representing some 300 different species. Some 30 or 40 are Australian and other foreign birds. The Chinese specimens, we understand, fairly represent the ornithology of those parts of the empire to which foreigners have free access. The taxidermist informed us that there are over 800 different species of birds in the country. Many of the specimens are magnificent in point of gorgeous colouring, the plumage of several "sparkling with unnumbered eyes."

In point of size, the emu in the Museum bears the palm—a veritable "Triton amongst the minnows," in fact. This huge bird stands over five and a half feet high, and must, we should say, have bestrode its "narrow world (in New Holland, whence it came) like a Colossus." The *Accipitres*, or rapacious order of birds, in the institution, number about fifty. There are some fine specimens of the eagle, that king amongst birds as the lion is amongst beasts. The imperial eagle, though not by any means so large as some of its congeners, has something noble in its expression.

Doubtless the imperial eagle got its title for its mental qualities.

There are two specimens of the vulture tribe in the Museum. Their expression is quite in keeping with their well-known rapacious habits. *Vultus est index animi*, says the Latin proverb. Everyone knows what an extraordinarily keen sense of smell the vulture possesses. Moore, in "Lalla Rookh," ascribes to them the faculty of being able to even scent their prey before life has departed. He says:—

"With that keen, second-scent of death,
By which the vulture sniffs his food,
In the still warm and living breath."

There is a good specimen of the eagle owl, with expanded pinions and bearing in its talons a hare. The great eagle owl, another specimen, looks comical in its sublime gravity of expression—

"The calm of heaven reflected in its face"

—and we feel sure that Nature must have intended this nocturnal marauder for the position of Mixed Court Magistrate amongst the feathered tribe in China, or at least for that of Assessor. Many of the pheasants are very beautiful specimens, the golden pheasant shining resplendently in its variegated gorgeous colouring. The "tragapan" is also a bird of very handsome plumage. But the "superb bird of paradise," a native of Java, is a host in itself. A fan-like feathery structure, closely resembling blue velvet, for which it could easily be mistaken, stands out prominently from the back of its neck, towards the tail, the ends extending some distance on either side of the body—a truly curious appendage for a member of the feathered tribe to have. The feathers on the top of the bird's head are tinged with green, of a metalic lustre, in many parts, giving the head the appearance of being studded with numerous small emeralds. These emerald-like spots are so radiant that they seem to scintillate. Another curious appendage this extraordinary bird possesses is a green feathery arrangement which covers the breast, the ends stretching out on either side. Altogether it is a truly remarkable specimen, and affords another illustration of the versatility of dame Nature in her manifold creations. Then there are specimens of the pelican, bittern, Manchuria crane, a veritable black swan, Indian tantalus, osprey, kestrel, albatross, cormorant, and a lot of other birds well worth seeing. The tantalus, with its very disproportionately long, thin shanks, looks like a "dwarf mounted on stilts." There is a *lusus naturæ* in the museum—a chicken with four legs. Strange to say, amongst all the numerous specimens of Chinese birds there are but some fifteen songsters. It may be that the excruciating discord called Chinese music has, in the course of centuries, operated unfavourably on the feathered tribe, changing, in the case of the birds most exposed to its harrowing influence, what might otherwise have been sweet, entrancing notes into an abrupt, unharmonious chirrup.

In the entomological department there are no fewer than 180 specimens of butterflies in infinite variety of gaudy colouring, 150 moths of various colours, and a large collection of beetles, as well as dragon-flies, &c., &c.

In the reptilian section there are twelve large snakes, including three cobras, and 23 small snakes, scorpion, &c., &c.

The mineralogical specimens, which embrace a large number from foreign countries, are very numerous, and include specimens of the lava and scoriæ of Vesuvius.

There are numerous and varied specimens of coral, those wonderful productions of the polypes. Some very handsome specimens of silicious sponges are also to be seen. Shell and other fish, shells, and a lot of other things are also represented. Those desirous of studying hornetorian architecture will find a huge hornet's nest in the institution, taken from the cornice of the angle of a wall at Foochow, 20 feet from the ground. Nor should any one miss the opportunity of seeing the chair of state formerly used by the Tien Wang (Heavenly Prince), the celebrated leader of the Taiping Rebellion.

We have in the foregoing alluded to all the salient features of this very excellent and valuable institution, the usefulness of which we should like to see extended by the addition of a zoological collection, however small. This, no doubt, would be well supported by the Chinese.

THE KIANG-SU ACID, CHEMICAL, AND SOAP WORKS.

THESE works, started by foreign enterprise, are situated on the north bank of the Soochow Creek, not far from the Upper Boat-house, and just opposite Messrs. Jardine, Matheson, & Co.'s Silk Filature, on the other side of the creek. The buildings are extensive, occupying a considerable area. A large capital is invested in the plant used for carrying on the various processes connected with the manufacture of sulphuric acid and the refining of silver, for which latter purpose the acid is principally used. Aerated water manufactories also take a considerable quantity of the sulphuric acid, of which some 8,000 to 9,000 lbs. are manufactured each day of 24 hours. Production goes on unceasingly day and night, as if, to adapt a quotation from Cowper, the works "dreaded an instant's pause, and lived but while they moved." It is only at the Chinese New Year that either the employés or the machinery get any rest, when they have a respite of eight or nine days. The silver to be refined is sent to the works in "shoes" by the various banking establishments all over the country, about 1,000 *pows*, or 50,000 taels in weight, being refined daily. The sulphur stones, or pyrites, used in the manufacture of the acid are obtained from England in monthly shipments of about 100 tons. Soap manufacture is also carried on at the works in a separate building. Some five or six tons of soap are manufactured weekly, for the European and Chinese markets; the article commanding a ready sale. The demand is increasing every day for the finer kinds, which the manufactory intends making a speciality. The machinery used in the soap manufacture is of the most modern description for producing soap in large quantity and of the best possible quality. In the acid works, silver refiner, and soap manufactory there are some 200 natives altogether employed, the combined establishments being under the charge of their able manager, Mr. F. Mann, who came out from England for the position, and who seems to us to be endowed with a marvellous amount of energy.

We will now endeavour to give the most intelligible account we can—remember, dear reader, we were not brought up in a laboratory, and are much better adapted for extracting cinders from the alembic than gold—of the various processes in the manufacture of sulphuric acid, silver refining, and soap-making, as carried on at the Kiang-su Acid Works, commencing with the first.

The sulphur stones, or pyrites, are first broken up, in the sulphur ore department, to make them the proper size for the furnaces, where they are burnt in order to extract the sulphur. There are eight double furnaces for the purpose, which are fed every two hours, about four tons of pyrites being burnt daily. The fumes pass upwards from the furnaces, through flues, into an iron column, where they meet and become mixed with nitric acid, and thence into a series of lead chambers, where they gradually condense into sulphuric acid. There are eight of these chambers made of lead, 10 lbs. to the square foot. The larger ones, of which there are six, are 25 feet wide, 17 feet high, and 120 feet long; the other two are smaller in size. The fumes, as they ascend from the furnaces, pass through each chamber in succession, where they enter into combination with nitric acid, steam, oxygen, &c., to form sulphuric acid, the resulting acid falling down like heavy drops of rain upon the floor of the chambers, five or six inches deep. Having passed through the several chambers, the fumes are finally compressed in the compressor before being allowed to escape as useless. There is no more sulphuric acid then to be extracted from them. Now, while the fumes pass through the chambers—which are set one higher than the other—from No. 1 to No. 8, the liquid produced travels in quite the opposite direction, from No. 8 to No. 1, by the force of gravitation, it being then drawn from chamber No. 1 by a pipe which carries it down to the concentrators. It is partially concentrated in the chambers, being finally concentrated in platinum vessels. As the acid leaves the chambers in a weak condition, not being then of sufficient strength for use, further concentration has to be effected, for which purpose it is first conveyed into lead pans. There are four of these, each being 20 feet long, 7 feet wide, and 1 foot deep, communicating one with the other, and each one slightly lower than the preceding, so that during the concentration the acid passes through the whole series. Near the lowest pan is a furnace, the flue from which passes under all the pans. A strong fire is kept up in this furnace. The acid is thus gradually concentrated, until it reaches the platinum apparatus, where the final concentration takes place. There are two platinum apparatus; one is 6 feet long, 2 feet wide, and 5 inches deep, and the other, 2 feet in diameter, and 2 feet deep, set in brick-work. In the first, the acid, after passing from the lead pans, is concentrated. In these pans, owing to the action of the acid on the lead, concentration can only take place to a certain extent. The acid then passes from the first platinum apparatus into the second, where the final concentration takes place. The excess of water separates, and is drawn off by a tube, leaving the acid of the required strength. The acid has now only to be transferred from the second platinum apparatus into the jars, in which it is kept for use and sale; but as it is very hot, it is drawn off by a long syphon, made of platinum, which is encased in a hollow tube, through which a stream of cold water is made to pass constantly, so that on its passage from the apparatus it is sufficiently cooled to be poured with safety into the jars. The platinum apparatus alone cost nearly £5,000 sterling; the first £1,700, and the second £3,000. There are two water tanks near the lead chambers, of 2,000 gallons capacity each, for use in case of fire; and in the event of any of the native employés breaking a jar of acid and spilling the stuff over his clothes, he can jump into a tank, thus arresting the action of the corrosive liquid. There is another large tank near the platinum apparatus, of 20,000 gallons capacity, for similar purposes; and there is a high pressure tank of 8,000 gallons capacity on the top of the building for supplying the works with water for ordinary purposes. The ore, after being burnt in the furnaces, contains about two per cent. of copper, for the recovery of which it is ground and treated.

We now come to the silver refining, a very interesting process, for which, as we have already stated, the sulphuric acid manufactured in the works is principally used. The "shoes" of silver are put into vessels, along with sulphuric acid, a high temperature being maintained by a fire underneath. The acid dissolves the silver, converting it into sulphate of silver. Whatever gold there may be present falls to the bottom of the vessel, being unaffected by the acid. The gold thus recovered is about sufficient to cover the expenses of extraction and leave a small margin. The silver in solution is then put into a reducing vessel, together with plates of copper. The acid, having a greater affinity for copper, quits the silver, which falls to the bottom, and fastens on the copper, which it converts into sulphate of copper. We have then metallic silver at the bottom of the pan, and sulphate of copper in solution, accompanied by any other base metals that may have been present in the silver. The silver is then taken out, having been purged of its impurities, and re-cast into shoes. The next thing then is to recover the copper which has been thrown into solution in the process of silver refining. This is done by placing old iron in the solution, by which the copper is thrown down to the bottom of the vessel, leaving the iron itself in solution as sulphate of iron, or copperas. The copper is then taken out of the pans, placed under a press, and pressed into blocks, after which it is conveyed to melting furances and re-cast into plates, ready for use, as before, in silver refining. A portion of the sulphate of copper, according to the market demand, is crystallised on wires in large tanks and sold for telegraph purposes. There now remains the sulphate of iron in solution to be dealt with. This product is conveyed to another part of the building and placed in large lead pans to be crystallised. As crystals form, they drop to the bottom of the pans, becoming what is known as copperas, or green vitriol. This is sold to Chinese, who use it for dyeing blue and black cloths. Some 200 or 300 piculs a week are produced, commanding a ready sale.

The fumes in some parts of the works affected our respiratory organs to such an extent that we were fain to indulge in a "Habana" to try and clear them out. The manager, however, informed us that we would be all the better for having our throat tickled by the vapours pervading the establishment; and he assured us there was not a healthier lot of men to be found anywhere than his native staff, who were constantly inhaling the fumes. Their appearance, certainly, would seem to confirm this, though, speaking for ourselves, we would rather not purchase health on such terms.

We will now describe the soap manufacture. The ingredients used are palm-oil, tallow, peanut oil, and other vegetable oils. The oils and tallow are first refined in the purification department by means of super-heated steam. They are then pumped into a large iron boiler, 15 feet deep and 15 feet diameter, where the alkalies are added, the whole being then boiled into soap. When this process is complete, the soap is drawn from a pipe, in a fluid state, and run into large iron boxes, where it cools and solidifies in four or five days. It is then taken out and cut up into large blocks, which are put through barring machines; these cut the blocks up into bars. It is now called palm-oil toilet soap. It is then stacked in a drying room heated by steam pipes. When dried it is ground between large granite rollers, the perfumes being at this time added, and made into bars again; then it is passed through a squeezing machine and made into blocks of the proper size for stamping. These are put into the stamping machine and made into cakes of any required size. After receiving the finishing touch in the perfuming line, the soap is dried again in another room. Here are to be seen the various kind—carbolic soap, almond soap, and other perfumed soaps. The carbolic soap, unlike that sent out from England, has scarcely any smell, pure crystalline carbolic acid being used in its composition. There are soaps made in the establishment containing respectively ten, five, and two per cent. of carbolic. The specimens we examined seemed to us to be of excellent quality and very pure, and we have no doubt that, when the article produced at the works becomes more widely known, the demand will be very large.

We have only to add that all these industries, as well as the match factory on the other side of the creek, nearly opposite the acid works, were introduced into China by Messrs. Major Brothers, whose energy and enterprise are deserving of every success.

THE MATCH FACTORY.

THIS local industry, as we mentioned in our article on the Kiang-su Acid Works,* also owes its existence to the enterprise of Messrs. Major Brothers. The factory is situated on the south bank of Soochow Creek, nearly opposite the acid works. The building is quadrilateral in form, and in the centre of the court there is a tank, or pond, for use in case of fire. Three sides of the premises are appropriated to the different branches of the industry, while the fourth is used as offices, compradore's room, &c. There are about 300 native hands employed in the factory, some 200 of whom are women, young girls, and children. A large number of Chinese families are also employed in their own homes in the making of match-boxes; and all around the village of Sinza and the Sinza Road the boxes are to be seen hanging out in front of the doors to dry. These people receive 170 *cash* for every thousand boxes they make, the factory supplying the materials; they have only to find the paste. The out-turn of the factory amounts to about 560 cases of matches per week, or nearly 700,000 boxes, for which there is a brisk demand all over China. The factory (wholesale) price is 2½ *cash* per box. Chinese shopkeepers retail the matches in Shanghai at 3¾ *cash* the box, and we hear that the price has sometimes gone as high as 5 *cash*.

A circular saw, worked by steam, cuts up the wood to be used for matches into blocks of a depth equal to the length of two of these blaze-producers, and about six inches square. These blocks are operated upon by knives, also worked by steam and acting vertically, which, with great rapidity, cut up the blocks into splints of the required shape and thickness. The splints are then made up in bundles and placed in the drying room to dry. After being dried, the ends are soaked, to a certain length, in a composition which imparts inflammability to the wood. The splints are then put by women into frames containing grooves, above a fifth of an inch apart, and sufficiently large to hold one splint. They are now ready for dipping, but before being subjected to this process, the frames are passed through a levelling machine. They are then placed on a revolving arrangement, something like a "wheel of fortune," from which they are taken by a man in an adjoining room, who dips the tips of the splints in the composition which produces the blaze on friction being applied. Another drying process is then gone through. If the weather happens to be damp, the frames are placed in the drying room, which is heated to about 100° Fahrenheit. After this the splints, each of which makes two lucifers, are cut in twain by knives operated by Chinamen. The match has now reached its final stage of perfection, and is ready for being boxed, packed, and cased. The various rooms are divided by fire-proof walls—a very necessary precaution where inflammable material is lying about in such profusion.

* These, with the match factory, &c., have been formed into a Limited Liability Company, with a capital of Tls. 300,000, divided into 6,000 shares.

It is quite interesting to watch the boxing and packing of the matches by the deft female fingers which perform this portion of the work. Through long practice, the women and girls can take up in their hand, the first time, the number of matches, within a trifle, required to fill a box. The boxes, when filled, are made up in packets of ten; these packets are then placed in zinc cases, hermetically sealed, to prevent damp getting at the matches. One young girl astonished us by the lightning-like rapidity with which she made up her packages. We are sure she would make a distinguished *prestidigitateuress* if she took up the profession. She is able to earn 10 cents a day at the work, which, as well as the filling, is paid for according to the amount done.

In the several female work-rooms, youth and old age, beauty (of the Celestial type), and ugliness are intermingled. Here you see a withered old crone whose summer of life is long past; there, a blooming damsel, bearing the rose of youth on her soft, velvety cheeks,—all toiling for one object, and all "as still as brooding doves;" scarcely a whisper is to be heard amongst them.

"Adam's children must work;
Eve's children must suffer,"

wrote Nilus. Such is the lot of humanity, and there's no escaping from it.

Insignificant as some may think the little thing known as a match, the lucifer was described by an English Chancellor of the Exchequer, in his Budget, some years ago, as "among the most splendid boons, though it sounds an humble thing in itself, which science has given to man."

A TRIP ON THE YANGTZE-KIANG FROM SHANGHAI TO HANKOW.*

WHEN Marco Polo visited Cathay and beheld the Great Kiang, or Yangtze-kiang, the impressions which were then formed in his mind, and afterwards given to the world in his wonderful book, still remain true in many particulars. He speaks of it as the greatest river in the world, which was in one sense true when he called it so, as the New World and its mighty rivers were then unknown. He said the Great Kiang "is in some places ten miles wide, in others eight, in others six, and it is more than a hundred days' journey in length from one end to the other." The length of the Yangtze is known to be about 3,000 miles, and though you can now do 600 miles of it, to Hankow, by steaming four days, and 320 miles from Hankow to Ichang, in two or three days we, guess the rest of the voyage, in native boats, would occupy several weeks, if not nearly all of the hundred days. The breadth of the river is said by some writers to have been over-stated by Marco Polo, but we do not think this is the case. The course of the river has changed since the great Venetian traveller sailed on its bosom; its banks are continually changing, and places which are narrow now might once have been very wide, or *vice versa*. The greatest width mentioned by Marco Polo is ten miles, and near the mouth of the river there are still ten miles from the mainland shores, but there are the large island of Tsung Ming and the smaller one Bush Island, in the centre of the river. From the rapidity with which the islands have grown there, by the enormous depositions of mud brought down the river, these islands must have been much smaller, even if they were in existence then; and there is no saying how wide the mouth of the river might have been in the days of Marco Polo (1274, A.D.), for, in speaking of its great width, he does not mention any particular part of the river. As to the trade on the river, Marco Polo says:—"I assure you that this river flows so far and traverses so many countries and cities that in good sooth there pass and repass on its waters a greater number of vessels, and more wealth and merchandize than on all the rivers and all the seas of Christendom put together. It seems more like a sea than a river." These statements cease to appear as exaggerations when we bear in mind the two facts that, at the date of Marco Polo's writing, China was more prosperous than now, and the fleets of Western nations were insignificant compared to what they are at present. In the "Middle Kingdom," Dr. Williams says:—"The assertion that there is a greater amount of tonnage belonging to the Chinese than to all nations combined does not appear overcharged to those who have seen the swarms of boats on their rivers; though it might not be found strictly true. Where Marco Polo estimated the vessels at ports on the Great Kiang in thousands and tens of thousands, they can be seen at the present day in hundreds and thousands. He says he saw 15,000 vessels at one city (at the junction of the northern section of the Grand Canal with the Yangtze, according to Colonel Yule's notes);

* Written for the *Shanghai Mercury* of 20th July 1880.

and he was told by "the officer employed to collect the Great Khan's duties on this river that there passed up stream 200,000 vessels in the year, without counting those that passed down!" The 15,000 sail at the mouth of the Grand Canal would not be beyond the range of probability in the heyday of China's glory; and the 200,000 vessels a year do not appear an exaggeration even now to any one who has sailed on this great river and passed through the fleets of junks and smaller boats which crowd its waters. For many years, since the Treaty Ports were opened on the Yangtsze, steamers have plied regularly upon it, and at present there are four companies running twelve or fourteen steamers in almost daily succession from Shanghai to Hankow. In May, at the opening of the tea season, about twenty large ocean steamers go up to Hankow to load. The traffic on the Lower Yangtsze is therefore very large, although the trade of some of the Treaty Ports has not developed so well as was anticipated. During the year previous to the time at which we write the total number of steamers entered and cleared at Hankow was 692, and their tonnage 671,120; and of steamers and sailing vessels 1,323, tonnage 733,335.

In the autumn of 1879, Messrs. Jardine, Matheson & Co. resumed their trade on the Yangtsze, after having withdrawn for twelve years by agreement with another shipping company, who on their part withdrew from the southern coast line. The s.s. *Kung-wo* was the pioneer boat of the new line, and one thing remarkable about the vessel herself is, that she was the first steamer ever built entirely in Shanghai; the rolling of the plates was the only thing done at home. She was built by Messrs. Boyd & Co., Shanghai, who have also built the second boat of the line, the *Fuh-wo*, and have a third and larger one in hand. We described the launch of the pioneer boat, the *Kung-wo*; we described her trial trip; and on her sixteenth trip to Hankow we had the pleasure of being a passenger, and of seeing much and learning a good deal of the Lower Yangtsze and the many interesting places on its banks. The *Kung-wo* was then commanded by Captain Popp, who has had long experience on the river, and a more genial and courteous commander would not be found. We left Shanghai about five o'clock on the morning of the 23rd March, when we were awakened by the shouting on board the steamer and on the wharf, and the cry of the mate "Let go," as we left our moorings. There was no inducement for rising so early, and we resolved to sleep on till we were past Woosung; and the movement of the steamer was so steady that we might have thought we were sleeping ashore. The next awakening we had was by the song of junk oarsmen while the *Kung-wo* passed through a fleet of junks at Woosung; the swinging song of the junkmen was loud and long, and the screeching of some voices bad enough; still it was not very unpleasant after all, and junk after junk passed, as we could tell by the song of one crew dying away, and another growing louder till they seemed to be shouting at the cabin window; then the noise died away, and anon we heard it louder than ever, as the junks passed in succession, and all their crews sang or yelled the same swinging oarsong. So close were they that some of them must have been nearly run down; quite a large fleet of junks had been right in the fairway of the channel. The song of the junk oarsmen passed like a dream, and by-and-bye our slumbers were again broken by hideous, unearthly groans; we could stand it no longer, for the cries of the leadsman, "N-o-o-o g-r-o-u-n-d!" and a "Qua-tah, sev-in!" and such like were more than anyone could sleep under, at least for the first time he tried it; so that when two and a half hours on our journey we got up, were soon on the hurricane deck, and gazed in wonder and admiration at the mighty Yang-tsze before us, and against whose strong current the *Kung-wo* was ploughing her way at good speed. When we first came on deck, we were near Lao Point, and remembered that we had been this length before when on the trial trip. "Where's that point?" "On the port bow; don't you see that dead tree in the centre of the clump!" "Why, there's any amount of trees there, but we don't see the dead one; and we don't see why you call that a point;" and we consoled ourselves by seeing, in an old pocket sailing directory, that the point is very difficult to distinguish when going up river. The appearance of the river banks—a thin green streak bordering the broad expanse of dirty-brown water—seemed to meet the Irishman's description of scenery: "Gintlemen, on the right you'll observe—nothing; and on the left a divilish sight less!" On the port side, the right bank of the river, there is the mainland; on the starboard side, there is Bush Island; and after we go further up the river widens, for we have passed Bush Island, and on the north side the thin green border is more distant than before. Surely that is the mainland on the north, and now we see the broadest part of the river? No, that's only Tsung Ming Island, and there's a big river on the other side of it,—the north entrance of the Yang-tsze. The general aspect of the river, looking ahead, is an immense expense of water, stretching away to the horizon before us, and it looks as though we were steaming up hill. The river is thickly studded with junks and smaller craft, and away in the distance, they appear only as small black specks. There is a long dark cloud of smoke wafted across the river from the steamer *Wuhu*, the biggest steamer on the river; she could be identified by her huge black funnel, though nothing else were seen, and sometimes she appears pretty much all funnel and smoke, her hull being of the same colour as the muddy water; when she takes the Langshan Crossing, we see her broadside, and again when in direct line with her we see nothing but her funnel and trail of smoke. We overtake one small steamer, bound up, deeply laden; and another steamer passes down towards Shanghai; there were thus four steamers in sight of each other here, and hundreds of junks and smaller native craft. These latter are chiefly fishing-boats; the fishermen go out with nets and lay them all over the river as thick as they can crowd them,—and the water appears thickly dotted with small black specks, which are the bamboo stakes attached to the fishing nets, and by which they are buoyed; and hundreds of fishing-boats are cruising about, laying out nets or hauling them in. The steamer goes right through a crowd of nets, and as a rule the nets go under the steamer without being damaged; but occasionally, and we saw an instance of it, the bamboo stakes get caught on the bow, the nets become entangled there and the steamer has to be slowed down to cast them off, for a big bamboo stake across the bow would impede the progress of a steamer against a strong current.

After we pass the end of Tsung Ming Island, we can barely see the mainland on the north side of the river, while away astern we look on the North Branch (42 miles in length), which leads out to sea, and down the other branch of the river, by which we have come up. An idea of the mighty expanse of water then in view fore and aft, cannot be conveyed in language,—it has to be seen to be realised; three quarters of the horizon are bounded with water, and the words of Marco Polo are certainly appropriate when he says "it is more like a sea than a river." Although the river is of enormous breadth, the navigation is very difficult in this neighbourhood, for the channel is only about a quater of a mile in breadth.

Confucius Channel is comparatively close to the south or right bank of the river; and there are numerous landmarks on the south bank, between Lao Point and Plover Point, which if not of any special interest, indicate at least by their names how little serves for a distinguishing mark for the trained eye of the pilot. There's Forked Tree,—which stands out a little from those around it, and is distinguished by two forked branches; One-arm Tree—which has one branch standing out like the arm on a guide-post; Great Bush—a tree with a bushy head, like a shock-headed Japanese student, in the distance; and Seven Poles—which are erected at a Chinese temple. The navigation of the river between Plover Point on the south and North Tree on the north side of the river, is more difficult than at any other part of the Lower Yang-tsze. The channel from the Actæon Buoy to the Centaur Buoy is only about two ship's lengths in width, and has steep banks on either side; after we come to the Centaur Bank, the channel, still very narrow, takes an angular course across the river to Langshan, and this is called the Langshan Crossing. When passing the Actæon Buoy we see in the distance the Langshan Pagoda Hill, on the north side of the river, and away inland from the south shore there are three small hills, which we take to be the Muirhead Hills. As we approach Langshan, we observe that besides the hill with the Pagoda on it, there is another close beside it; both are marked on the chart, the Pagoda Hill as being of 376 feet, and the other a few feet higher. For lack of any more striking objects in the range of vision, we watch these hills and try to make out of what configuration they really are. At first they seem to be two hills joined in one, with only a small ravine half way down between them; one hill seems perfectly hemispherical, and the other conical; then they open out till we can see through between them, and the river appears to wash round and round their base; but when we come up abreast of them we find there are really three hills, a long distance between the 376 feet one and the other that beats it in elevation by four feet only; and they were not islands at all, but all three on the mainland, though quite close to the bank of the river. On Langshan Hill, the pagoda rises out of a clump of trees on the summit, and on one steep side of the hill a belt of trees extends down to the base; that side of the hill is dotted with white buildings,—temples most probably,—and the face of the hill next the river has no trees, but some white buildings; while the third side which comes into view is a rocky precipiece. The largest of the hills is quite barren, and is capped with a low square of white buildings. The pagoda is very ruinous in appearance. After taking the Langshan Crossing, the channel is comparatively close to the north bank of the river; here there is a landmark called the North Tree, and a beacon also. Steamers always leave Shanghai for Hankow early in the morning, so that the dangerous channels we have now safely navigated may be passed in the daytime; and on the return voyage to Shanghai, steamers anchor at the North Tree over night, or time their speed so as just to reach it at daylight, as they cannot take the Langshan Crossing and the other dangerous channels below it in the dark. In passing the North Tree this time, *we* were comfortably anchored at the saloon table for tiffin.

While steaming onwards and keeping close to the north bank of the river, we had the first distinct view of the agricultural pursuits of the Chinese, as hitherto the shore was too far off to see anything except the trees, and here and there the roof of a small thatched hut. Along the bank there are cultivated fields, extending inland for a quarter of a mile at some places, at others a less distance, and the background is closed in with thickets of bamboo and clumps of trees which preclude one seeing further into the country. The small houses of the farmers are scattered here and there, some gathered in groups and forming small villages; the houses are chiefly built of bamboo wickerwork and mud, although some have brick walls and tile roofs, but nearly all of them have their roofs thatched with reeds and straw. At some places, Celestials in blue cottons stand on the bank of the river, and relieve the monotony of their toil in the fields by gazing awhile at the passing steamer, and over the green fields you see blue specks here and there—the patient labourers stooping down to their work with the hoe, or some other celestial implement of similar kind. For several miles we keep close to this shore, and the scene is the same all along. The bank of the river is about fifteen feet above the level of the water, and quite perpendicular,—a clay bank which is continually being washed away by the strong current. Now and then we pass the mouth of a creek, chock full of small boats, and a long way up the creek there are hundreds of boats, as we judge by the bare masts which are all that is to be seen of them; they are stranded in the creek, and are waiting for a rise of water to take them into the interior. Grave-mounds are also very numerous along the bank, some of them within a few feet of the river, on a falling bank, and when the water rises in summer floods the Celestial remains will have a watery grave. At four o'clock in the afternoon we passed the town of Kiang-ying, on the south shore, where there is a pagoda some distance inshore; mud forts are erected on the top of the low hills which rise on each side of the swamp and creek leading up to the town. It was quite cold in the evening, and there was nothing of interest to be seen as we stayed inside the saloon.

Now we may say a few words about the leadsman, the man at the wheel, the crew and the Chinese passengers. There are six Manilamen on board, of the rank of quartermaster, whose duties are to take turns at casting the lead, and at the wheel. There are chain platforms on the port and starboard bows, in which the leadsman stands when casting the lead on either side as may be ordered by the pilot. The Manila quartermaster gets inside the chains, and has a Chinese sailor to pull in the lead for him. The quartermasters varied not so much in personal appearance as in voice; it was not at all unpleasant but rather somewhat romantic to hear one man calling out the depth of water found, while another at the same work gave unearthly yells calculated to wake anyone from sleep and make the hair of one's head stand on end. None of them, however, came up to Mark Twain's description of the man on the Mississippi boat, who sings out "No sound, no ground, no bottom to be found, with a long, long, pitch, pine, pole." The Manilaman cries "N-o-o-o g-r-o-u-n-d," and the way he drawls out the "o" in the first word, and grinds the "g-r" in the second, is perfectly hideous and unearthly. Or when he finds a bottom at seven and a quarter fathoms, he shouts "And a qua-tah, sev-in!" singing the first word with a peculiar drone, then hurrying on to the "sev," and drawling out the last syllable as long as the lead-line. "And a half sis" (six), "Deep sis," "By the mark five," "Deep four," and half and quarters for each of them, are all given with distinguishing peculiarities, but which are too difficult to express in print. We never got into water shallow enough to hear him call "By the Mark Twain." In the wheel-house on the hurricane deck, the Manilamen are seen at the wheel, two of them together, and when the pilot calls out the course to be steered one of the men at the wheel repeats it, with "sah" (sir) at the end of everything. "Nor.-east and by east," says the pilot, and the wheelman responds "Nor'-east and by east, sah!" "Steady!" "Steady, sah!" The crew, with the exception of the Manila quartermasters, are all Chinese sailors, and they work well, although there is not very much for them to do on a river steamer. The Chinese passengers enjoy a trip on the river immensely; they have a large saloon filled with sleeping bunks, three deep,—and about 150 passengers in the one saloon; there are other smaller apartments with only six bunks in each. The steamer takes about 200 native passengers, and while some are booked through from Shanghai to Hankow, the most of them are for way-ports, and dozens come in at one port and go out at the next, so that on the round trip perhaps 1,000 passengers may be carried. The Chinese passengers on the river steamers travel as cheaply as any one possibly could do; it is questionable if there is such cheap travelling in any part of the world. A Chinaman pays $5 for a passage from Shanghai to Hankow, of nearly 600 miles, less than a cent per mile; it occupies four days, and during all that time he is supplied with as much chow-chow as he can take; if that isn't cheap living and cheap travelling we don't know what to call it. But more than that, there is no restriction on the amount of baggage which a Chinese passenger can take on board, free of charge; as most of the passengers from port to port are bent on little commercial ventures, everyone generally has about a ton of baggage with him.

At midnight we reached Chinkiang, the first treaty port on the Yangtsze, and anchored alongside the hulk *Orissa*, an old P. & O. boat; and where, from early morning till 9 a.m., we discharged cargo, and at the latter hour proceeded on our voyage. Our brief stay at Chinkiang on the upward voyage, and a few hours' stay on the way home, was sufficient, when the two were put together, to convey some idea of the beautiful situation of this port. In the morning when we lay alongside the hulk *Orissa*, near the north bank of the river, we could see little or nothing; after we got underweigh, the whole scene opened to our view; but on the return journey when we came into port on a bright afternoon, we had a firstrate opportunity of witnessing the fine scenery, and we will therefore from memory describe it as approached from the west. The most attractive object in the scene is the high conical rock known as Golden Island, but which no longer is an island, being connected with the shore by low ground, occasionally flooded. The rock is surmounted by a small open pavilion of circular shape; and on a cleft in the side of the rock, near the summit, stands a seven-storied pagoda, now in ruins, stripped of all its ornamental work, and its crumbling stones moss-grown. Several temple buildings, some painted white and others red, lie round the base of the rock and to the west or shore side. The tall, fantastically shaped rock, with trees growing here and there in its clefts, and the old ruinous pagoda, stand in bold relief against the barren range of hills which roll on from the west, and between which and the river there is a broad alluvial plain; the channel of the river is said to have once been over on the other side of this plain and close to the base of the hills. A large barren and rocky hill forms the end of the range, and a steep and rugged escarpment descends to the bank of the river, while from the water's edge up the steep rock, and away over and along its ridge there is an old brick wall,—a part of the wall of the ancient city of Chinkiang. Substantial and well built white mansions are seen on the rising slopes of the hill facing the harbour; the most prominent of the buildings being the British Consulate; while the foreign settlement, a goodly range of white bungalows, stretches along the shore, sweeping round to the base of another hill which closes in the further side of the harbour. This hill is surmounted by walls and forts, and another hill seen at greater distance has also a cap of white-washed walls. Looking in over the foreign settlement, we see the old city of Chinkiang, or all that remains of it, nestling at the base of hills which rise up on every side, and zig-zag walls are seen rising over rugged spurs, steep ascents, and along the ridges. A hill at the back of the city is surmounted by a fort, and red triangular flags are waving over the walls; if we judged from the bright array of flags, the celestial war paint, we should say there was enough there to be a terror to Western nations; but although Chinkiang is admirably situated for erection of fortresses, there did not appear to be any in existence that would be capable of opposing resistance to an invading force. The harbour, opposite the bund, is occupied by several hulks, alongside of which the river steamers discharge their cargo, and there are numerous native craft about, particularly at the mouth of the Grand Canal, which is full of junks. On the opposite shore there is a long range of dilapidated white cottages of foreign design; these we are told were built by foreigners when they first settled at Chinkiang, but the foreign settlement is now on the city side or right bank of the river; a large number of native houses, small hovels with thatched roofs, extend along the left bank beside the old foreign residences, and the whole place there has a ruinous and dilapidated appearance; but still there are signs of traffic on this side too, for a very large number of *papicos* are moored here; the *papico* being a boat considerably smaller than the large trading junk, but still large enough for river and coasting trade. Away far down the river we get a glimpse of the large hemispherical island, known as Silver Island, which stands out of the water like a huge bee-hive. It it covered with rich foliage, and white temple buildings are seen amongst the trees, and glistening in the rays of the setting sun. Of such islands as Silver Island, Golden Island, the Little Orphan, and other places on the river, Marco Polo remarks:—" There are at many places on this river hills and rocky eminences on which idol monasteries and other edifices are built." Then in his quaint style he adds regarding any place he is describing: " The people are idolaters, and subject to the Great Khan, and use paper money."

Chinkiang is a about 150 miles from the mouth of the Yangtsze, on the right bank, and the southern section of the Grand Canal enters the river to the east of the foreign settlement. This port was captured by the British in 1842. The Taiping rebels occupied the city from 1853 till 1857 and it was utterly destroyed by them; even now the desolation is apparent, for although the foreign settlements and foreign trade on the Yangtsze have brought new life to the place, the native city will never be what it was before the rebels destroyed it. The best description ever written of Chinkiang, and a very interesting one indeed, is that by Mr. Laurence Oliphant, the historian of Lord Elgin's Mission to China and Japan in the year 1857-9. Lord Elgin's Mission ascended the Yangtsze to Hankow, and several days were spent at Chinkiang (in September 1858), just after the rebels had deserted the place. Mr. Oliphant explored the ruined city, and also visited the monastic island rocks, of which he gives interesting particulars, and from which we will quote a few sentences. The first view of Silver Island is thus described:—" Presently we sweep round a bold projecting bluff, and Silver Island opens to view, with its quaint temples embowered in autumnal foliage; their white walls are gleaming, and their frowzy priests are basking in the midday sun. Beyond, a noble reach of river curves beneath the swelling hills which rise from its margin, their

CHINKIANG.

summits crowned with the irregular wall of Chinkiang, and their slopes strewn with the debris of that once populous city; while in the distance, as though rising from mid-stream, stands a precipitous rock called Golden Island, with its tall pagoda pointing to the skies. The scene is of such surpassing interest and beauty that it rivets our gaze." Of his visit to Silver Island he says:—" The island itself was little more than a tumulus rising out of the centre of the Yangtsze to a height of scarce two hundred feet, covered with the richest foliage, at this season of the year a blaze of fiery tints. Its highest point was still crowned with a small edifice, pagoda-shaped, but which contained nothing more interesting than the somewhat unimaginative inscriptions of the British sailor:—most of these bore the date of August 1842." Golden Island is thus described:—" As we approached it we discovered, to our astonishment, that it was no longer an island. Flourishing cabbage-fields now occupied the space marked on the chart as a channel, with four fathoms of water in it. We landed on this recently-formed peninsula, and walked across it to the rock. Climbing up the steps hewn out of the living stone, we reached the base of the pagoda, shorn now of those external decorations which once rendered it celebrated, but still standing, a battered monument of its own departed glory, and of the beauty by which it was surrounded. Heaps of unsightly ruins marked the spot where once was grouped a picturesque collection of temples and pagodas. Sir John Davis thus describes the impression produced upon him by a distant view of it, obtained years before: " The celebrated Kinshan, or Golden Island, which, with its pagoda and the ornamental roofs of its temples and other buildings, looked like a fairy creation rising out of the waters of the Kiang. This picturesque place is celebrated all over China."

Steaming onwards from Chinkiang, and leaving its picturesque island rocks and white buildings shining on the face of the hills, we find on the right bank of the river a rich alluvial plain extending away to the base of the receding range of cloud-capped hills. On the north bank we pass the mouth of the Grand Canal which leads to Peking; there is a large fleet of junks in it, and a foreign-built steamer, a small paddle-wheel revenue cruiser, owned by the mandarin in charge of the entrance station of the Canal, who might correspond to the official who was at this same place interviewed by Marco Polo,—the man who collected the duties of the Great Khan, and who told the Venetian traveller of the 200,000 vessels that went up river in one year. The mandarin's yamên at the mouth of the Canal is a prominent building, comparatively speaking, for all the other houses near it are very small. The town situated near the mouth of the canal is named Kwa-chow, and a few miles further up is the city of Yang-chow, which can be seen from the top of the hills at Chinkiang. After steaming a few miles, we see ahead of us a very large fleet of small boats, with square white sails shining brilliantly in the bright rays of the noon-day sun; and still further ahead we see the bank of the river lined with a forest of junk-masts, which are laid up at the salt-junk station of Eching. This place is also a passenger station for the river steamers, where native passengers are taken on board, but no cargo is ever taken for these stations, as they are not treaty ports. While we were approaching Eching, we observed a small open boat pushed out from the crowd of junks, and coming down the river towards us; an old man stood in the stern, and worked a pair of oars with great vigour; a very strong current was in his favour, and the boat came down at a high speed. Another old man in the boat held a long bamboo pole in his hand, and the Ewo flag (Jardine, Matheson & Co.'s), the St. Andrew's cross on blue ground, was flying from it. The old man waved his flag in a frantic manner, as if he desired to stop the steamer to warn her of danger from torpedoes or a pop-gun on a salt junk. The officer on deck wondered what the devil was wrong with the old standard-bearer, for he was a long way down from the place where passengers are usually taken on board. The steamer was slowed down, to see what the old man wanted; the small boat passed by on the starboard side, severely tossed on the waves caused by the wash of the steamer, and the oarsman and the standard-bearer both fell on their backs in the bottom of the boat, the one nearly losing his flag and the other his oars. The old man with the flag, as soon as he recovered himself,—and when his boat was washed close up to the bank of the river, and the steamer was at a stand-still,—commenced shouting in Chinese to the compradore of the steamer, and the officer on deck shouted to the compradore to ask the old fellow what he wanted. What do you think he meant by making all this fuss, endangering his life, and stopping the steamer? He said he only came down to tell us that there were some passengers up at the station waiting for the steamer! As we steamed ahead, the officer held up a broom handle and shook it at the old fellow in the boat, the gesticulations meaning that he ought to be bambooed; while the old fellow looked disappointed and must have thought that his well-intentioned efforts were not appreciated. In passing the junk station of Eching, we saw that the junks were laid in tiers of six or eight abreast, and they lay along the bank for such a great distance that it was impossible to count them exactly, but on a rough guess there were at least 300 of them. A native builder had several junks drawn upon the beach in front of his yard, and a large number of men were engaged repairing them. We stopped opposite the junks for a few minutes and several boats came alongside, from which passengers were taken on board. All the steamship companies trading on the river are represented at Eching (as well as at other similar passenger stations) by small Chinese houses where the passengers are booked; in front of these shipping offices there are look-out stations, which consist of four long bamboo poles, rising to a considerable height, and a ladder leading up to a platform on the top of the poles, where the look-out man goes up to watch for steamers approaching from Chinkiang or for others coming down the river; and from the top of each look-out perch, the flag of the steamship company is flying. Besides the shipping offices, which are small white-washed cottages, there is a long range of low-built houses stretching along the bank of the river, but almost hid from view by the forest of junk masts. The boat which we described as coming down the river to meet us, was the first in which we noticed a provincial difference from any boats seen on the lower reaches of the Yangtsze, or on the Whangpoo at Shanghai. The *yuloh*, for sculling, was the only oar we had seen used at any other place (except the long oars and poles used in junks), but here at Eching, oars of another shape are used; in the larger boats, there are three or four oarsmen, but in a small boat there is only one, sometimes a man, but perhaps more frequently a woman; the oarsman stands in the stern of the boat, looking forward, and works a pair of oars, by pushing them backwards and forwards before him; the oar is made of a long narrow plain board, lashed to a pole, a handle stuck on the end of the pole, and the oars meet and cross each other before him. Leaving Eching and its salt junks, our course up the river for hours brought us through innumerable fleets of small boats, the only remarkable thing about them being that their sails were very white and appeared to be quite new, whereas the most of the boats further down the river had dirty, black, tattered and torn sails, some of them having only a mass of rags and patches stretched on bamboo ribs, and of little use for holding the wind. On the right bank of the river there is a great expanse of green sward, where natives have been stacking reeds, and the blue cottons are dotted over the fields like scare-crows. There are also large herds of buffaloes grazing, and the stooping Celestials toiling in the field are barely distinguishable from young buffaloes, except that one is blue and the other black. At short intervals along the bank there are dip-nets for fishing,—the dip-net so well known to everyone here, but which strikes a stranger as the most peculiar mode of catching fish ever invented; the large net is suspended from a horizontal frame of bamboo poles, and by means of a lever it is lowered into the water or hoisted up, and when a fish has come into the net it is scooped out by a small net on the end of a long pole; but although we saw hundreds of these nets, and natives hoisting them up every now and then, we never saw anyone rewarded with success, or having occasion to use the scooping-out net; they toiled all day and caught nothing. Several boats are seen loading reeds, and others afloat are like huge stacks of reeds on the water. On the right hand a range of hills is seen dimly through the mist; and by-and-bye the hills come out more distinctly; there are three ranges rising one behind the other; and on one hill, seen a great distance off, there is a pinnacle like the cairn of stones on Birnam or Dunsinane, but on examination with a field-glass, it is seen to be a large pagoda. The range of hills on the left hand is still a few miles from the right bank of the river, but instead of the green plain between us and the hills we have undulating ground, covered with trees and brushwood. The opposite mountain ranges seem to close in upon the river a long distance ahead; a prominent and rugged hill in the range on the left hand is Single Tree Hill, which stands at a bend in the river, and the Yangtsze sweeps round its base. The hill takes its name from the large tree which stands on its summit; and near which there is also a small square tower. From Single Tree Hill, a mud flat or alluvial plain extends for miles, and it is thickly covered with herds of buffaloes; young boys are gamboling on the green plain, or riding on the backs of the buffaloes, while the latter move slowly over their pasture ground; there is a young boy in blue cotton for every buffalo on the ground; the great animals move about altogether heedless of the little boys perched on their backs, and can scarcely be conscious of their existence there, except that now and then the boys may give them a whack with a stick. A fleet of boats loaded with stacks of reeds pass down the river, with the boatmen lying on the top of the stack, which is built up nearly to the top of the mast; the reeds are built on planks and project over the sides of the boat; no oars can be used, and the mast is buried in reeds so that no sail can be set; but no sail is required, for the huge stack presents such a broad surface to the wind that the boat is sent onwards at good speed.

The next object of interest is Mud Fort, thirty-eight miles from Chinkiang. The fort stands on low ground on the left bank of the river; it consists of a large square enclosed by a wall of brick and mud, and the only objects seen over the wall are a large four-legged stand for a look-out station, and several triangular flags hoisted on poles are flying in the breeze. Opposite this fort, on the right bank of the river, there are several ranges of small hills, coming out at right angles to the course of the river, with steep precipices of limestone rock; there are also forts on the summits of the hill next the river in each range, and forts in the horse-shoe valleys formed by the base of the hills. None of the forts appear to be of great strength, but their situation is good, and a few guns mounted in them could command the river. On the hills and between the forts there are well-made roadways which lead over the hills, presumably for the accommodation of the gallant Celestial soldiers when they desire to retreat, as it is the first care of the Chinese military engineer to make a good back road for retreat from every fort before he thinks of erecting the battery. We have pleasant sailing in a fine open reach above Mud Fort, where we pass through myriads of wild duck floating on the bosom of the river; now and then a covey of them rise and fly further up the river, rest again on its waters and come down on the swift current; and as the steamer ploughs on through the dirty brown water, but which before us is almost covered and black with game, the birds float down till they are a few yards from the bows, and then rising they fly further up the reach, only to settle again on the water and take another sail. If there had only been some keen sportsmen on board, armed with good duck guns, they could have shot hundreds of birds, but the difficulty would be to recover them from the water after they had been shot. A story was here told of a passenger on a former trip who tried to shoot duck at this part of the river; he fired with a revolver at a crowd of birds on the water some distance ahead; they all rose, but *one* black speck remained on the surface, and the sportsman shouted with delight that he had killed at least one of them; but when the black speck came nearer and passed close by the steamer it was seen to be a decayed plant, nothing more nor less than a cabbage. From nearly opposite Mud Fort there is a channel or " less cut off " which goes right up to Nanking; it is a fine channel of deep water, but rather narrow for large steamers; it was used at one time by the river-steamers, but so many junks were in the way, and a few of them sunk, that the Chinese authorities prohibited the use of this channel by steamers, so that the junks have it all to themselves now.

At four o' clock in the afternoon of the second day of our trip, we came in sight of a bold headland on the left bank of the river, with a tall pagoda on its summit. This is directly opposite the city of Nanking, and the pagoda occupies what would be a very good site for a lighthouse; in fact, if the monastic tower now in ruins were converted into a lighthouse, it would be of more service in the future than it has ever been in the past. When we come up nearly abreast of the pagoda, we observe that it stands on the very extremity of a long range of hills, not of great height, and of very irregular configuration. There are five or six small hills to the south-west of Pagoda Hill, all surmounted with forts,—these fortified hills are all flat on the summit, and naturally adapted for works of defence; all we can see of the forts, however, are the white walls standing on the summits and facing the river; whether they are strong fortifications, it is impossible to tell by a distant view of them; but one thing is quite evident, that is, their position is one of great advantage. The slopes of the hills are covered with blue smoke curling slowly and fantastically in the still air; the smoke rising from fires where the natives are burning charcoal at the base of the hills and along their slopes. On the flat ground between these hills and the river, there are numerous conical erections shining in the sun, and at first sight they looked like a cantonment where Celestial soldiers might be camping out; but any such idea formed at first sight was rudely shattered when we discovered that they were nothing more nor less than heaps of reeds. So much for the left bank of the river opposite Nanking. As we approach the ancient city, we have on the right bank the continuation of a broad, flat plain between the river and the "cut off" from Mud Fort; all of which plain is covered with buffaloes grazing or Celestials stacking reeds; and just at the corner, before we come to the mouth of the "cut off," where it joins the river, we noticed a variation in the animals on the pasture, for the pilot pointed out a donkey, calling it a "buffalo with a cross on its back," and near by there was a herd of black pigs, which he called "Irish policemen from Donnybrook fair." We now have the first view of the wall of the ancient and far-famed city of Nanking,—the splendid "southern capital," now desolated and ruined, a city from which the glory is departed never more to return. The wall is of great height, built of dark blue bricks, blackened by the storms of centuries; it rises over the spur of a hill and stretches far away in a mountainous region, visible here and there on the brow of a hill, and then lost to view in the valleys; a wall of 23 miles in circumference and enclosing several large hills, with peaks rising to the clouds; and at the base of which, but now hid from view, stands all that remains of the great city,—what was once perhaps the greatest city in the world. In the foreground between the river and the wall are the remains of what might once have been a flourishing suburb; now there is only a small bridge of one arch, with a little tower on the centre of it, and the roadway over the bridge is covered with turf, and the stones are green with moss; a few brick cottages stand here, one with walls painted white, a door painted yellow, and two windows painted black, but not a living soul about the place; and beside the cottages there are some dilapidated huts of bamboo and reeds. Two Chinese gunboats are anchored in the river, close to the shore; and they appear to be Foochow specimens of the naval power of China. We pass close to them; the few guns seen on deck are of small calibre, and on the first boat two or three coolie-like Chinamen are leaning over the bulwarks, while on the other boat three celestial warriors are performing acrobatic feats on the jibboom. A little further up, a mud and brick fort, covering a large square, stands close to the bank of the river, with a wall of about 20 feet in height, full of embrasures; and flags—the usual triangular blood-red flags—are waving from poles inside the fort. A look-out post, erected on four poles and consisting of two platforms, with ornamental roof, is all that is to be seen over the wall. On the west side of the fort a small tower is built into the wall, and outside the fort there is a large open court, surrounded by a small wall, the gateway leading into the court-yard being close to the river; the gate itself is of iron and foreign in style, but the usual Celestial portals of red poles and an ornamental roof with turned-up corners stand over the gate. Further up the river bank there are four or five small cottages, used as booking-offices for the native passengers on the river-steamers, and a boat-load of passengers are already alongside our steamer, and clambering in at the large port-hole on the main-deck, frantic with excitement in regard to their luggage, of which there is an enormous quantity. A short stone pier comes out into the river, nearly opposite the fort, and on the extremity of the pier there is an old rusty field-gun, lying on the stones, and only worth its weight in old iron. A few minutes' stay is made until the Chinese passengers are all on board, and then we go ahead again. The city wall is seen to extend for miles along the right bank, but gradually receding till it is lost to view amongst the far-off hills. Inside the wall, as far as we could see, there was high ground,—a small ridge close to the wall,—while over it the heights within the extensive circumference were seen, some prominent points being crowned with fortifications and towers. For a brief moment we catch a glimpse of the roofs of houses in a thickly built corner at the base of one of the hills, which showed the position of the city itself.

While on the homeward voyage, there was no particular incident at Nanking worth mentioning, except that about twenty Chinese passengers disembarked, and they half-filled one large boat, the other half of that boat and two other large boats were full of luggage, so that there were two-and-a-half boat-loads of boxes and baggage for twenty passengers, or about half-a-dozen boxes for each passenger,—and all conveyed at less than a cent per head per mile. Some of the baggage fell into the river, and there was great excitement in rescuing it.

When eight or nine miles above Nanking, we passed the mouth of a creek, full of boats, which leads up to the city; two or three miles further up the river we passed a small island rock, with a white-walled joss-house on it; and here for the first time we saw an example of raft navigation on the Yangtsze; the opportunity was a very favourable one, for although we saw dozens of rafts further up the river, on this first one certain manœuvres were being carried out which we did not afterwards see at any other place. These rafts are composed of a large number of trees or poles lashed together; they are brought down chiefly from the Tung-ting Lake, above Hankow; some of the rafts go as far as Shanghai, others are broken up at Chinkiang, and the wood sold there, and taken by canal or river to various places, the poles being used for house-building and some of them also for junk-building. The poles are from twenty to thirty feet in length, and there are such a large number of them lashed together that the raft has a draught of six or eight feet, while its breadth varies from ten to twenty; each section is just the length of the poles, but four or five such sections are generally attached together, forming one long raft; and in some cases, the rafts are of enormous size, perhaps a dozen lengths of poles, and of considerable breadth. On the top of the raft, matsheds are erected for the accommodation of the raftsmen, and the larger rafts have the appearance of floating villages, although the top of the raft is only about two feet above water. On this first raft we saw there were more than a dozen small huts, in two rows, capable of accommodating a large number of raftsmen and their families. While we were watching it, an incident occurred which showed the peculiar manner of navigating these rafts on the shallow waters. A small boat was sent out from the raft, with a tow-line of twisted bamboo fibre, and when the boat was about 200 yards from the raft, down stream and a little to the right side of the river, a drum or tom-tom was beaten loudly on board the raft, at which signal the men in the boat threw overboard a huge piece of wooden frame work, about ten feet in length and four in breadth, and which is called a "drake." They sunk this "drake," and then all hands in the raft were called to work at a windlass, by which they took in the line and pulled the raft up to where the "drake" was sunk, and in this manner they managed to clear the raft of a shoal on which they were in danger of being stranded. The windlass is a clumsy reeling machine, worked round an upright post.

The next point of interest on the river is Wade Island, a long mud flat, named after Sir Thomas Wade, late H.B.M.'s Minister Plenipotentiary at the Court of Peking, who accompanied Lord Elgin, as Chinese Secretary, during the trip up the Yangtsze in 1858, after which event, we suppose the name was given to the island, as we find other islands on the river which also bear the names of members of Lord Elgin's suite; "Oliphant Island," below Kiukiang, being named after Mr. Laurence Oliphant, the historian of Lord Elgin's Mission. Late in the evening, when fifteen miles below Wuhu, we passed "The Pillars,"—two large conical rocks which stand out of the water, near either shore. These miniature "Pillars of Hercules" have been called by someone "the gate of the Yangtze;" but, as Captain Blakiston remarks, "you might as well have a gate half-way up a carriage drive." "The Pillars" are near the city of Taiping, where the rebellion broke out, and the whole district here is famous for the exploits which took place in it during the progress of the Taiping Rebellion. We arrived at Wuhu about half-past ten o'clock on the second day of the voyage, and anchored in mid-stream, towards the north bank. Nothing was seen of the town of Wuhu, on the south bank, except a large pagoda whose outline was dimly visible under the moonlight, and of the town itself its location was only distinguishable by several lights along the shore. The pagoda at Wuhu was destroyed by the Taiping rebels, but we were told it has since been repaired. On the homeward voyage, we again passed Wuhu in the dark, so that we had no opportunity of seeing what the place is like. Wuhu is 460 miles from Woosung, and from the Customs reports we learn that the tides are perceptible at this port from the middle of December to the end of April (during the low winter level of the river), and the rise of tide varies from six inches to two feet. We only made a short stay at Wuhu to discharge Chinese passengers, who went off in large boats, taking an enormous quantity of baggage with them; and just about as many passengers and as much baggage came on board, the shouting and yelling of the passengers and boatmen alongside the steamer being something dreadful, the more so as it was dark and they did not see very well what they were doing; so that those already in the boats had to keep a lookout in case some fellow still on board the steamer did not throw his boxes on their heads. The oars of the boats differed from any farther down the river, in that the oarsmen sat down on a cross seat in foreign style, and pulled two long and heavy oars; although the boats were large, clumsy, and heavy-laden, the oarsmen pulled with a long and strong pull, and the boats with their noisy freight quickly disappeared, going across the river to the town; and the *Kungwo* was soon under way again. By the morning of the third day, we had passed Point Haines, Pan-tze-chi, Two-fathom Creek, Walled Village, the passenger station of Tatung, and then came Fitzroy Island. Opposite this island, a remarkable sight was witnessed on the left bank of the river. An embankment, of considerable height above the surrounding fields, lay from the riverside away inland in an angular direction, and the ridge was thickly covered with coffins, lying close, side by side, and in two rows; some of the coffins had been long exposed to the weather, and the thatch on them was nearly worn away, but others appeared to have been recently covered with straw. The sight of coffins above ground is a common one; in almost every field they are to be seen here and there; but we 'never saw a large collection of them exposed on the top of a bank in this way before. Along an extensive low-lying meadow on the right bank, there was an innumerable herd of buffaloes grazing, and we had some fun watching one buffalo who came careering along the bank of the river, at times coming to a dead stop and staring wildly at the steamer; perhaps the red funnel was the object of his wonder and admiration, though he couldn't see very well how to get at it.

The steam-whistle was blown, and the buffalo went racing wildly over the plain, causing considerable commotion among the herd; then he would stop and look round, till on hearing another blast of the whistle, he threw his tail in the air and rushed off for the hills at the other side of the plain. In the channel here between Fitzroy Island and the left bank, several boats were being "tracked" up stream; a long bamboo fibre rope is thrown out to coolies and boys on the bank, and they pull the boat up against wind and current. Further up the river, there's a pretty view on the left bank; a broad creek comes out at right angles, and looking up it you see a host of junks and small boats; while at the base of a hill not very far distant, and up to which the water-way leads quite straight, there is a large village; and away in the distance at the base of another hill there is a range of white houses which form a bright speck in the picturesque landscape. After passing Tai-tze-che Rock, with its joss-house and beacon poles standing out of the centre of the river, we approach Hen Point, a difficult and dangerous part of the river, where a nasty turn is made, the north bank sweeping round in quadrant form, and the south bank running out to a sharp point, while from the latter bank three quarters of the bed of the river is full of sunken rocks, on one of which the steamer *Kiangloong* was lost on the 2nd March, 1873. While yet a great distance off (as far probably as the Prodigal Son was when his father first saw him), the pilot notices that a raft is stuck on the top of the *Kiangloong* wreck, for the wreck was never cleared away, and part of the steamer is still hanging about the rock. The raft was a pretty good mark to warn the navigator of the dangerous rocks, and a raft or something else better suited should be kept over the rock always; there is only a beacon on the north bank. On the stranded raft there were about half a dozen houses; no one was seen on board, but the raftsmen were evidently still there, for some of them had just been hanging out blue cottons to dry; so that in their weary waiting for a rise of water they had so far forgotten themselves, or become so unlike their brethren, that they had actualy been washing their clothes. The story of the *Kiangloong* wreck is that she was drawing ten feet, and went full speed on a sunken rock, nine feet under water. From this rock to the south bank, or three quarters the breadth of the river, there is a series of low rocks. When the wreckers were salving the *Kiangloong*, having recovered most of her cargo, they were told by a Chinaman that, up to twenty-three years before 1873, there used to be a sampan buoyed over these rocks, and an old man on board exhibited a feeble light, a paper lantern of course. These precautions were for the benefit of the junkmen, and the man who kept the boat was recompensed by receiving from every salt junk which passed one handful of salt. But by and bye, the junkmen failed to appreciate the services of the old lightkeeper, and they first neglected and then refused to pay the small handful of salt to him, so that the old man gave up his philanthropic post, unmoored his sampan and sailed away, leaving the rocks without any signal of danger to the navigator. The sunken rocks were not discovered, although foreign steamers had traded on the river for years, till the *Kiangloong* made the discovery and was lost in doing so, becoming a total wreck. Such was the story told us by an officer of the *Kungwo*, who was one of the salvage party at the wreck of the *Kiangloong*; but if the rock on which the latter vessel was lost was unknown until she struck upon it, there must have been a general knowledge of the rocky bar which crosses more than half of the river here, for we find it referred to in Mr. Oliphant's history of Lord Elgin's Mission, is 1858, or 15 years before the wreck. In regard to Hen

Point, and the "48-chang or 180 yards' passage," Mr. Oliphant says:—"The river is here barred more than half across its width by rocks which rise out of it like stepping-stones." On the occasion of our trip, in March, the rocks were all submerged; and it is difficult to see how in September 1858 (as in that month the river should be at a high level) Mr. Oliphant could have seen the "rocks like stepping-stones," unless they have now sunk much lower than they were in that year. He continues:—"It is called the Lan-kan-ke, or "Bar river hen," and derives its name from the following legend, as graphically narrated to us by our communicative pilot:—"In former days the scenery at this place was very beautiful and romantic, gigantic rocks being strewn over the surface of the country. One day a bonze saw in a dream a quarrel arise between the beneficent spirits of the air and those who resided in the rocks. The presiding spirit of these was a rock in the form of a hen; and the result of the quarrel was, that, to give vent to their spleen, the rock-spirits determined to block up the passage of the river. In pursuance of this ill-natured design, off started the hen-rock, followed by all the rocks in her train, when the priest awoke, and, perceiving what was occurring, with infinite presence of mind commenced crowing like a cock. This so fascinated the leading hen-rock that her progress was arrested in mid-channel, on which the goddess Kwan-yin was invoked; then the people subscribed together, and while the hen-rock was thus enthralled by the well-sustained crowing of the priest, they succeeded in cutting her head off: this effectually checked the progress of herself and attendant rocks, and there they remain to this day!" In the reach above Hen Point, the river is a little less than half a mile wide, and here the banks are much steeper and higher than at any place farther down, where the river is broader. There are extensive brick-fields and lime-kilns on the right bank, before we come to Jocelyn Island.

We were now approaching the city of Nanking, the capital of the province of Anhwei. A Chinese sailor came and reported to the officer then on the bridge that "Passaga hab got too muchee bokasa; wanchee two piecee flag!" which being interpreted meant that the passengers from the provincial capital had so many boxes with them, that two boats would be required, and two of the "Ewo" flags had to be hoisted as a signal to those at the passenger station to send out two boats. The city stands on the left bank of the river, and just before coming up to it, we passed a large number of floating villages on rafts, with their bamboo fibre ropes drawn up on the shore and fixed to stakes. There is a fine broad sandy bank, like a sea beach, and on it a large number of children were playing. A splendid view is obtained from the river of the Pagoda of Nanking, the finest of the many to be seen on the Lower Yangtze, if not now the finest in China, it being in a good state of repair. The pagoda is octagonal, and eight storeys high, the walls painted white, and the balconies and the turned-up eaves on each storey are all of a yellowish brown. The pagoda towers above the centre of a large block of buildings, which rise in terraces from the river bank, some with white-washed walls, and others painted red, all·having ornamental tile roofs; these buildings are temples and other houses connected with the "idol monastery." The pinnacle of the conical roof of the pagoda is surmounted by six huge balls, decreasing in size in their order upwards, and between each ball there is a circular frame-work of iron. The lowest ball is seen to be of very large diameter, and the others above it decrease in size till the smallest one on the top looks liks the size of a cannon ball. Iron rods or guys stretch from the pinnacle rod above the highest ball, coming down in graceful lines to the corners of the roof ; these rods are strung with small bells, and larger bells are suspended from every projecting corner on the many ornamented eaves of this beautiful building ; and as we glided past the pagoda and came to anchor quite near it, a gentle breeze kept the hundred bells swinging to and fro, and their merry jingling broke very pleasantly on the ear. The city of Nanking was for three years in possession of the Taiping rebels, and some severe fighting took place round its walls. It was captured by Li Hung-chang (now Viceroy of Chihli), who earned fame during that rebellion ; Nanking is his native city, and, at the time we write, his mother still resides there. The Imperial troops having been baffled many times in attempting to capture the city by making breaches in the walls, the pagoda, which is outside the city walls, was made use of by Li-Hung-chang ; he shelled the city from the top of the pagoda, and on account of the facility which the sacred edifice thus afforded the Imperial troops, the pagoda was thoroughly repaired and is kept in good repair still, and may be considered a monument to Li Hung-chang more than anything else. The city wall comes round to the river, passing behind the pagoda, and stretching away up the river bank a great distance, but there is a considerable space between it and the river,—a space broad enough to have a small suburb of a double row of houses outside the wall. On the long sandy beach there are a large number of big boats, loaded with reeds, and many stacks of reeds are on the beach ; hundreds of Celestials—men, women, and children—are running about, most of them engaged in unloading the boats or building the stacks of reeds. The walls of the cottages on the top of the bank, and some protection walls, show the marks of former floods, the highest water mark being about 30 feet from the present level of the river. A small range of cottages of a modern foreign style are conspicuous by the whiteness of their walls and their generally neat and tidy appearance,—one of them especially approaching to something stylish in verandahs and green-painted blinds ;—these are the shipping offices for booking native passengers, for Nanking is only a passenger station, and not a port open to foreign trade. The opening of these passenger stations is owing to a stipulation in the Chefoo Convention, although it is still unratified. The "two piecee flag" brought out two big boats for our native passengers and their tons of "bokasa ;" and here again there was a provincial peculiarity in the boats and the manner in which they were propelled ; the oarsmen stand up on one side of the boat, and works a long oar, fixed by a piece of leather to a pin on the other side of the boat and which serves for a rowlock. In going ahead under full steam, we see that for about one mile up the river bank from the pagoda, the scene is the same all along,—hundreds of boats drawn up on the beach, huge stacks of reeds, and bundles of the same stuff scattered all over the ground, a range of small white cottages on the top of the bank, and the high and grim-looking city wall behind them ; while inside the wall there is nothing to be seen except here and there the ornamented roof of a temple, and aloft there are several kites flying in the air, with which the children, or perhaps the old men of the city, are amusing themselves. Then the city wall, at a corner about a mile, as we roughly judged, from the pagoda, goes inland from the river, mounts over rising ground, and winds round some of the small hills within its circuit till it is lost to view. Away in the background there is a high mountain range with craggy peaks, only dimly seen through the hazy atmosphere. Nanking is a great military post, and while taking a last look at the city as we were fast leaving it behind, we were struck by the appearance of a large square block of buildings outside the city walls on the west side; the buildings were decidedly of foreign style, and they stood on a slight eminence surrounded by a strong brick wall; a small chimney sent forth a column of black smoke; and the buildings appeared to be a small arsenal. Another prominent building near this corner of the city is a richly ornamented Chinese house standing on high ground, and surrounded by a high circular wall of brick; it is possibly the residence of a mandarin, and in its fine, airy situation commanding a view of the reaches of the river both above and below Nanking, and also of the vast tract of country stretching away to the hills, it is a more desirable residence than anyone likely to be found inside the city walls.

We experienced a slight sandstorm in the afternoon, just a little after leaving Nanking, but it was not of much account. About five o'clock we passed the town of Tung-liu, on the right bank; a dilapidated and ruinous eight-storied pagoda and some temple buildings are all that are seen inside the city walls, the town itself being hid from view. Then there are great tracts of flat ground on each side of the river, with herds of buffaloes grazing, and little boys in blue cottons perched on their backs. While there is a great extent of meadow there is also plenty of cultivated patches, most of them with young green crops,—wheat probably,—and here and there a yellow patch of rape-seed plants, relieved the monotony of the green fields. The sun went down "in a blaze of luxuriant dyes," and the full moon shed her soft lustre on the mighty river, a streak of silvery light stretching from the right bank to the port bow of the steamer, while the dark shadow of the hull, masts, and funnel lay across to the further side of the river. When passing the range of hills on the south of the river, near the Poyang Lake, a beautiful scene was witnessed. The full moon rested her "broad circumference" over the summit of the hills, and lurid flames, like a wall of fire, were seen leaping up the slope of the hills, in zig-zag directions, and spreading further and further till the whole hillside seemed to be ablaze; the brilliant illumination of the mountain range being produced by the fires lighted by Celestial charcoal burners.

The entrance to Poyang Lake, and the little Orphan Rock several miles further up the river, were seen with all the weirdness imparted by moonlight, but a much better view was obtained on the return journey. Poyang Lake is a very large expanse of water, lying to the south of the Yangtze, in the province of Kiangsi, and receives all the drainage of the rivers of that province, which it discharges into the Yangtze. It communicates with the river by a long and comparatively narrow neck of water, three miles long and one mile broad, and debouches into the muddy flood of the Yangtze at the city of Hukow. On the right bank of the river, below the confluence of the lake waters, there is a long range of sand hills, which rise higher and higher till those rolling inwards towards the lake form a very bold range, but unlike the others they are partially covered with green vegetation, and with rocky ravines. Away far into the lake, and barely visible except on a very clear day, a huge rock stands out of the water,—another of those "rocky eminences with idol monasteries," as Marco Polo calls them. This one is known as the "Big Orphan;" and its brother the "Little Orphan" is a rock of the same kind some distance away,—the latter on the river and the former on the lake. The city of Hukow stands in a very romantic situation; the most striking feature is the high rock rising from the waters of the channel between the river and lake; the summit of the rock is fortified, and contains the residences of some big mandarins. Down behind the rock lies the city, and the range of hills already spoken of stands in the rear.

On the opposite side of the channel from the city of Hukow, the Lewshan, or "Mule Mountain," rises to a height of about 5,000 feet. The Little Orphan Rock stands in the middle of the Yangtze, the fantastic rock towering to the height of 300 feet above the river level. As seen coming down river, there are three or four small blocks of buildings, rising higher and higher behind each other, and each range standing on a narrow cleft of the rock. The other sides are bare, perpendicular, and rent surfaces of grey rock.

Early on the morning of the fourth day of our trip, we arrived at the treaty port of Kiukiang, of which the old native city and the foreign settlement stand on the right bank of the Yangtze, 445 miles from Shanghai. When approaching the port, there are various objects of interest on the bank of the river,—the foreign cemetery, a small hill with pagoda, two or three small round forts outside the city walls, the wall itself riding over a rocky spur close to the river bank, and extending onwards towards the foreign settlement, where it sweeps round and inwards away from the river. The most prominent object inside the city is a very tall pagoda, now in ruins. The foreign settlement, as seen from the river, forms a fine range of bungalows and two-storied houses of neat design, embowered amongst a profusion of beautiful green trees; and lines of trees also extend along the whole length of the Bund. On account of the extraordinary rise and fall of the river during a year, it is necessary to have a bund wall of great and very substantial construction. From Customs reports we learn that on the 11th January 1878 the level of the river was 37 feet below the level of the Bund, and during several days in August of that year the water was one foot above the level of the Bund! Several hulks lie moored in the river opposite the Bund, for steamers discharging and loading. There is a good amount of foreign and native trade at this port, and it is chiefly noted as the depôt for the famous King-te-chin porcelain. At the western extremity of the settlement there is a creek full of native boats, and on the other side of it, on the corner of an alluvial plain, stands a small Chinese settlement, chiefly devoted to the boat-building trade; a lot of native boats are lying about on the bank, bottom up, some of them put in that position for repairs, others fixed permanently,—at least as long as the planks hold togther,—to serve for a house; the ricketty shanties on the bank at this corner are ruinous and miserable. After leaving Kiukiang, there is a fine view obtained of the bold range of mountains, between which and the river there is a vast alluvial plain, covered with buffaloes, ponies, and Chinamen. The highest peaks of the mountains are about 4,000 feet above sea level, and amongst the slopes of this range the foreign residents of Kiukiang have good sport hunting wild boar.

The next point of special interest on the river is the passenger station of Wusueh, 25 miles from Kiukiang, which is an important place in the native salt trade, and the large salt godowns form a striking contrast to the small hovels of which the rest of the town is composed. Wusueh is on the left bank, and the river there is only about a quarter of a mile broad, but of extraordinary depth, soundings of thirty fathoms having been obtained towards the right bank at the base of the hills. From this point we enter upon the grandest scenery of the Lower Yangtze. Opposite Wusueh, the first of the hills on the right bank are small and hemispherical, a large group of them lying close together, with deep ravines between;

behind these small hills a higher range is seen, and behind it again still higher peaks rise boldly against the blue and cloudless sky. A large hill, with steep slope full of gullies descending down to the water's edge at the narrowest part of the river, with a small village at the bottom of one of its ravines, has a very imposing appearance; further up the river a shoulder of this hill slopes gradually down till the base forms one side of a small round valley, with two or three hills rising on the other sides, and behind them still higher peaks. Another hill of most remarkable configuration on the right bank of the river is in the form of a long ridge running in the same direction as the river, and the slope coming down to the river is composed of about twenty deep furrows and ridges. The groups and ranges of hills extend for nine miles on the right bank till Split Hill is reached; and the most remarkable feature of these hills is that,—on those next the river at least,—every available inch of ground is under cultivation, the industrious and economical Celestial farmers having cut out terraces on the hills from base to summit, wherever it was possible to do so, and all the hillsides are covered with little terraced patches of cultivation. While on the one hand there is this extensive and varied mountain range, on the north side, or left bank of the river, the scenery is also very imposing. For the first mile or two above Wusueh, there is low-lying flat ground, and a bold range of hills is seen some distance inland, and rolling onwards till it closes in upon the river further ahead. By-and-bye we come to a point where the hills are quite close to the river on both sides, and the appearance of those on the left bank is most remarkable. In the foreground there are several red sand hills, with slopes like the face of a pyramid, and behind them there is the bold and rugged range of rocky hills, full of precipices, and the slopes covered with huge boulders of a blueish tint. Among some of these hills of Hupeh, mining engineers have been prospecting for coal, but with little success as yet. A large amount of limestone rock is in these hills, and along the bank of the river there are numerous lime-kilns, the kilns being formed by huge baskets of bamboo wicker-work. Split Hill is of remarkable appearance; the face of it is a sheer precipice of rock at a point where the river makes a sharp bend, and the side of the hill first seen is terraced from base to summit with patches of cultivation. After turning Split Hill the river sweeps round till it is like a semi-circular bay, and the right bank a sandy beach. Up from this crescented bay there is a beautiful expanse of green and yellow fields, and the further side of the valley is closed in with a small hemispherical hill, terraced round and round from base to summit, and as neatly done as though it were a Christmas cake. Further on, after passing through this bend of the river, terraced hills are seen on one side and rocky hills' on the other, this romantic and grand scenery continuing to present new charms and additional features of interest for miles still further up the river, till at last the rocky ranges on the left bank recede inland and a broad expanse of flat ground lies between them and the river.

When we approach the city of Keechow, on the left bank, the Ruined Fort, which stands in the river about 150 yards from the corner of the city wall, is the first object which attracts our notice. The fort evidently must at one time, probably not long ago, have been connected by land with the city, although now the strong rolling currents sweep round it. At the level of the river when we saw it, the rock on which the fort is built was barely visible; all that remains of the fort itself is a large mass of solid brickwork, then standing twenty feet out of water, and the side against which the current breaks is semi-circular, while the other walls are square. On the top of this ruin, the Imperial Customs officials have placed a red-painted tripod, with beacon, and between the three legs of the stand there is a small box, which at first sight did not appear big enough for a dovecot, but which is the only shelter provided for the lightkeeper, and we could scarcely have believed that a man could have got into it unless we had seen an old Chinaman coming out.

The wall of the city of Keechow is quite close to the river bank, mounting over a rocky knoll at a corner opposite the Ruined Fort, then extending up the river bank for some distance, and sweeping round two or three small hills which are included in the city boundary of moss-grown brick and mortar. The city appears to be a pretty large one, and away to the right the houses are densely packed. At the corner, outside the city wall, and shaded by the small hill, stands a white joss-house, with a large camphor tree behind it; at nearly all the Chinese joss-houses this tree flourishes in prominent positions. Further up the river a creek goes round by the wall, and on the bank of the creek a large suburb stands, the most prominent building being of the design of a mandarin's yamên.

On a fine, broad sandy beach, some miles above Keechow, an interesting sight was witnessed, being no less than a travelling theatrical company, who had pitched their tents on the left bank of the river. The main structure was fixed up by a large number of huge poles stuck in the sand, and cross beams between them supported a platform or stage, which was next the river, and about ten feet above ground; the pit of the theatre was on the further side, and all enclosed with canvas. Around this large tent were many smaller ones probably the sleeping quarters of the theatrical troupe, or possibly the big show had several satellites crowding round it, just as a travelling circus at home is accompanied by small penny shows. The approach of the steamer brought a crowd of several hundred Celestials out on the beach; and on the platform at the end of the large tent we could see the actors in all their gorgeous robes, pushing themselves half way through between the torn canvas to see what the matter was. The appearance of the actors at that part of the tent at once indicated that the elevated stage was at that end. Some of the actors were very gorgeously dressed in bright-coloured robes, and apparently done up for emperors, generals, and mighty big mandarins. It was a puzzle to understand how the approach of a steamer could have brought all the people out of the theatre, but still it did so, and the only thing that can be inferred is that, if the play was actually proceeding at the time, it did not say much for the interest or excitement of the piece if the red funnel of a steamer was a greater attraction. The only noise we heard from the shore, save the playful shouting of children, was the beating of a gong by the only member of the orchestra who stood to his post.

The next affair which attracted notice was a raft, high and dry on a shoal, towards the south side of the river. This is frequently the fate of the raftsmen, so that it is well they have houses on board, for that same raft we now saw had been stranded for several months, and would remain there more than six weeks longer, till the water rose in the summer floods. A raft stranded in the middle of the Yangtze all winter and spring is not a very pleasant situation for those on board; and some of the raftsmen, if not all, are obliged to remain on board, else the raft would soon disappear bit by bit. On the one we saw there were signs of life, for blue smoke was curling upwards from a small stove-pipe chimney in one of the huts.

Towards sunset on the fourth day of our trip, and when entering on the last hundred miles of the journey, we witnessed the finest scenery of any part of the Yangtze between Hankow and the sea. In the last hour before sunset, after passing the Ruined Fort and the old city of Keechow, the scenery was charming indeed. A series of small hills extends along the left bank, beginning several miles above Keechow, and terminating at the bend of the river opposite Cock's Head. These hills are arranged in groups, and each succeeding group seemed to be a duplicate of the one just passed; if there was any difference at all, it was only that they appeared to grow more beautiful as we glided past them. The hills are of no great height,—only a few huudred feet to the summits of the highest of them; they are set in horse-shoe groups, with a little round valley formed at the base of four or five hills; the bluff rocks which come close to the river's edge, and which are cut by the current, showing the high water mark, are about a hundred yards apart; the small hills next the river are backed by slightly larger ones, and still larger hills close in the further side of the valley. The slopes are terraced and cultivated at some parts, at others they are covered with shrubs; here and there a peach tree is seen in full bloom; and nestling in the cosy shaded nooks at the base of the hills, a few cottages of bamboo and thatch, or occasionally of brick, show that each quiet valley has its own peaceful tillers of the soil. The flat ground between the hills is all under cultivation, coming out to the bank of the river and occupying the full breadth between the rocky bluffs; the crops show their soft green blades only a few inches above ground, and look like a carpet; the green patches next the river are on the lowest level, and yellow plots of rape rise behind them, with green fields again in the rear, and covering the whole of the valley up to the base of the furthest hill. We passed about half a dozen groups of hills, forming as many small valleys of this description, and as we remarked at the time, "What a pity there are not some such lovely spots about Shanghai." While we had this fine scenery on the one hand, the prospect before us was delightful. Cock's Head is a bold rocky eminence standing on the right bank of the Yangtze, at a point where the river takes a sharp turn, and when viewed from a distance the outline of the rock resembles a cock's comb. The face of the rock, as seen when coming up the reach, is a sharp rugged line descending to the water; the side next us, and back from the perpendicular face, is a very steep slope covered with trees and brushwood; the summit of the rock, about 500 feet high, is also covered with foliage. Near the bottom of the slope, and almost hid amongst the trees, stands a small white joss-house. As we approached Cock's Head, the setting sun gilded the bosom of the Yangtze, so that the water was not seen in its real colour of dirty brown, but shone brilliantly in reflecting the rays of the sun. Foreign and native craft lent a charm to the scene, and a striking contrast was presented between steamers and rafts. The China Merchants' Company's steamer *Kiangyung*, a paddle-wheel boat of the American river style, all brightly painted, came down the river and passed us on the starboard hand; her decks crowded with Chinese passengers looking at the *Kungwo;* and the decks of the *Kungwo* crowded with Chinese passengers watching the yellow paddle-boat sweeping past us; and from the bridge of each vessel, white handkerchiefs were waved as friendly salutes between the officers. The *Kiangyung* had just passed, when we saw ahead of us, in the reach beyond Cock's Head, first one, then another, a third, and again a fourth raft or floating village of bamboo huts coming down the swift-rolling current. A minute or two later we were passing the huge rock, and looking upwards at the sheer precipice of 500 feet. Our attention was called to a hermit's cave in the face of the rock, and sure enough there it was,—an arched entrance, and in the opening we could see a rudely-built hut of bamboo and mats, elevated a a few feet from the bottom of the cave, and a three-stepped ladder leading up to the hut. "Is there really a hermit living there?" "Yes, I have seen him; he sometimes comes out and sits on the rock fanning himself." "How does he get his food?" "Oh, he can walk on a narrow ledge round to the joss-house at the other side of the rock." While the hermit and his cave were the subject of conversation, we looked through a glass, and saw an extremely narrow ledge in the rock, by which it would be possible, but not very safe, for a person to make his way from the cave round to the other side of the rock. The high-water mark on the face of the rock seemed to be only about fifteen or twenty feet above the level of the river that day, but we were assured it was between thirty and forty feet; and the hermit's cell was about fifty feet above the highest water mark on the rock. It was but a brief moment that elapsed while we were passing the rock, and besides the cave there was something else to occupy our attention, for the steamer's whistle was blown several times, so that we might hear the echo, and the loud and long blasts of the whistle were clearly echoed; but the whistles and their echoes did not fetch the hermit out to see what the matter was; he had never heard the song "Whistle and I'll come tae ye my lad." We were looking towards the face of the rock, and had forgotten all about the floating villages, but though the whistles and echoes were loud enough, we just then heard excited shouting in Chinese, and looking down from the port side of the hurricane deck we saw the four rafts coming sweeping past us at a terrible speed; they were all in a crowd and seemed as if they would smash against each other; the raftsmen were all "on deck," some with long poles and oars in their hands, though neither poles nor oars were of any use on the breast of such a current; others were running about on the rafts as excitedly as though they "expected every moment was going to be their next;" the rafts and their huts—quite a small town on the four of them—swept past at a good distance from our steamer, and the current took them just as if they were to be dashed on the rocky face of Cock's Head; but no, they could not have touched the rock even if they had tried, for the peculiar set of the current took them close to the rock but still quite safely past it, and the huge rafts and all their superincumbent huts and trappings rushed onwards to the broad reach below. Rocks, hermit's caves, rafts, and echoes, were compared to what followed. We had just passed the rock, when we were delighted with most fragrant perfumes which were wafted on a gentle breeze, and casting our eyes eastward we beheld a lovely sight. From Cock's Head, a range of hills sweep round till they come to the river's edge nearly a mile further up the river. Between the right bank and the base of these hills there is a beautiful and fertile plain, which lay there covered with lovely green crops, and behind this green carpet rose the steep slopes of the hills, which from base to midway up were literally white with peach trees in full bloom; and from these myriads of blossoms, shining in the last rays of the setting sun, came that sweet-smelling fragrance which so delighted us.

The scene as above described closed the fourth day of the voyage, and next morning we found ourselves at Hankow, the *Kungwo* being moored alongside a hulk in front of the Bund. We made a stay of about 36 hours at this port, but the writer, being then an invalid, was unable to go ashore, and therefore cannot say as much about Hankow as he would have liked, having only seen it from the river; most of the time was pleasantly spent in the company of Hankow gentlemen. The foreign Settlement of Hankow extends along the left bank of the Yangtze for about half-a-mile, and has the finest Bund of any port in China; the Bund wall being of extraordinary height, which is rendered necessary on account of the great rise and fall of the Yangtze during a year. The river here is nearly a mile wide, and there is a difference of about 60 feet between the lowest winter and the highest summer level of the water. When we were there (in March) the river was 13 feet above the lowest level of the previous winter, and still from the hurricane deck of a steamer you could not see level with the roadway of the Bund. The massive wall of masonry, with sloping base, is ascended from the hulks by long bridges and gangways, which rise and fall with the flood. On the Bund there is an avenue of tall green trees, and behind it a range of fine buildings standing in gardens or "compounds." The river Han joins the Yangtze to the west of Hankow; on the other side of the Han stands the town of Hanyang, and on the south side of the Yangtze is the city of Wuchang-fu, the capital of the province of Hupeh. This latter city has a very picturesque situation, the town itself and its pagoda standing on the slopes of a small hill, close to the river bank, while the city wall sweeps away round, over high ground, to the base of hills in the rear of the city. A large fort, said to contain 400 guns, stands on the bank east of the city, and directly opposite Hankow. The background is occupied by a bold range of hills, on one of which there is a large pagoda, and we presume it is the site upon which Captain Blakiston stood when he witnessed the panorama of mountains, plains, rivers, and lakes, which is thus described by him in his book "The Yangtsze:"—"Hankow is situated just where an irregular range of semi-detached low hills crosses a particularly level country on both sides of the main river in an east and west direction. Stationed on Pagoda Hill, a spectator looks down on almost as much water as land, even when the rivers are low. At his feet sweeps the magnificent Yang-tsze, nearly a mile in width; from the west and skirting the northern edge of the range of hills already mentioned, comes the river Han, narrow and canal like, to add its quota, and serving as one of the highways of the country; and the north-west and north is an extensive, treeless flat, so little elevated above the river that the scattered hamlets which dot its surface are without exception raised on mounds, probably artificial works of a now distant age. A stream or two traverse its farther part and flow into the main river. Carrying his eye to the right bank of Yang-tsze one sees enormous lakes and lagoons both to the north-west and south-east sides of the hills beyond the provincial city." While we were at Hankow, the large fort on the opposite side of the river presented a very gay sight, as its long yellow walls, full of embrasures, were covered with a grand array of brightly coloured flags. We have since heard of a curious accident to this fort, which puts one in mind of the story about the walls of Jericho. It is said that when the American gunboat *Monocacy* visited Hankow this summer, and when the Viceroy of Hupeh came from Wuchang-fu to visit her, a salute was fired in his honour, which had a most disastrous effect on the fort. The vibration of the air caused by the firing of a few blank charges, half a mile or more from the fort, is said to have broken down a large portion of the walls of the fort; perhaps the foundations had been damaged by floods, but at any rate it does not say much for the stability of Chinese forts.

We left Hankow about eight o'clock one evening, and arrived at Kiukiang next morning; Nanking was passed in about twenty-four hours from Hankow, and Chinkiang reached in another twenty; we left that port after a few hours' stay, and steamed slowly so as just to reach the North Tree and Langshan Crossing at daylight; and we arrived in Shanghai eight and a half days from the time of starting. The voyage down river, with the strong current in favour, is made very much quicker than the upward voyage. The fastest time in which the voyage from Hankow to Woosung was ever done, we believe, was by the *Glenartney*, one of the tea steamers in 1879, the time taken for the 600 miles being 37 hours; but then she made no stoppages. River steamers generally do it in about 60 hours, but a large portion of the time is spent in stoppages at the way-ports; and it takes about 100 hours for an average passage up river from Shanghai to Hankow. Having included in our narrative of the upward voyage the description of some places seen on the way down, there now remains nothing to add except to conclude the sketch with an acknowledgment of thanks to Captain Popp and the officers of the *Kungwo* for their courtesy during the trip.

A DESCRIPTION OF PEKING.

ON arriving from Tungchow and nearing the southern gates of Peking, the first object that strikes the view is the beautiful tower erected on the top of the wall. The wall itself is from 40 to 50 feet high, and from 30 to 50 feet thick. The facings are of fine large bricks, with which also the top is covered. The wall is fully 16 miles round, or rather square. There are in all nine gates: three in the south, two in the north, and two in the east. The gates are all well constructed, with an open space between the two doors. The *Chie-men*, or front gate, is the best and largest. It has three pairs of doors or entrances. Through the middle doors, and quite opposite, is the palace entrance, where only the Emperor passes. At ordinary times this middle gate is always shut and locked. All the gates are shut shortly after sunset, except on New Year's Day, when they are kept open a little longer. After the gate is once shut no persuasion or money can open it till the morning. The front gate is open at midnight for a short spell, in order to let the mandarins come in who have to attend the meeting of the State Council at the Palace at 4 a.m. Peking, seen from the top of the wall, looks like a grand garden, at least from some parts. The yellow roofs of the Imperial Palace buildings are seen in the distance, glittering in the sun, with their so-called golden chairs suspended at each corner. At short intervals along the walls guard-houses are erected, in which soldiers are said to be always stationed for the protection of the city. Judging by the braves on the look-out from the wall, but actually only one or two men are to be seen in each guard-house. Although entering Peking over the walls means death, and going out the same way banishment for life, a good deal of smuggling in this manner goes on every night, apparently unknown to the authorities. Peking is built in a perfect square, and all the principal streets run from north to south, or from east to west. The Hata-men Street, running from the Southern Gate, straight to the northern wall, where it terminates a little to the east of the Anting Gate, is the longest street in Peking, and measures about four English miles in length. Most of the streets are very broad and would make splendid promenades or drives, were it not for the many encumbrances one meets in the road. Every Chinaman seems to use the street as he likes without apparent interference from the police authorities, and filth, dirty water, and refuse of all descriptions are thrown openly into the public thoroughfares. On each side of the road, the pathways, which should be used solely by pedestrians, are monopolised by booths and stalls in which a large retail trade is carried on, reminding one very much of the appearance of a fair at home. Sometimes, when a big funeral is at hand, a great catafalque may be seen obstructing the road for weeks at a stretch. The carts and horses make a circuit without a demur being uttered. The sacrifices to the dead, burning of big paper houses, horses, carts, figures of all sorts, and paper money, are performed in the middle of the road, to the no small inconvenience of passers-by. The streets are always very muddy or dusty, and although $500,000 are said to be paid annually on their improvement, nothing is ever done in the way of effectually cleaning them. When the Emperor or Empress Dowager goes out, the streets are strewn with red earth, which gives them something of the appearance of a circus track, and all traffic, vehicular and pedestrian, is prohibited over these patched-up thoroughfares, until the Imperial journey is ended; but the moment this takes places, the street returns to its old condition. The heavy, springless carts are enough to ruin any thoroughfare. Once an attempt was made to introduce the jinricksha, but the carters combined against the innovation and threw the unwelcome vehicles into the moat outside the city. In a word, when the weather is wet, the Celestial capital may be described as a mud hole, and in dry weather a dust bin. The numerous sewers in Peking, which were once praised up to the skies by a former French Consul at one of the open ports, are useful in many ways. From time to time in the spring they are emptied into the streets under which they run, breeding disease freely in the surrounding neighbourhood, and all the year round their filthy water is used for keeping down the dust in the streets. No wonder that so many people of the city suffer from sore eyes and sore throats in windy weather when the dust is blown about. The cleansing of the sewers is generally in charge of a high Mandarin, who pockets the money and lets a deputy look after the work. The deputy performs his duties by going into the shops and telling the shop-keepers that unless they give him a bribe, the sewers will be opened in their houses or before their shops, thus putting a stop to their business for a considerable time. In the rainy season some of the streets are utterly impassable, the water coursing through them like a rapid river. It has often occurred that carts have been upset and the occupants drowned in the streets of Peking in wet weather; and yet, notwithstanding the filth, the climate of Peking is not considered unhealthy, except in summer. The dust-storms, which usually last for three days and nights, and carry the yellow dust from the Western Desert, purify the air and dispel all harmful odours. The Chinese houses are all very low, and, as a rule, without an upper story. As buildings, they leave much to be desired, for, in rainy weather, hardly one of them does not leak. The shops in some quarters have magnificent gilded and carved fronts, which contrast oddly with the filthy streets in which they are situated. The Forbidden City, where the Emperor resides, occupies an immense tract of ground. Formerly a roadway led from the Imperial City over the Marble Bridge, but of late years this means of access has been closed, and now a circuit has to be made to the West City. The Foreign Legations are mostly situated in the southern part of Peking, in the *Chia-mi-hsiang*, or so-called Legation Street. The French, English, and Russian Legations occupy former ducal palaces and are very large. A chapel has been built in each of these edifices, and suitable accommodation is provided for the large staffs. The Missionaries, both Protestant and Roman Catholic, are scattered all over the city, the Catholics having four large churches, in the north, south, east, and west quarters of the city respectively; in the latter is the Cathedral,—a fine church, standing in extensive grounds. The lighting of the streets is far from perfect. There are a multitude of lanterns provided for this purpose, with paper facings, in which a small oil-lamp burns, but their light is very feeble, and as they are generally lighted only on bright moonlight nights, when the Mandarin in charge of this department may be expected to make his tour of inspection, the system is far from a satisfactory one. The Customs people only have gas in their houses.

TEMPLE OF KWANG-TI, PEKING.

IT is often said by persons who ought to be well acquainted with the subject that the ordinary Chinese people have no religion, and if they have one they do not practise it except at funerals, when the priests, both of Taoist and Buddhist cult, unite to perform the necessary rites for the dead and to the departed spirits. Such statements may be true to a certain extent, but they hardly hold good for the mass of the people. Europeans who have studied the language of the Chinese and have lived among them for a certain number of years, and observed their ceremonies, their manners, and customs, can certainly testify to the contrary. We may simply state a few facts to prove that idolatry has certainly a greater hold on the Chinese people than is generally supposed to be the case. Not far from the back gate of the British Legation in Peking, in a side street leading to the Mongol market, a beautiful new temple has been erected, principally dedicated to Kwang-ti, the God of War. The owner of the temple is a Chinese merchant, who, having failed in business, employed the wreck of his capital to erect a place of worship and make a living out of his superstitious countrymen. No priest is seen in this martial temple. A couple of ordinary Chinese coolies keep the place clean and assist in the worshipping at the same time. Besides the image of the God of War several other idols are set up at the back of the principal hall. The God of Medicine sits here enthroned next to his colleague the God of Wealth, and in a row with the House God and the divinity of Medicine. Before the last one a candle is kept burning, at a certain period of the year, probably because at that time of the year his aid is mostly sought for. On the walls in the courtyard pictures are painted, giving scenes from the history of the three kingdoms, representing the hero Kwang-ti in his martial exploits. Presently a Chinaman enters the temple with a little boy of some seven or eight years of age. They go straight to the medical god and buy from the attendant coolie a bunch of incense sticks, which the coolie lights at the candle. When well lit he hands it to the little boy, who prostrates himself several times, with his head to the ground. Now the incense is placed in a vase on the altar before the god. The coolie, by the way, has all this time been striking a bell placed on a near table, in order to call the attention of the divine Esculape. The coolie then takes a bamboo receptacle with numbered sticks, somewhat the same as used by the Chinese in gambling for cakes. He passes it through the flame of the incense and then lets the little boy draw one of the sticks. The boy hands the stick to the coolie, who looks at the painted characters and selects a paper bearing the same number. It seems that the little boy has been suffering from a cough, and curiously enough the paper selected contains a prescription, which the coolie tells the father of the boy, if purchased of a chemist and religiously taken, will cure him completely. The father hands 15 cash to the coolie and carries the prescription to the chemist in the city. So it goes on every day. Especially during certain seasons of the year, certain temples in and outside Peking are visited by crowds of believers, many of whom have travelled for days on foot to reach the holy place. Some, perhaps, perform a pilgrimage for a sick friend or relative, while a great many women visit the temple to beseech the deity concerned for a son. If one sees the number of scrolls put up outside the door, on the temple walls, or on the wall in the vicinity of the temple, it is evident that convincing proofs are not wanting of the idolatrous habits of the Chinese people. In Wo-fou, in the temple of the Sleeping Buddha, one may see numerous pairs of boots, large and small, presented to the idol. In a temple just outside the North-eastern Gate of Peking, people have contributed a large collection of silk cloth and paper eyes. In the Yung-ho-kung, the large Llama temple near the Anting Gate, Northern City of Peking, the large wood and clay image of Buddha (standing figure, some 70 ft. high) has its large toe of the right foot nearly kissed away, like the toe of St. Peter's image at Rome. Countless examples of the deep-rooted hold which the superstitions, almost amounting to a religion, of the "joss," *fêng-shui*, and kindred occult influences, have upon the commercial classes of Chinese—merchants, compradors, boys, shroffs, clerks, and others in the employment of Foreigners,—might be quoted from the daily experience of every Foreign resident, which would go to show that, though the average Chinaman may not be endowed with what Western people term the religious or spiritual cast of mind, it is a great mistake to assume that he is the thoroughgoing materialist and sceptic he is so often represented. His ancestors in remote ages worked out his religious system, such as it is, and the Chinaman of to-day is well contented with it. His spirit is anything but of an inquiring turn; he is not troubled with mental searchings and doubts, or if he is, he keeps such phenomena to himself, and goes in the ways of his fathers, worships their gods, pays his offerings and knocks his head dutifully before the clay images that have formed the pantheon of countless generations of his ancestors. Doubtless in ordinary circumstances, the average Chinaman troubles his head very little about spiritual things, but in time of trouble he is very like the ancient personage of whom Hudibras says:

> "When the Devil was sick,
> The Devil a Saint would be;
> When the Devil was well,
> The Devil a Saint was he."

A JOURNEY TO THE WEST OF CHINA.

"ICHANG, a small place on the way to Chungking." Such was the adequate description of a Shanghai journal: but that was in the olden days when life in Ichang was synonymous with exile. Now, however, since the "latest riot" has brought the little port into prominent notice, and the ordinary Foreigner has, by the aid of "the last revised" atlas, discovered where Ichang really is, matters have changed. So, at least we found it, when, after a pleasant trip from Hankow, during which we received many courteous favours at the hands of Captain Cain and the officers of the *Tëhhsing*, we anchored opposite the dingy building that does duty for the British Consulate. While speaking of steamers, it is impossible not to express delight at the change from the time when the Hankow-Ichang traffic was practically in the hands of the Company that flies the Dragon Flag. Then travellers and some shippers knew what carelessness, tinctured with insolence, meant, but happily that can be avoided now (1892). The business of Ichang was in full swing; junks bearing the different house flags were lying abreast of the steamer, some just arrived down the river, others preparing for the up journey. Quite recently the Customs staff received extensive additions, the question of "quarters" being solved by hiring large Szechuen junks for the more recent arrivals, as well as for two missionaries who have returned to resume the work interrupted by the riot. Our business in Ichang was to prepare for a journey to the west, and the object of these notes is to give some of the impressions received by the way. First, then, a boat must be obtained. This is by no means so easy as may at first appear. Owing to increased traffic and the demand for large boats at Ichang, prices have advanced considerably, and the traveller is lucky if he can strike a fair bargain within the first twenty-four hours. The usual plan for amateurs, globe-trotters, and the like is to utilise the services of someone's house-boy, who can retail enough "pidgin English" to make himself dimly intelligible, and he receives the commission to get a boat "chop chop." Sometimes the steward of the steamer "runs the thing," which he is perfectly willing to do with the greatest courtesy, providing, of course, that he has a hand: one such venture is well within memory. Some enterprising travellers from far had come to "do the Gorges." It happened to be a late season and the water was yet high even in late September, but a boat was hired at an almost staggering price, and a start made. The first half of the first Gorge was made all right and then a mere temporary stop of three days, to await falling water, was indulged in to the chagrin of the tourists, whose temper rapidly became worse as the days dragged on. On the third day the boatman was called, and, by the help of the "English-speaking" cook, was informed that "a start must be made to-morrow morning." The boatman expostulated strongly and longly, but ultimately succumbed to the inevitable and prepared for the start. In the morning all hands were duly fed, put ashore, and a long rope paid out; then the boat was pushed out from the little cove, and gradually came into the full force of the current swishing at the base of a magnificent cliff. The trackers stood in a small recess, on a scanty ledge of rock (the proper path being submerged) and pulled for all they were worth. There were a few moments of suspense; then with a smart snap the rope parted, the boat swung out into the river and commenced a series of rotary movements, which seemed somewhat childish in a boat of its build and proportions. After a rapid run for a long distance down-stream, the shore was finally reached and a mooring place found. By this time the boatman was pretty well scared and the tourists badly enraged. Scene:—Boatman with profuse prostrations begging the "great Foreign man" to stay till the water should subside; Foreigner, with fists up and a strong vocabulary—wealthy in expletives, demanding that the boat set out again at once or "he'd knock fits out of him"—a friendly blow or two being thrown in by way of emphasis. Well, this continued, with some variations, for three days longer, and travellers set out for Shanghai, leaving the boat hands, middlemen, and sundry hangers-on to enjoy their gains.

The ruling prices at time of writing (spring of 1892) for ordinary four-roomed boats, capable of accommodating from three to five persons, is from one hundred and fifty to one hundred and sixty-five taels. Three-roomed boats will go for about one hundred and ten to one hundred and twenty taels. This includes boats, trackers, wine money, extra trackers at rapids and all incidentals. When one considers that a crew of thirty all told is needed for a month, besides a small boat to act as consort, having six more men, the marvel is that it can be done so cheaply, yet time was when Foreigners even could command prices ranging from twenty per cent. cheaper than these.

The river has apparently grown busier. One sees flags that promise to become familiar,—such as Butterfield & Swire's, Jenkins' and others,—flying at the stern of the huge, well-manned junks that in this case must act as pioneers to the long expected "fire-wheel ship" unless the "fire-wheel carriage" happens to come along first, and thus verify the hopes of some ardent Chinese.

"How far to the rapids?" is the ever recurring question. It is difficult to say anything about these rapids that will not conflict with what someone else has already said and, perhaps, written. One man will insist that there is a "direct fall" of 10 feet, while another avers that there is no fall at all; but the fact is the aspect of the river changes, and what may be true of one season of the year will not be equally true of another. The fact is that at this time of the year there are some pretty respectable rapids that would be difficult of navigation by any kind of craft. Notable among these are the "Shin," the "Yeh," and "Sha Ma" rapids. At these we added from fifty to sixty men, put out double ropes, and were prepared for squalls generally. These rapids present the greatest problem in the increasing traffic in this upper river. For example, at the "Shin" rapid there could not have been less than one hundred junks, large and small, waiting to be towed up. A moderate "wait" is from twenty-four to thirty-six hours, the average crew would be about thirty men,—thus there are, approximately, three thousand persons lying idle from one to two days, to say nothing of the delay of goods in transit and damage to the boats by the pounding and scraping while all are jammed together at the foot of the rapid. There are many rapids to be ascended, and delays longer or shorter occur at all. What is needed is some uniform plan, rigorously enforced, to get boats up quicker; a good energetic man to regulate matters would greatly facilitate this business and remove a great nuisance from the road. At the entrance to the province of Szechuen one finds the "new road," of which so much has been said about, 6 feet in average width, solidly faced with stone and raised to a considerable elevation above the river; this road should be a valuable means of communication when the waterway is impassable. It was a huge undertaking. At places the whole roadway was blasted from the solid rock; the overhanging cliff now forms a roofing above the road; chasms had to be bridged, steps built, and other difficulties overcome, till the cost must have been enormous; but much of its value is neutralised by the fact that it is incomplete. The provincial authorities of Szechuen have done their part; the road is built quite level with the boundary between that province and Hupeh, and there it stops short. The Hupeh powers appear to have done nothing; so the thing remains a practical failure as a means of intercommunication.

There is no difference in the attitude of the people towards us; in the main it is friendly. The same old stories about the "precious treasure" are retailed. One man gravely told us that some Foreigner had offered three hundred taels for a cave in the mountain side, but could not procure it, because it was filled with treasure, though only a Foreigner could get it. To-morrow we expect to reach Kuei-fu, the great *likin* station and point of delay to boats in general. It will be interesting to see how they treat boats with the Foreigners aboard; rumour speaks of such delay of cargo junks ordinarily as to be more than a nuisance.

At Kuei-fu the west-bound traveller leaves the Gorges and emerges into more open country. The river, as it rushes through these narrow channels is unquestionably very fine, and impressive. Gloom generally lends its aid to heighten the effect, yet, as a rule, the Gorges are too short for effective grandeur: one is just beginning to feel a sense of wonder and solemnity and is prepared to have it deepened to any extent, when a sudden turn opens out a new and wider reach ahead and the previous effect is spoiled. This is specially the case should there be a good wind blowing and the boat making better time than the trackers could do. The sense of wonder is too brief to leave a deep impression.

Leaving the "Wind Box" Gorge the most prominent feature is the cluster of mat huts partially enveloped in steam and smoke, which occupies a sandy beach about a mile from the city. This is the point where brine is obtained and evaporated for the salt it contains. At high water all this place is submerged, and as the Chinese have no way of preventing the brine from flowing into the fresh water around it, the whole is lost for a considerable portion of the year. The officials at the "likin" (Native Customs) station were very courteous and caused us no delay at all; in this they differ from the practice in by-gone days. After a brief delay to change the small boat and "swap" useless men, we got away most expeditiously. By the way, it is said, a sharp letter of reproof was received by the official in charge of the *likin* sometime since on the subject of delaying freight junks unnecessarily, so that may have improved matters. Between Kuei-fu and Tünyang-hsien are some very dangerous rapids at low water, where, strangely enough, there is only the usual strong current in the high water period. One now begins to notice the climate characteristic of Szechuen. Misty, gloomy days, in which one scarcely sees the sun, clouds lying around on the mountain sides as if waiting to precipitate themselves in rain upon the already well watered fields. As a natural consequence every growing thing, from the bamboos waving on the slopes to the vegetables that cover the fields as a carpet, is gleaming with a brilliant green. Snow lies upon the higher mountain-tops, but apparently does not reach the valleys or river; here it comes down in rain.

A very common feature of this part of the river are the little straw shanties and the rude apparatus of the gold-washers. The men engaged in this occupation are all, apparently, very poor, only scraping a bare subsistence from the sand and gravel in which they seek the precious metal. Where the shore is gravelly, the apparatus is a basket on rockers, in which the gravel is washed, the fine sand, in which are the particles of gold, being caught on a screen beneath the basket, and afterwards collected and treated by the quicksilver method, thus separating the metal from the sand. Where there is only sand, a wooden tray is used for washing, and the gold collected from the fine, black sand left in the bottom of the tray, by the same method used in the other case. The washers informed us that the gold sells at from two hundred *cash* per *fen* and one man could make two or three hundred *cash* a day at the work. There is little to attract attention between Wan-hsien and Chungking, a journey of from twelve to fifteen days, usually. The land is cultivated to the water's edge. As soon as the receding water leaves a little patch of sand long enough for it to dry, the farmer comes along with a hoe or plough and makes a place to put in the seed, such as wheat, peas, and turnips, while in most places one may see little clusters of the opium poppy gradually crowding out other things and becoming more plentiful as one goes farther west. What ultimate effect this home production of the drug may have upon the Indian trade, is still problematical, but one thing is sure, it is having a marked effect upon the people in this province. The article is cheap, is easily procured, and hence very widely used among all classes of society. It is one of the most saddening sights to be met with, the steady decadence of persons who use "the pipe" and gradually come under its overmastering influence. The habit begins insidiously—often in fun, because one asks another to "play awhile," and assures him no harm can come of "a pipe or two." So the "play" commences, which too often ends in misery, not seldom in tragedy. One hears sometimes of the great desire in official circles to check the opium traffic. Such a sentiment does not seem to obtain in this part; often the "yamêns" are the worst offenders in this, as in other malpractices. One I was in some time since had six ordinary Chinese beds at the entrance room, and every bed had its pipe and smoker, yet from that same "yamên" had just issued a stirring little proclamation against opium-smoking, while "all the world" knew perfectly well that the "venerable sage" who sent it out himself was addicted to the forbidden pipe. The most acceptable bribe to the officials is generally a bowl of opium. Being out at dinner with a rising young gentleman, who has aspirations to the official chair, I was surprised to see one of the literary lights of the place adjourn from the dinner table, lie down upon the divan, take his regulation dose, and then resume his eating. The pipe was offered to each of the guests in turn, as if it were a common custom. I have met several men who contracted the habit while yet in school, the example of the teacher being quoted as a sufficient reason for the practice. The shame that used to attach itself to a confirmed smoker is passing away, because now they say "eight tenths of the people smoke."

We arrived at Chungking without serious mishap and found a noisy mooring-place at the confluence of the two rivers, outside the Tsao-tien gate. Chungking would probably be a pretty place if one could see it, but it appears to be wrapped in perennial fog, thus the grandeurs of the situation are lost to the observer. Once inside the city one observes nothing but the interminable stairways and the abominable mud that bespatters one if any walking is attempted. The refuge of a sedan-chair does not afford the usual relief. In going *down* one sees a long stretch of muddy, slippery stone steps away beneath him, while holding on with precarious tenure lest one misstep of the bearers should land him in some hideous puddle, to the great amusement of all the spectators. In going *up* one struggles against the tendency to fall out at the back of the frail chair, while the swinging motion imparts a sensation as of incipient sea-sickness, that makes one long for the ground in spite of the mud. Chungking is undoubtedly a thriving city. The evidences of prosperity are many. Large, well-stocked shops occupy the principal streets, provisions of every kind abound, while the bustling activity indicates a large and thriving trade. The Foreign community has increased of late, but is so scattered in different parts of the city (some even being across the large river) that visiting is a difficulty should one's time be at all limited. This city is the great distributing point for west, south, and some places north; the traveller going farther west will probably make a change of boats here and accommodate himself to a somewhat different order of things even in boat life.

From Chungking upwards the river is shallower, more cultivation is seen, and the long sandy (or gravelly) beach becomes a prominent feature in the landscape. Large orange orchards may be seen along the slopes on both sides, and fine fruit obtained very cheaply. Coal and lime abound in places and every sign indicates a rich, prosperous country. The people are civil, and their pretty white-washed houses, sheltered in clumps of bamboo, charm the eager traveller, who is on the watch for every pretty bit of scenery with which to help to make a good account of a strange country. But let him push his acquaintance no farther than a distant view, if he would carry away good impressions of that which close inspection would surely render distasteful, not to say odious. Adobe walls, floors of virgin earth, dust-laden furniture, and that civilised smell inseparable from the vicinity of Chinese dwellings—one not desirable anywhere, except in poetry, where they sometimes serve "to point a moral or adorn a tale." Luchow, a fair-sized town, about ten days above Chungking, is a principal telegraph station for the west. The clerks in this department of the government service are singularly intelligent and courteous gentlemen, whom it is a pleasure to meet. Turning into the smaller river at this point, an easy and enjoyable trip may be made to the celebrated salt wells, one of the glories of Szechuen. The journey may be made by boat to Fu-shun and thence to Tz-liu-jin (the self-flowing well) by chair, or on foot, over a good road, beside a stream with a greenish hue, said to taste strongly of salt. On the afternoon of the second day one comes to a large straggling town (or series of towns) lying on both sides of a small river and branching off into the adjacent valleys. The whole forms a most striking scene, —the most un-Chinese scene perhaps in the west. The river is literally lined on both banks with salt boats, the hill-sides covered with buildings from which a thousand chimneys pour forth as many streams of smoke, and between the buildings are the derricks for raising the brine from the wells. The well-owners are an obliging class of men and willingly show one around their establishments, apparently proud to show "the lions" of the place. The wells seem to be anywhere, principally along the course of the river, however, and the town has to accommodate itself to them; so one sees buildings of all kinds packed together in a most promiscuous manner, the only bond of similarity being the inevitable derrick over the wells, around which all else must centre. Entering one of these interesting places, one is met by the courteous owner who draws attention to his fine herd of buffaloes, tied up in open sheds at either side of the yard; sleek, well-fed animals they are, much better cared for than the herd of coolies which take the place of buffaloes in some of the establishments. Beyond, one sees a clumsily constructed derrick, from 30 to 40 feet high, with a rude iron wheel at the top, over which a raw-hide rope runs, connected at one end with a bamboo tube which goes down into the well, and at the other with a huge windlass, which is used for raising and lowering the tube. The well itself is a small opening, of, say, 5 to 7 inches in diameter, and if one may believe the statements of the owners, from 2,000 to 3,000 feet in depth. The bamboo tube is lowered by simply releasing the windlass, which flies round with increasing momentum till the rope is all paid out. The tube fills with the brine, and, by a self-adjusting arrangement, the water is prevented from flowing out, and the ascent begins. In some places buffaloes are hitched to the sides of the windlass, and slowly drag it round, winding on the rope at a pace exasperating, because so slow. In other places from thirty to forty men and boys are hitched up, in place of the buffaloes, and perform the same work. When at length the rope is all wound in, the tube, now dangling from the top of the derrick, is seized and the brine runs out into a cistern, constructed to hold the brine till it can be conveyed to the evaporating sheds, which are often at a distance from the brine wells. In the process of evaporation, advantage has been taken of the natural gas which abounds in this neighbourhood, thus giving it a distinct advance over the salt region near Kiating (some hundred and fifty miles to the west), where soft coal has to be used, increasing both dirt and expense. The gas is conveyed from the wells where it is obtained to the place where it is used in bamboo pipes, which are braided with straw in order to prevent leakage in transit; but it is obvious that a great waste will take place with such poor methods. In the sheds where the evaporation is carried out, one sees parallel rows of shallow iron pans fixed over large jets of gas; a constant supply of brine flows to the pans from reservoirs placed in convenient positions, the flow being regulated by a poor process that involves a great waste. There does not appear to be any method for checking or increasing the gas supply, so one may see rows of gas burners, intended to light the building at night, flaring away in broad daylight, when they are worse than needless. The owners are eager to hear of Western ways of doing such things, and one could but wish for them that some competent helper were at hand to show them a better way—but, then, what good? They would probably admire, and withdraw.

Well-drilling exhibits at once both this splendid persistency of the Chinese in the face of obstacles and their clumsy force-wasting methods, in a striking manner. A place is selected for a well: now begins the task of realising in fact what has been planned in hope. A heavy wooden frame is erected, and a large beam is attached leverwise to one side of it; he longer end of the beam is inside the frame, the shorter one is heavily weighted and under it is the apparatus connected with the drill. When all is ready, five or six men arrange themselves inside the frame and step simultaneously on the longer end of the beam, which descends with great force under the combined weight of the men. When the beam reaches the limit of its descent, the men slip off at once, and it flies up, the weighted end striking the drill with great force. This goes on from day to day till years are spent, and a fortune too, in finishing the boring of a single well. Energy certainly is not lacking in Tz-liu-jin, but it is sadly wasted; yet the industry pays fairly well; some get rich, so rich that the Emperor *borrows* occasionally from some of the wealthier nabobs (how euphemistically the supple Chinaman can " put " some unpleasant things !) while a multitude of poor folks find work at the wells. It is said that many of the men employed are virtually slaves, death only can release them from allegiance to their masters. One is glad to note in many places excellent asylums for the aged poor. The one personally inspected had accommodation for "several tens" of indigent persons, who each had a little room and comfortable surroundings in which to pass their declining days. There are also orphanages for pauper children, and, so far as one is able to observe, others beside paupers avail themselves of its advantages.

Szechuen presents many delightful features to the traveller, none more pleasing than the civil, industrious people who, however eager they may be to see the "Ocean man," will seldom wantonly outrage him.

About one hundred and twenty *li* below the site of the present city of Luchow is a decayed place called Old Luchow. The Natives say that in the Ming dynasty the charter of this city was withdrawn because of an offence, which is very heinous in Chinese eyes, and the place where such a crime could occur fully merits its punishment. At an uncertain date in that dynasty a lad ("wa wa") of uncertain age beat his grandmother to death. To save the reputation of the city the plea of insanity was set up on the boy's behalf. In order to test the validity of such plea, the District Magistrate called the boy into his presence and finally had a meal of rice put before the culprit, "because," said the official, "if he eats with the right ends of the chopsticks he is sane, but if he should reverse the usual order, and eat with the *square* ends that would prove his insanity beyond doubt." This course was taken, and unfortunately for the city, the boy ate his rice in the ordinary manner, with the result above indicated—the city lost its charter, the boy lost his head. Comparing the national advantages of the two sites, however, one cannot be far wrong in supposing that this crime was but the occasion used to get the city removed to its present favourable situation, where it commands the waterway to the "salt wells" and has excellent mooring places for junks at all seasons of the year. There is a similar tale about a city further up the Yangtze, with this exception, the occurrence took place quite recently. In 1890 a son killed his father at Lan-chi-hsien in the Sui-fu prefecture. The Magistrate and towns-people were much alarmed and at once started a subscription, got together a good round sum of money, with which the official proceeded to the provincial capital and succeeded in buying up the Viceroy, who failed to report the murder to Peking, thus the Magistrate saved his button and the city saved its charter. So "money makes the mare to go," or otherwise as may be desired.

Sui-fu lies at the confluence of the Fu River with the Yangtze. It is a busy city and particularly friendly towards Foreigners. South-west from this point the road goes to Yunnan, while north is the road to Chentu, Kiating and the famous O-mi Mountain, the sacred mountain of the west. Two days, directly west from Sui-fu, beyond the point where the road diverges to Yunnan, one reaches the country of the "Man-tsi," the name by which the Chinese designate the hill tribes, who occupy so large a tract of Western Szechuen, and where they maintain a disputed independence, to the detriment of the over-lordship of China, who is constantly subduing these despicable "wild men" and ever finding them unsubdued.

The Chinese profess to loathe these outcasts who love to dwell in their mountain homes, and avoid the city where Chinese congregate. "The Man-tsi have no doctrine" is the contemptuous reference to these rude children of nature, but no steps have been taken to give them that "doctrine" the exclusive right to which inheres in a Chinaman's nationality.

Above Luchow many minor differences are seen by the traveller accustomed to down-river travel. At quite frequent intervals one may observe little stone pillars, crowned with a rudely carved head, with the cabalistic sign "O-mi-toh-fu" carved below. They are characteristic of this part of Szechuen, and perhaps serve to indicate the general prevalence of Buddhistic practices and influence as we near its chosen home in the indefinite "West." Also one observes new temples or shrines built at dangerous spots along the river, for the protection of travellers, while an attendant priest stands by the water's edge, armed with a small net attached to a long pole with which he collects cash from the boatmen, to repay the guardian care of the interested idol. A much more sensible proceeding is that of the erection of flag-signals in the river to indicate the situation of dangerous rocks, to the down-coming boats. At one point below Ho-jiang there is at this season a long rough dangerous rapid;. at one point in the rapid a large timber raft on its way down stranded on a reef of rocks and went to pieces,—a grand field-day for the small boats lying below the rapid, whose owners enriched themselves at the expense of the unfortunate owner who stood on the shore, showing his empty cash pocket and sobbing out the story of his great loss. It was probably ruin to him, poor fellow. Two other boats lay partially submerged near the shore, while their disconsolate owners sat on the shore surrounded by the few remnants of things they were able to secure from the wreck. One meets with many pitiful cases like this along the whole course of the river. One large cotton boat we saw was blown clean over, and lay with her mast pointing towards the centre of the river, while part of her cargo was eddying about her in the little bay.

Leaving Sui-fu by the Fu River (called Min on the maps) one travels through a delightful country in a northerly direction, passing fleets of small boats and bamboo rafts. These latter are made expressly for the navigation of the Ya River to Yachow, a prefectural city, some one hundred miles north-west from Kiating. They are of very light draft indeed, being merely a row of large bamboos bound securely together with strips of green bamboo, having a little platform raised some few inches, down the centre, on which the goods are placed. They carry mainly wine and cotton up river, and lumber, medical plants, and such like articles down stream.

In the tall rock cliffs along this part of the Fu, one noticeable feature, is the number of Man-tsi caves cut into the face of the rock. Mostly square, from a distance they look like the entrance to some royal tomb. In those inspected, there was a main entrance, and branching off from this, many collateral passages, some of great length. It must have been a gigantic task, the making of these caves, even though the sandstone be soft and to our ideas easily worked, and prove the Man-tsi to be intelligent folks for "wild men," as they are styled.

The approaches to Kiating are very pretty indeed. The country is broken and picturesque, and the city occupies a most advantageous position, at the confluence of the Ta, Tung, and Fu Rivers. Below the city about ten miles, is a brisk prosperous place, where brine is obtained in something the same manner as at Tz-lui-jin, but on a much smaller scale. Here only soft coal is used in evaporating the brine, and in consequence, a dense pall of smoke lies on the surrounding hills. The people in this region are not quite so pleasant to deal with as is general in Western Szechuen, but do not seriously object to the presence of the Foreigner.

Opposite the lowest point of Kiating is a gigantic image carved into the face of a magnificent cliff. The idol is said to be three hundred feet in height, is in a sitting posture, and so covered by weeds and shrubs as to be almost indistinguishable at high water, when the nearest point of view is nearly one mile distant, the intervening space being filled by a raging rapid, which the idol is said to control, alas! for the control or lack of it. Continuing along the bank of the Fu beyond the wall of the city one comes upon a well-built, clean street, which is the centre of the silk manufacture for which Kiating is noted. Sleek, well-dressed merchants are to be seen in the stores, where one may see a display of silk of many shades, patterns, and prices. Kiating is a city well worth more than a passing glance. From here we made a trip to O-mi-shan, the celebrated sacred mountain, and later to Ta-chien-lu, the "port of entry" on the Chinese-Thibetan frontier. Kiating to O-mi-shan is a romantic journey and well repays the toil of ascent and hard fare by the way.

From the wall of Kiating, looking westward, in clear weather one sees a striking panorama. In the near foreground are the united waters of the Ya and Tung Rivers, flowing through a fertile, picturesque plain, graced with the feathery bamboo and heavier foliage. Farther away is a mass of hills rising somewhat abruptly from the plain, the distinctive outline of each shaded in softening blue. Above all the nearer and lower hills, the clear cut profile of sacred O-mi emerges above a sea of billowy clouds; off to the left two other peaks attract attention and are described as O-mi number two and number three.

Sedans are plentiful, and although Kiating coolies have sharp tongues and quick tempers, and an exasperating way of sticking out for more cash just when one is in the greatest hurry, they are mostly efficient, and by their help one may make the journey to O-mi-shan pleasantly, even should the time be that of the summer pilgrimages.

Passing out of the city under a newly-built gateway the traveller finds himself upon a pretty roadway, well kept, much travelled, and should he be curious at all, there is much to allure one to linger in exploration, to say nothing of the tempting fare on the roadside stalls, that in appearance promise so much to the clamouring calls of a healthy appetite, but yield so little to fulfil the promise. A few miles out brings one to the banks of the shallow, babbling Ya River, making its way fussily to the larger river below. Across both Ya and Tung, chairs, coolies, and the miscellaneous remnants of the party, such as yamên runners and hangers-on, are poled and rowed at a pace that makes patience grey. At thirty *li* from the city we strike the busy little town of Su-chi. The situation of this place is very pleasant, and might be made attractive in the hands of a more imaginative people than the Chinese. As it is, while nature has lavishly done her part with river, hills, trees, and a teeming wealth of insect and bird life, the towns-people have done nothing to help, but all to mar, the prospect. Poor, dirty dilapidated houses, filthy streets, and the ordinary heterogeneous crowd of "wonks," hogs, fowls, and beggars. One is constantly struck with the air of content, not to say enjoyment, evinced by the people in the midst of surroundings that appear to be utterly unendurable. Perhaps it is that "they are native and to the manner born," else how do they live and multiply in what are considered to be fatal environments to the stronger European nations?

There is a fine bridge made of large stone slabs, resting on pillars of the same material, spanning the broad stream, giving ready access to the pretty village and country on the opposite side.

About fifty *li* more and O-mi-hsien is reached, the way lying through a fertile plain, rich in everything we are accustomed to associate with rural wealth and beauty. The people are well behaved, courteous, too much used to the sight of travellers to pay any heed even to the Foreigner. One spot by the roadside remains in mind,—a clear indolent stream, fringed with drooping willows and grassy banks, too like an old-time summer scene away among the Norfolk broads, to be passed unheeded. The sun was veiled in white massy clouds, everything seemed to rest, save now and again the leaping of the fish to the surface of the quiet stream, almost the only reminder of active life in the dreamy daylight hush. Such spots are too rare where paddy and opium hold sway to be readily missed.

O-mi-hsien is a long, straggling town, with a more than ordinary number of Romanists, who, indeed, are numerous all through this section. Few Foreign articles are for sale in the shops,—incense bags, incense sticks, map of the sacred mount, and other trifles used by the pilgrims, are the most conspicuous objects for sale. The inn we stayed at was over-crowded; insects were numerous and lively—the night was hot and—well, the morning was never more welcome. We got off in the early light somewhat ahead of the sun, while the dew was yet hanging heavily on the pendant rice ears—off to O-mi-shan! Pilgrims of all classes were even now out upon the road and the beggars too were out in force, lining the road on either side at a spot some little distance outside the gate, all bent on "making hay while the sun shines." Beggars, indeed, of every degree of need as to clothes, soap, and medical attendance; disgusting diseases, mutilated limbs, and such like valuable (in a beggar's estimation) appendages, were exhibited with as much pertinacity and success as a quack medicine advertisement in a religious newspaper. Entreaties of all shades,—vociferous, pathetic, half-humorous, ultra urgent,—filled the air. There were children of what we call "tender years" whose most prominent feature was a shock of tangled hair (or was it a gorze bush?) full of—crawling sensations at the distance of two yards. What a mission of mercy lay right here at the very [door of Buddha the Merciful and Kwang-yin the Pitiful. Among the thousands whose lives are given to the worship of the associated deities that crowd this far Olympus, there is surely one who could give his life to caring for and training in some better way this crowd of infant starvelings.] But perhaps it is too much to expect a *Buddhist priest* to give himself to the practice of mercy and benevolence in any substantial form. True they will climb out of bed in the morning's grey mist to strike the bell and light the incense in front of some gaudily painted idol; they will make long pilgrimages to distant shrines and make themselves a nuisance as beggars on the road; they can find leisure and strength to chant their meaningless litanies in the house of the dead; if only the "consideration" is sufficient; they will even find time and place for cards, opium, and gambling, to speak of no worse things; but who ever saw the touch of a priest's ministering hand by the sufferer's couch, or heard him soothing the dying man's latest hours with hopes of some coming bliss in the land where Buddha sits eternal? when we see this, perhaps we may hope also to know of some such scheme as is hinted at above. Anyway there was the need in that crowd of growing idlers, whose leisure will probably be spent in the opium shops and thieves' dens of the neighbouring cities.

The mountains had seemed to be so near the previous day that, as we wound in and out among the paddy-fields, bordered now with the pretty white wax trees, coming no nearer, it seemed, to our mount of hope to "freer skies and airs" than the plain could furnish. One often called querulously "Where are the hills?" "How far yet to O-mi?" In reply to which the coolies would purse up their lips, elevate their chins, and direct one's gaze forward. It was always ahead, if one could only tell which way that was, so woefully crooked were the roads. At length we began to rise, and reached the crown of a range of low hills, when, suddenly, as we came to the gap in the range through which the road passed, we saw before us a valley filled with the low branching white wax trees, which are a characteristic feature of this whole neighbourhood, but flourish especially in this lovely valley. The wax for the most part had been gathered before this date, but some lingering specimens gave us a fair impression of the appearance of the whole, which indeed must be striking and unique. The branches, of what looked to be a kind of mountain-ash, with stem cut short off, crowned with a coronal of green, sprouting boughs at the point of decapitation, were covered with a thick coating of "hoar frost" that sparkled in the clear sunlight. This white glistening substance is the famed white wax so widely known and used in China.

From this point the road rises, and each successive point gained gives a clearer outlook, and reveals magnificent heights beyond. Very soon we leave the "paddy" zone behind and beneath; maize now takes the regnant place, tall obstructing stalks line the roadsides and cut off the view. At one point we cross a clear mountain stream, by a suspension bridge that looks so slender and oscillates so disagreeably, as to make solid ground on the other side both welcome and desirable. At an altitude nearly four thousand feet Wan-nien-sz (the Monastery of the Myriad Ages) is reached and completes the first part of the journey.

This monastery with adjoining temples, outbuildings and numerous accessories, covers a large space of ground, indeed almost the entire summit of a somewhat isolated hill in a superb position. The flora is semi-tropical in character and luxuriance, and the whole environment is of great natural beauty. The temples themselves are sorry structures, and cannot fail to disappoint anyone, who, having heard of O-mi's sacred attractions, has come expecting to see something more than the ordinary mud and paint embodiment of the superfine ideal so inordinately embellished in "The Light of Asia." It may as well be said here as later, that the attractions of O-mi, sacred as it may be in the eyes of a scarcely discriminating Chinese public, will be found to lie in the beauty of the natural surroundings.

In one of the most recent works on Szechuen, in which a section is given to an elaborate description of O-mi, there is a drawing of a sacred bronze elephant, in a wonderful structure of brick and stone, the elephant's head apparently protruding from the inside of a not too commodious house, which has been erected over his sacred carcass. We started out in great expectation to find the said quadruped, hoping, of course, that we might perhaps see something which both author and artist had failed to emphasise in a "thing" so interesting. And surely we did, or rather the point lay in what we failed to see. After a hasty search we found the elephant, not standing out in the open as we had supposed, with his noble head in full view of the searching daylight, but, by the aid of a couple of friendly young priests and so many candles, we saw the noble form rudely enclosed within a strong high stone balustrade, so protected by the joint aid of the darkness and stone palings, that at no point could a comprehensive view be had of this unique treasure. It is very disappointing to have to say this, because we were quite prepared to be romantic over the pet. There were a few desperate pilgrims crowding round the spot, where by the help of a long arm and perseverance one might touch the surface of the bronze body, on which these ardent pilgrims were rubbing ordinary copper cash in order to brighten them, when they are said to act as very potent charms. Many of the idols in the temple were new, and some tolerably good-looking, but nothing more than may be seen at a score of places on the coast. One figure there was decidedly indecent, so that some one had draped it in a piece of red cloth, but the good intention was entirely frustrated by an officious urchin who stood near and obviously gloried in his office of exposing to the gaze of all comers this, the only indecent item in the show. In another building we were informed, that Buddha's tooth was on exhibition, and were invited to see it. The priest in charge had a face that would have been a fortune to a professional diplomatist. He could coax, scold, wheedle, and enjoy his own verbosity in a high degree. The precious tooth lay on a small side table, covered with a piece of dirty yellow cloth. Descanting on this precious relic with the view of rousing us to an adequate interest in it (which was quite superfluous, as we were ready for a tolerably smart shock), the priest at length uncovered the object of our seach—" Buddha's tooth, gentlemen !" A tooth indeed ! and of magnificent proportions, worn smooth and bright by the affectionate caresses of successive generations of wondering pilgrims ; but when it was suggested that " if this were Buddha's tooth, then Buddha must have been an elephant"—the ensuing laugh was too much for the oily priest, and he nearly forgot his customary politeness. Taken as a whole, the priests at Wan-nien-sz are an agreeable class of men, and do their share towards the comfort of their guests.

From Wan-nien-sz to " the golden summit," as the top of O-mi is euphoniously styled, is an interesting and enjoyable trip, even though it be a little hard on the poor pedestrian who essays it for the first time. At times the road leads up a violent ascent, which makes frequent resting a necessity, again it descends just as abruptly that one fears the wrong road has been taken. Temples are placed at about five *li* apart all the way and afford good resting places and decent hostelries, should the traveller need to put up for the night. Changes in the flora are observed at succeeding stages of the journey, and much of the teeming life of the lower heights is soon a minus quantity. Less than twenty *li* from Wan-nien-sz marks the limit of cicadas, whose deafening chorus is one of the unpleasant features of that luxuriant spot. Birds become fewer, and there are fewer varieties of butterflies and other insects. At the "Elephant's Bath Temple" there is a fine growth of trees—almost a forest; and here one sees a small dirty looking pool in which the elephant that brought the celebrated god Pu-shien to O-mi is said to have bathed; hence the name. The road all the way up may now be called good, some pious Buddhist having just completed the paving of it at a great expense (there are miles of stone steps) for which he was thanked by some who were not of like faith with himself. At some places by the way there are grand views—above, beneath, and around. Looking down through an opening in the foliage by the road side, one sees far beneath a matchless panorama, outspread in the winding valley. Dizzy depths that seem to fascinate the beholder. Then around one and above is the silent majesty that can be felt, but never expressed. Just as we emerged upon the plateau on the threshold of the summit, a spectacle opened to us that exceeds the power of this untaught pen to portray. The sun was westering and lay embedded in a vast ocean of billowy clouds. They appeared to hold and temper the glory of his powerful beams, while themselves were aglow with the golden light. They seemed indeed to act as a grand artistic shade to the great sun, and the deflected rays shot far up into the boundless blue above us and also down upon the mountains, that seemed to be not far beneath—the far-famed snow mountains of Eastern Thibet. They lay in perfect form and brilliance, the glistening ridges well defined by the dark patches of bare ground hue and that between—it was a scene of entrancing grandeur that we did not see again in such perfection. The artist has ye to be, who will do justice to the beauties of "the golden summit." No account should be taken of the barn-like structures called temples, the only good point about them is—they afford a lodging for tourists, otherwise they are a blot on Nature's proud escutcheon. They are the valleys, the woods, the clouds, the eternal snows to be seen off across the distance, the precipice, and "the glory." This last we did not see in perfection, I judge, but what we did see was something like this. The face of the famous precipice is toward the east. Frequently the whole valley beneath will be filled with what seems to one above it a dense impenetrable mass of white clouds firm enough to work upon. If this should occur in the afternoon while the sun is shining, the outline of the mountain is thrown in shadow upon the cloud surface. Just at the point of contact between shadow and cloud, one sees a luminous ring, diverse in colour, much like the nimbus (which somebody has irreverently styled a soup-plate) round the heads of mediæval saints in mediæval pictures. This is a "Buddha's glory," and so striking is the effect on the heightened imagination of sensitive pilgrims that often some impetuous soul will leap over the precipice and, of course, into "the glory." The priests have tried to stop this by stretching an iron chain, plentifully spiked, along the face of the cliff, but "where there's a will there's a way," and this is still the direct road to happiness to poor deluded victims. What a number of pilgrims one meets here at certain seasons, and from far they come. Aged women on bound feet are to be met trudging up and down these torturing steps; some parties seem to be "personally conducted" by the "befrocked priest" from some local temple. This unsatisfactory sketch of a wonderful place would be incomplete, inexcusably so, were no mention made of the young priest who lives in the furthest temple on O-mi. The other priests on the mount all appeared to be eager for the riches which they profess to have abandoned. Lying, cheating, and simple fraud are not strangers among them, but this young fellow, only twenty-six struck one as being different from all the others. He lives alone and is in process of becoming a Buddha himself. He has travelled extensively; knows Shanghai, Hangchow, Peking, and so forth, but here he is practically immured in his youth for the object named. He and his gods—which he called "likenesses of the unseen"—live together in this little temple, far removed from the arena of human sorrow and suffering. Much as one found to admire in his present position for the purpose of becoming better, who would not rather have seen him a man among men, bearing his share of the great world burden which presses heavily on so many? Tigers and fire are the two forms of evil most dreaded on O-mi, if one may judge from the frequent recurrence of shrines to these two objects, yet in the early months of last year a fire ravaged the summit, burnt down eight of the ten temples there, consumed gods, furniture and all but the priests themselves. This is the answer given by the priests when taunted with the inability of the fire-god to save either himself or them: "It is the custom to clean the house you live in sometimes; isn't it? Well! every thirty-third year the fire-god comes with a besom of fire and cleans out the accumulated filth in the temples of the gods. This was the proper year, and so he came "— thus the sceptic is "hoist with his own petard," and the priest is triumphant!

Kiating is also the point of departure for Ta-chien-lu, the little known emporium of Western Szechuen. As far as Yachow, four good days' travel, the road lay along the banks of the shallow, noisy Ya. The country is pretty and fertile, low hills abound, just enough to pleasantly diversify the scenery, and as to what may lie beyond them, one is left to wild conjecture, thanks to the natural mistiness of the Szechuen atmosphere, which effectually shuts all from view but that lying immediately around one. Boats are rare in this district, their place being taken by bamboo rafts of shallow draught on which goods from below are hauled as far as Yachow, which is the great distributing point for places more remote. The Chinese tell "tall" stories of the dangers to be met with on the road to Thibet of hardships to be encountered, which, together with the natural exaggeration of inexperience, gives one a strange tingling of curious excitement, with a shade of foreboding— not that the stories are confined to the "travelled Chinese," for the stories of some enterprising "Foreign guests" in the pursuit of discoveries in the "bug kingdom" were quite as "tall" as the others were high. The first day's journey from Yachow takes one over a rough pass, quite tiring in the blazing August sun, but, as it subsequently proves, only a prelude to the grander heights beyond. Chun-jin is reached at the end of thirty miles, *long* miles too they seemed, and here the sun seemed to be hotter than ever. This thriving city is the centre of the "compressed tea" trade with Thibet. From this point westwards one meets constantly long trains of pack-laden ponies, while the road is literally "occupied" with the long procession of tea-carrier coolies, but one remove from the beasts of burden, with which they often have to contest the road, and not much better cared for, save that they are able to speak and thus more able to look after themselves. One meets them of all ages, the father with an adult load, and after him his boys with loads graded to their capacity, and also, one sometimes sees the mother toiling on in the great procession, though personally the sight always was a painful one, children of tender years, and what should have been a tender woman, impressed into such a service as this. The remuneration is woefully small, so that, though they carry heavy loads (some strong men "back" a load of quite four hundred pounds English weight), and live on the coarsest food (large cakes made of maize or buckwheat flour, hard and heavy) they can only make a living without a surplus for old age and sickness. It will be easily seen that the cost of transport for goods by this route is heavy, and it would tell greatly on the Chinese-Thibetan trade, were a quick, efficient route opened to the south, connecting with the Indian system and thus with the sea on that side. This possibility has been most prominent in the minds of the Chinese statesmen who were sent to negotiate the Sikkim Treaty with British officials in India. One of the principal mandarins engaged in this treaty-making remarked to a well-informed Foreigner at Ta-chien-lu that, if the British should push their claims in the Sikkim Valley and connected it by rail with Darjeeling, it would give a mortal blow to Chinese trade with the lower half of Thibet. Were such a railway built, it would be but a matter of some days overland to Lhassa—the golden city—and, with one exception, there are no natural barriers in the way; while from the Chinese side it takes months to reach that point, and the passes over the mountains are in some cases stupendous, bad roads, and only imperfect security. India has tea in abundance at hand there, and Thibet has wool, hides, tallow, and so forth, to give back in exchange.

So we found ourselves in this procession westward, toiling to such fine altitude that we shivered in spite of wearing our entire wardrobe in the month of August. In the eventide, when compelled to sleep on some of the passes, we would sit wedged in between the good-natured coolies around a smoking wood fire, listening to "the short and simple annals" with which they beguile the gloaming hour, after which they unroll a straw mattress on the floor and "turn in" to a well earned rest. The traveller here must carry his own provisions, the host at the wayside inn provides fire and water (*such* water! cool and sparkling from the snowy reservoirs beyond); the traveller finds the rest of the fare.

At Tuting-chow we cross the famous suspension bridge over the Tung River; the bridge is, perhaps, three hundred yards long, formed of five iron chains stretched side by side, with boards fastened across. A couple of chains are also suspended on either side, in order to keep the passengers from being precipitated into the roaring torrent below—and indeed there is need of this precaution. The bridge is subject to violent oscillation, whenever any number of persons cross at the same time, so that one needs a guide on whom to lean, and ordinary coolies have to employ a specially trained Native for the transit. One of our fellows begrudged the ordinary fee to the ready porter, who offered to take his load across and himself, boldly started, but long before one-third of the distance was accomplished he was sitting on the roadway of the bridge, his load upset, and himself a picture of misery and object of ridicule, till he was rescued for the sum of five *cash*, by the one whose services he had previously scorned. Ta-chien-lu lies in a cramped position, shut in between lofty mountains, and divided by a rapid stream, lashed to foam in its sharp descent by its rocky bed. What a babel of tongues assails the ear, and what uncouth attire one sees on splendidly athletic figures. Men with earrings, women with large (quite large!) feet. Men with "tails" twisted around their heads and adorned with large silver rings above the forehead, women with fearless, attractive faces, walking out on the streets with the greatest freedom. And then what a display of supplies—beef, butter, cheese, bread; we see all this in a hurried run through the streets and make mental notes for the future! We found a welcome from the Thibetan women at the "yang lama" and soon had a table full of provisions furnished by their ready hands.

The population of Ta-chien-lu is a shifting one—Chinese merchants going in to transact business at certain seasons of the year, Thibetans coming in from the other direction with pack trains of goods, some of which are destined for Shanghai. Every one is courteous, some became familiar. An interesting afternoon was spent with M. Dejean, the courteous priest in charge of the Roman Catholic house and premises outside the North Gate. We saw his garden, his poultry, and a most pathetic sight, that could not fail to arrest attention. All round the upper edge of the garden is a fringe of graves, the resting-place of the Native Christians, laid side by side, their modest graves marked with the cross—that cherished symbol of a faith dear to many. That row of graves is a silent witness of a change being surely effected even in these remote districts.

The situation of the city is most salubrious, being at such an elevation (8,400 ft.), and with good rapid connections, would be a favourite resort in the summer heat. There is generally a breeze blowing through the valley, as one observed, whose observations of natural phenomena were more exact than his knowledge of the English tongue, "Ja-chien-lu is like one cup, the wind he blow, he blow, he blow for ever," and so it seemed, so far as we could observe.

The Thibetans in their garments of wool seemed to be literally steeped in the odour of "tsamba," their natural beverage. Tea and butter, churned to a uniform consistency, may seem to be a peculiar mixture, yet it becomes palatable, and when mixed with the roasted meal with which a kind of porridge is made, it has become an object of desire to weary travellers.

The little we could see of the neighbourly Thibetans made us wish for the day when they no longer shall be a "hermit nation."

THE HILLS-FUNG-WANG-SAN.

A HOUSE-BOAT TRIP TO THE HILLS.

FOR those who cannot spare the time for a holiday jaunt through Japan, a week-end house-boat trip to the hills—known as Fung-wang-san—makes a welcome break in the often dreary monotone of life in our Far Eastern Settlement. A short and pleasant drive to Jessfield, and at mid-day on Saturday, and we find the house-boat moored alongside the tracking-path ready to depart. No fancy vessel, built on airy lines, but a large flat-bottomed boat, some thirty-five feet long, the greater portion covered in, the stern occupied by the yulohing crew and lowdah (captain); the forecastle giving pleasant space to sit in the open, enjoying the air and passing scenery.

Entering, one finds a good room, some 8 feet high, 10 feet wide, and 15 long, half of which is taken up by two huge bunks, one either side, with a passage between, at the end of which is a door leading into pantry, kitchen, and cook-house, where not only is our food prepared but both "boy" and cook find sleeping accommodation. The fore part of this saloon is at present taken up by a table laid ready for tiffin by the waiting-boy, who has also undone our bags and packed everything safely into the many and spacious drawers beneath the bunks. This saloon is cosy, hung with curtains which not only drape the windows on either side but, hanging at the foot of each bunk, hide them effectually from view. Easy chairs, gun-racks, and an imposing array of bottles in the racks testify to our intention to enjoy ourselves, whilst a stove standing beneath the mantelpiece, although not in use, adds a homely touch to the appearance of the place, which is finished off by the mirror overhead, and the curios, pictures, and nic-nacs all round the "walls." After our morning's work in office we are to do justice to the meal before us, and whilst we replenish our inner men the vessel starts, with a crew of eight men in all for us two passengers. The motion is gentle, but tide and wind are in our favour, and we go pleasantly along the creeks, past waving cornfields, with goats and kids innumerable, and many sheep, grazing here and there in the green pastures bordering the water's edge. Strange antiquated sights meet our eyes, reminding us that the English-looking farms and thatched roofs belong to Eastern climes. Now we pass the Soochow mail-boat, a long, low, oval flat, mat-roofed canoe, in which the master of the mails sits lazily in the stern working a yuloh with his feet and steering the paddle-rudder with his hand. Although many steam-launches run daily between Shanghai and Soochow, the Native post goes by these slower boats, so that even steam has not accelerated communication by letter a jot in this queer corner of the world. On the bank of the creek there is a group engaged in threshing with a bamboo rack, on which the corn is beaten by holding a bunch of stalks in the hand and bringing the ears down with a swish on the slanting rails; a little farther and a bamboo flail is used instead.

The crops in this part of the country are home-like and familiar,—wheat, barley, and broad beans occupying most of the ground. Every fifty feet or so, chain-pumps made of bamboo, the wooden endless chain of small, square, upright blades working in a bamboo rough, the motive force a water-buffalo, blinded by two tortoiseshell blinkers, which goes continually round and round under the cone-shaped, clean, thatched roof, driving a 7-foot wooden cogwheel. But meantime we have got on deck. The ice-chest makes a convenient seat in front, and our flagstaff at the stern is ornamented with a life-buoy.

So we go gliding quietly along, enjoying the fresh and cooler air, feasting our eyes on the trees, filled with the song of many birds, until we are strongly reminded of China by the foul odour of a flat, low-lying manure boat, which we pass on its way with its fetid cargo from Shanghai to some up country paddy-field. But in a moment or two our attention is more pleasantly absorbed in a boat bearing down on our left with cormorants aboard. Six of the black and gloomy-looking birds sit, as if stuffed, along each gunwale, facing one another, while two more occupy the bow lower down; they will go fishing for their master, who now is taking his feathered servants to their hunting grounds. Occasionally we pass a group of women, seated on low bamboo stools, at work in the fields, who stop to gaze at the Foreigners, who now are no uncommon sight. Coolies sometimes shout "*La-le-loong!*" or thief; but more often half-naked youngsters run along the banks airing their only English—" I-say ! " .

A fine, sunshiny, cool, and breezy day, with a temperature at 78° in the shade, we enjoy the sight of wild-flowers—roses and honeysuckle. In the distance the dirty light-blue clothes of the Natives harmonise and lighten up the landscape.

But evening is coming on as we near Wongdoo, and see on our right the mud forts, with soldiers in their gorgeous red and blue, loose-fitting clothes. Glancing through the openings in the apparently very solid walls we see two huge, hideous, and strikingly-painted lions,—meant to strike with terror all onlookers. But, like the mud fort itself, all is "look-see," real strength being absent. In front of us towers up the apex of a triangular bridge, solidly built in huge blocks of well trimmed and carved stone, passing over a huge central semi-circular arch, flanked on each side with a smaller arch of the same shape. Here our sail has to be taken in and the mast lowered to allow us to pass through the arch. A few miles farther on—we are the only boat in sight,—we come to an anchor, the writer fishing for an hour, in vain, whilst his companion, attired in the blue cotton knee-breeches and "kakee" drill coat, topped by an ancient, brown slouch hat, goes forth for a walk. But what care we, not toil, but pleasure, rest and recreation are what we came for,—so once more we are on the move, sometimes along creeks arched over by drooping trees, the only blemish being the foul odours from huge pits of manure which lies rotting in them on the banks,—native sewage-farms, which purchase excreta and night-soil at Shanghai and other towns, storing it, to afterwards retail it to surrounding farmers. Ere long, however, we are past all this, and by 8 o'clock sit down to enjoy with heartiness our dinner, in which Boston beans and pork figure largely. Every meal appears as punctually served, and as well as if we were on shore, the only sign of rustication being the absence of the cruet, through the "boy's" forgetfulness; but an old tin canister serves for pepper castor and egg-cups for salt and mustard. The evening meal over, we light our cheroots and, donning heavier coats, sit on the forecastle in easy chairs, indifferent to the heavy falling dew, drinking in the soft scenery lit up by the silvery light of the moon-rays glint on the stream; no sound to be heard but the croaking of the frogs or the ripple of the water round the yulohs astern. Fair tide and wind have favoured us, for with sail set for a great part of the trip we are up to the smaller hills by 10 at night; and at last convinced that all China is not a flat and dreary plain, intersected by stinking ditches, we bid adieu for the night to the clear, dark stream below us and the moon above, turn into our pyjamas, falling quickly into sound slumbers until early dawn. " Up with the lark," we shout to wake the boy for the inevitable morning tea and toast, and thus fortified go on deck to find we are moored in a little bay beneath the shadow of the Catholic Monastery Hill, and behind us are two other house-boats which have arrived during the night. Tumbling into the lavatory, which is at the fore-end of the cabin, we quickly wash and fling on our clothes, losing no time in getting on shore to enjoy a walk before breakfast, for everything points to a hot and scorching day. By half-past six we were climbing up the Monastery Hill, whilst the bell was calling worshippers to matins; reaching the top we flung ourselves down on the rocks at the back of the Roman Catholic Church to breathe in the gloriously fresh morning air.

This church is situated twelve miles north of Soongkong, and twenty-five miles south-west of Shanghai. Early in 1867 the Rev. Father Desjacques, later well known in Shanghai, built a small chapel in honour to " Our Lady, Help of Christians." The present church, built after the plans and under the supervision of Brother Mariot, S.J., was completed in the beginning of 1870. It was constructed after the massacre of Tientsin, in thanksgiving for the preservation of Shanghai for the Kiangnan Mission.

The view was splendid: about half-a-dozen hills here and there, jutting out from a level plain of green and black fields reaching as far as eye can see, the winding glassy creeks shining in the morning sun. Around us the birds, with joyous notes, sang their morning hymn; below the patient buffalo was working at the pumps, and the blue-coated Natives hoed and dug their crops. But, as the sun gained in strength, we had to wend our way downwards, past the ruined old pagoda, on which, long years ago, bells tinkled in the gentle breezes, reminding the country-folk of some departed benefactor. Reaching the boat, we, with hearty appetite, demolished a substantial breakfast, lolling on board the remainder of the day in restful ease, till evening, when, raising our anchor, we turned homewards, passing through the Siking Reach—as fine a stretch of water as any rowing club could desire for their annual regatta. The next morning we awoke to find ourselves in the narrow creek bordering the Sicawei Observatory, the rain pouring in torrents. Landing, we got into 'rickshas and rode to the Settlement,—the trip over, but we refreshed and re-invigorated for another week's work.

www.ingramcontent.com/pod-product-compliance
Lightning Source LLC
Chambersburg PA
CBHW031818220426
43662CB00007B/706